D1232098

Body, Sex, and Pleasure

Body, Sex, and Pleasure

Reconstructing Christian Sexual Ethics

Christine E. Gudorf

The Pilgrim Press
Cleveland, Ohio

The Pilgrim Press, Cleveland, Ohio 44115
© 1994 by Christine E. Gudorf
Paperback edition 1995
All rights reserved. Published 1994

Printed in the United States of America on acid-free paper

00 99 98 97 96 95   5 4 3 2 1

Library of Congress Cataloging-in-Publication Data
Gudorf, Christine E.
Body, sex, and pleasure : reconstructing Christian sexual ethics /
Christine E. Gudorf.
p.   cm.
Includes bibliographical references and index.
ISBN 0-8298-1014-5 (alk. paper)
ISBN 0-8298-1062-5 (pbk.) (alk. paper)
1. Sex—Religious aspects—Catholic Church. 2. Sexual ethics.
3. Catholic Church—Doctrines. I. Title.
BX1795.S48G83 1994
241'.66—dc20   94-5008
                                                CIP

Dedicated to Frank, with whom I discovered much of what I know about the grace and power of sexuality, on the occasion of our twenty-fifth anniversary, with gratitude for his help and understanding.

Contents

1. *The Necessity for Reconstructing Sexual Ethics*

For at least two decades, there have been voices calling for the development of a sexual theology which would reject body/soul dualism and do justice to the Incarnation. Ethicists have made many contributions to the beginnings of such a theology of sexuality with significant contributions found in the work of people like James Nelson, Beverly Harrison, and Andre Guindon. Unfortunately, most of this work is not readily intelligible to the general Christian public still blinkered by the traditional code of Christian sexual ethics which has formed its understanding of both sexuality and morality.

Our society is in a crisis over sexuality, in part because the churches have been paralyzed by fear of stepping away from the confines of the Christian sexual tradition to develop a responsible sexual ethic which not only accords with our scientific and experiential insights into sexuality, but which better accords with our understanding of the central revelations of the gospel. Society looks to the churches to provide moral guidance for public policy in many areas, but especially in sexuality, since the churches have long claimed proprietary interest in sexual behavior. The unwillingness of the churches to risk abandoning a familiar but unworkable sexual ethic has left the broader society without effective moral guidance on sexuality at a time when more and more public policy issues involve sexuality.

The Dutch Reformed Church of South Africa is today being called to repent and renounce its traditional teaching on apartheid; the Catholic church at Vatican II felt required to repent and renounce its historic anti-Semitism. The same kind of renunciation of traditional teaching in sexuality, followed by repentence, is necessary on the part of all Christian churches today in response to the suffering and victimization it has long supported and legitimated.

Churches can no longer justify presenting inherited Christian treatment of sexual ethics with only piecemeal modifications or critique. It is past time that we admit that the reason so many differ with specific conclusions of inherited sexual ethics is that the entire approach of Christian sexual ethics has been and is grievously flawed. Gradual, piecemeal revision is not sufficient.

Traditional Christian sexual ethics is not only inadequate in that it fails to reflect God's reign of justice and love which Jesus died announcing, but its legalistic, apologetic approach is also incompatible with central Judaic and Christian affirmations of creation, life, and an incarnate messiah. Because the Christian sexual tradition has diverged from this its life-affirming source, it has become responsible for innumerable deaths, the stunting of souls, the destruction of relationships, and the distortion of human communities. The Christian sexual tradition uses scripture and theological tradition as supports for a code of behavior which developed out of mistaken, pre-scientific understandings of human anatomy, physiology, and reproduction, as well as out of now abandoned and discredited models of the human person and human relationships. The churches are still today teaching theological conclusions originally based in ignorance of women's genetic contribution to offspring, ignorance of the processes of gender identity and of sexual orientation, and of the difference between them, and ignorance of the learned basis of most gender differences—ignorance which has allowed and supported patriarchy, misogyny, and heterosexism, the assumption that heterosexuality is normative. We are still teaching a sexual code based in fear of the body and of sexuality, in understandings of sexual virtue as the repression of bodily desires by the force of the rational will, on physicality, especially sexuality,[1] as an obstacle to spirituality, and on women as lacking reason and only possessing the image of God through connection to men.[2] The churches have disowned the Mosaic law's assumption of male ownership of women and children,[3] Luther's understanding that women are like nails in a wall, prohibited by their nature from moving outside their domestic situation,[4] and Aquinas' teaching that females are misbegotten males, produced from male embryos by physical or mental debility in the father, or by moist winds off the Mediterranean.[5] But we continue to teach most of the sexual moral code which was founded upon such thinking.

Beginning with Sexuality, Not the Christian Sexual Tradition

The first step in restructuring Christian sexual ethics is to understand as best we can human sexuality itself, and in this day and age this means consulting both biological science and social science, as well as the experience of human individuals and communities. I do not suggest that Masters and Johnson or Bell and Weinberg[6] replace the Bible, church fathers, and the classic theologians as more or less infallible authorities. Sexuality is a social construct in which biology is only one part. Neither are the social sciences of themselves capable of defining or interpreting human sexuality. But we must take seriously the broad areas of scientific consensus regarding reproduction, sexual response, sexual difference, and the development of sexual identity and orientation. It means, for example, that we admit into our discussions of what is "natural" sexual behavior the fact that human infants' second instinctual physical feat, after satisfying oral gratification, is manual genital stimulation, and that infants under one year are observed to produce all the signs of orgasm through self-stimulation.[7]

As in other areas of ethics, we need to begin doing ethics with a description of the reality of our situation. Only after this can we turn to theological reflection regarding the meaning and significance of the various factual elements we have described. To do social analysis—the investigation of the surrounding reality—in sexual ethics will involve using not only the tools of social science that we are accustomed to using in social ethics, but the biological medical sciences as well. For the influences on sexual behavior include our individual genetic inheritances, the worldview and customs inculcated by our specific culture and society, the shape of the economy and political system in our society, and our social location within that society.

It is often mistakenly assumed that the hard sciences are normative in a way that the social sciences are not. But it is not the case that medical-biological research describes the givenness of human sexuality, and social sciences such as sociology and psychology only present facts about changeable responses of human persons. The biological sciences are fallible even in the twentieth century. Until relatively recently medical science taught that there were only two sexes, identified by an XX or an XY pair of chromosomes. Now we know that there are over 70 sex chromosomal abnormalities; that within the human population are numbers of persons with triple X, XYY, and single X chromosomal make-up—information with tremendous importance for human sexuality.[8] How can the biological sciences be both foundational and fallible? Because the findings of scientific research must be interpreted in order to be assembled into larger models of reality, and the human reason which performs the interpretation and assembly is fallible. Despite the large number of scientific experiments—flawlessly repeated—which demonstrated that humans who exhibited male body characteristics turned out to have XY chromosomal structure and humans who exhibited female body characteristics turned out to have XX chromosomal characteristics, it subsequently became clear that interpreting these as the only two patterns was not justified. We must always work on the basis of what we can know at the moment, recognizing that there may always be missing pieces which, when known, will significantly alter the general interpretation. But the very history of recent scientific work in sexuality should serve as a constant reminder that science is one, often fallible, tool for understanding creation, and not a method of defining, much less controlling in any final way, any aspect of God's dynamically developing creation.

In sexuality as well as other areas of human life, we must steer a course between, on the one hand, the human arrogance that causes unforeseen disasters by impelling intervention in systems incompletely understood, and on the other hand, a rigid refusal to accept the human role of co-creator through responsible intervention when necessary. At the present moment in the AIDS crisis, for example, the global community must resist the temptation to regard the pandemic as the hand of God at work in the world against which human efforts are both sacrilegious and ultimately doomed. At the same time the global community must resist two related temptations. The first is to assume the possibility of a technological fix which removes the need for rethinking and resocializing global patterns of sexuality. The second is to assume that since a technological fix is possible, any shortcuts to that fix can be morally justified, even morally required, despite their danger to specific communities.

The social sciences provide additional limits to moral reflection on sexuality: it is social science which has illustrated the tremendous influence of culture on sexuality, an influence which extends into every area of sexual organization and behavior, as well as determines understandings of the significance of sexuality and sexual relationship.[9] It is social science which has demonstrated the folly of assuming any universal, natural code of sexual morality.

Once we have discerned contemporary scientific consensus regarding the general parameters limiting the social construction of sexuality, we can begin to ask what reflection on our Christian experience has to say about sexuality. Christian experience is a broad, multifaceted reality which includes the experiences of the early church recorded in scripture, the teachings of later church communities and of theologians of different cultures and races up to the present, *as well as* the contemporary experience of people today all over the world.

Lisa Cahill, in *Between the Sexes*,[10] proposes four sources for a Christian sexual ethics: scripture, theological tradition, philosophical accounts of the human, and descriptive accounts of the lived reality of persons and societies. While I appreciate her nuanced understanding that none of these sources is either determinative or always primary, and that the weight of each source will change in particular cases depending on how its direction agrees with or diverges from those of the other sources, I am dissatified with the disproportionate weight given the traditional Christian religious sources. That is, the anti-sexual attitude of the Christian West permeates the theological and Christian philosophical traditions as well as much of the New Testament, and a related misogyny winds through these three and the Old Testament as well. The fourth source—"descriptive accounts of what is the case in human lives and societies"—is often too insufficiently developed to be able to counteract this inherited anti-sexual and/or misogynist bias in the other sources.

This fourth source is not precise enough. It collapses the most objective knowledge we have—e.g., of the human reproductive process—with the evaluations of individuals, of academic disciplines and professions, and of entire societies regarding the interpretation and value of sexual activity. We should not either absolutize science as the interpreter of sexuality, or treat science or scientific method as infallible. We must maintain an understanding of sexuality, and of human nature, as social constructions limited by biological/psychological realities. We must preserve a critical approach to the inevitable ideology present even in science, despite continuing popular and professional assumptions that science, both hard and soft science, is value-free. But Christian ethics cannot responsibly ignore or deny the general areas of scientific consensus regarding sexuality. Once those parameters are established, ethical reflection can proceed to discern "meaning"—to look at interpretations and evaluations of sexuality in scripture, in theological tradition, and in contemporary theological, philosophical, and literary, as well as general popular, thought. It seems incontestable that science—all the scientific disciplines together—has replaced philosophy as the privileged discipline for describing humanity, in this case human sexuality. Science is no more infallible than philosophy was in interpreting human sexuality, and the time may come when scientific understanding of humanity, like philosophy at the dawn of the scientific age, becomes less fruitful than other paths of investigation. But for the moment, despite the arrogance and presumption of contemporary science, despite all its limitations in defining the human, we are forced to acknowledge that the sciences have revolutionized human understanding of our sexuality in the twentieth century, and, at least for the present, continue to add more pieces than any other sources to the puzzle that is human sexuality.

Christian Experience Regarding Sexuality

In doing sexual ethics, or any other Christian ethics, we must be both consistent and explicit about our use of scripture. Most Christian ethicists, by training, turn to scripture as a primary resource in doing ethics. There are a number of different approaches to scripture among Christian ethicists and even some who seldom make explicit reference to scripture. Though it is possible to address sexuality meaningfully in Christian terms without reference to scriptural texts, and though a strong case can be made for scripture being largely unhelpful in sexual matters, I agree with Elisabeth Schüssler Fiorenza that popular attitudes toward scripture as revealed truth make it necessary to deal with scripture if one is to address the majority of Christians.[11] However, it is not enough to demand that ethicists address scripture in treating sexuality or other contemporary ethical matters. Frequently the only ethicists who clarify their approach to scripture are those specifically addressing the methodological relationship of scripture to ethics. Ethicists addressing other issues, about which scripture is a source, seldom explain what degree of authority they ascribe to scripture, or whether that authority is equally distributed among all texts, much less the justifcation for that authority or the criteria for discerning what is authoritative within specific texts. Some of this silence stems from a failure to comprehend the profound degree of ignorance about basic scriptural scholarship which characterizes the general Christian audience; many ethicists have so thoroughly absorbed scriptural criticism and have lived so long in universities and seminaries that they miscalculate the needs of their audience and thereby reinforce many of the very attitudes towards scripture which they oppose. Some ethicists select texts which support their particular interpretation; some ethicists survey scriptural texts dealing with their specific topic and point out problems with interpreting them or contradictions between them. Sometimes this latter involves limited exegesis demonstrating that the text has been misinterpreted or was influenced by prevailing customs of the time (as if all texts were not influenced by the culture and history out of which they emerged!). None of these approaches tackles the authority question directly; virtually all assume a "hermeneutics of consent," rather than the "hermeneutics of suspicion" which Elisabeth Schüssler Fiorenza suggests is appropriate in approaching scripture.[12] Most Christians tend to approach scripture as revealed truth and to assume that the truth scripture reveals is ordinarily self-evident. For this reason, when ethicists treat scripture as a primary source, but fail to make critical distinctions regarding the authority of scripture, they reinforce in the popular mind the tendency to revere all of scripture as revelatory.

Since the majority of scripture scholars seem to regard scripture as a kind of intricate historical and anthropological puzzle to be explored, and are impatient with demands that they discern what contemporary meaning can be found in scripture, ethicists must, for the most part, use a great deal of discernment in using scriptural scholarship. Nevertheless, scripture scholarship is far beyond the point where we can ignore the fact that scripture is not only revelatory, but also counter-revelatory. That is, there are clear scriptural messages which run counter to the character and will of the God we worship. This is a far more important issue than the evidence of historical inaccuracy in scripture, or the evidence of differing accounts of the same event, from creation to the accounts of the Resurrection. It is not enough to say that scripture is conditioned by the person and context of its writers. We need to admit that sometimes the scriptural authors/redactors and their communities either misinterpreted or completely reversed the content of God's revelation. It is not enough to point out that two texts contradict one another, for so strong is confidence in the revelatory character of scripture that audiences are fully capable of concluding that we are not able to reconcile the texts, but that such a task is possible, given another perspective or a more gifted interpreter. We need to connect contradictory texts to the conflicting acts they legitimate in order to demonstrate the necessity for choosing between the meanings of texts.

Arguably, sexuality is the area of ethics demanding the greatest clarification in order to show the general Christian audience that scripture is sometimes counter-revelatory, that not only are some direct scriptural imperatives and statements of theological fact mistaken but the message conveyed in countless stories is also false in terms of human experience of God. There can be little doubt that the authors of Genesis 34, Judges 19, and II Samuel 13 meant that the accounts of the rapes of Dinah, the Levite's concubine, and Tamar were to be a clear message to the reader that injury in Israel was to be avenged in order that God's justice prevail. Yet as Marie Fortune makes clear, the primary message of these passages conveyed to readers today, which was an unreflected assumption in the authors' societies, is that women were property whose welfare was not important in itself (for nothing was done to redress their loss).[13] The injury to the welfare of these women was important only as an affront to their male owners and their colleagues, who take revenge on the women's attackers. And today we wonder why it is necessary to counsel so many fathers and husbands of rape victims that their primary role is to deal with the hurts and fears of their daughters and wives, rather than to dedicate themselves to personal vendettas against the rapists?

Similarly, the author of Leviticus 18:6-18 presented the law against incest as one against sexual union with near kin, because that would be union with one's own flesh, a practice which was to distinguish the Canaanites from the Israelites. Yet when the author cites a long list of persons with whom a man is forbidden sexual congress, it includes not only his parents, his sisters, his aunts, and his granddaughters—his blood kin—but also his sisters-in-law, his daughters-in-law, and his aunts by marriage, none of whom are blood kin. However, Fortune notes that few commentators have noted that the list fails to mention a man's closest blood kin, his own sons and daughters, in the list of kin with which he is forbidden sexual congress.[14] As Fortune points out, the inclusions and omissions of the list are much better explained in terms of respect for the ownership rights of men over women and children than in terms of respect for the sexual integrity of near kin.[15] All those named in the list, though they may be under the practical control of the patriarch of an extended family (in the case of the patriarch's father, the father may be helpless and senile from old age), are nevertheless formally recognized as responsible to themselves as men or to some other man. The major effect of the incest taboo here was to limit the sexual prerogatives of the patriarch, and to protect the property of other men in the family. The emphasis given men's property rights in women and children and the general failure to attribute any sexual autonomy to women elsewhere in the Old Testament give indirect support to such an interpretation.

Judges 11 presents the unnamed daughter of Jephthah as pleasing to Yahweh because she agrees that she should be sacrificed to Yahweh to satisfy her father's vow in return for Yahweh's having allowed Jephthah's victory over the Ammonites.[16] When we fail to point to these stories, and to point out what acceptance of such stories as revelatory says about the character and will of the God they supposedly reveal, we promote idolatry—the worship of a false God.

Because of the patriarchy and misogyny which permeate scripture, it is crucial in sexual ethics that we do not merely select the more positive texts, or merely point out biblical texts which conflict with each other, but that we are clear that not all of scripture is revelatory, that some is counter-revelatory. This is as true of the New Testament as of the Hebrew Scriptures, as we shall see.

This need points to a second, closely connected proposal. We should not be surprised that a great deal of the theological tradition, as well as scripture, which deals directly with sexuality is not revelatory. Schüssler Fiorenza, dealing with women's leadership in the New Testament, suggests that it is the liberatory *practice* of the New Testament community, which the texts attempt to reverse, and not the practice urged by the texts themselves, which is revelatory.[17] This is a very effective way to deal with the issue of revelation regarding some scriptural issues. However, Schüssler Fiorenza never proposed universalizing this approach. The scriptural texts depicting women and children as property of men did not have that property status as the point of the texts, but as the taken-for-granted background of the texts. The intended messages of these texts did not concern the status of women and children, but rather concerned the status and relationships and rights of men vis-à-vis other men.   *but does this create a canon w/in a canon?*

The dismissal of texts as revelatory must be done on a text-by-text basis, but it is apparent to all persons not blinded by idolatrous, uncritical worship of scripture or theological tradition that both are permeated not only with patriarchy and misogyny but also with anti-sexual attitudes which are in conflict with the central messages of the gospel. James Nelson has made clear that the foundational meaning of the Incarnation—the complete unity of human and divine natures in the fully embodied Word—is nullified if we accept the Gnostic-influenced, anti-sexual attitudes of the Fathers and their theological successors.[18] The anti-body, anti-sexual attitudes which have predominated through most of Christian history are at curious odds with Christian insistence that Jesus Christ was fully human, born of a human mother, suffered bodily pain and death, and was bodily resurrected. One would expect that Christians, compared to other world religions, would be clearest about the goodness of the body and most accepting of embodied expressions of love.

Traditional acceptance of patriarchy and misogyny in the churches undermines both Jesus' insistence on a discipleship of service, not domination, as well as his parables and example establishing radical inclusivity as the symbol of the reign of God.[19] What records we have of Jesus tell us virtually nothing about his approach to sexuality, either personally or pedagogically, except for his radical openness to women which he demonstrated in the inclusion of women in his travelling band, contrary to the practices of the day (Lk. 8:1-3), in his inclusion of parables from women's activities such as housecleaning (Lk. 15:8-9) and baking bread (Mt. 13:33), in his refusing Martha's request to make Mary accept women's domestic role rather than join Jesus and the disciples (Lk. 10:38-42), and in his disregarding customs limiting women's social intercourse with males to family members (John 4:7-29, esp. 9 and 27). The later excessive weight given to sexuality—and to very negative approaches to sexuality—in Christian discipleship is not supported by what we know of the life and teachings of Jesus Christ.

I do not advocate setting aside the Christian sexual tradition on the grounds that it doesn't appeal to us today, or that it is historically conditioned. Of course it is historically conditioned, as is all scripture and theology, including our own. But we are compelled to jettison large parts of the Christian sexual tradition for two interconnected reasons.

First, large parts of the Christian sexual tradition are incompatible with the God we experience and worship. The discovery of such incompatibility has been the source of innumerable changes in the Christian tradition from its very beginning. In the Acts of the Apostles, for example, the apostles and elders of the church in Jerusalem were initially certain that Jesus' teaching that he had been sent to the Jews constrained the church to insist that the Gentiles convert to Judaism in order to become followers of Jesus. Nevertheless, they were later persuaded by arguments such as Peter's—that since faith was God's gift, and since their experience was that the gift of faith was already present among the Gentiles, *God* had evidently decided to admit Gentiles to the Christian community.[20] Experience is always open to fallible interpretation, but the bottom line is that experience is, and always has been, the most reliable source for discerning God's will. Today it is experience of sexuality within the contemporary church which has led many to question or reject those aspects of the Christian tradition which present sexuality as morally dangerous or sinful, devoid of the capacity to reveal God. In constructing ethical and theological arguments supporting such rejection of the anti-sexual tradition, equal stress should be given to the experiential basis of the rejection, rather than focusing exclusively on locating supportive texts from scripture or the classic theologians.

Rejection of anti-sexual attitudes in the tradition should not be primarily based on intra-traditional grounds (if it were, the rejection would have taken place centuries ago) but rather on positive experience of sexuality.

Secondly, internal contradiction, beginning with the New Testament itself, forces us to set aside large parts of the Christian tradition. There can be little doubt that contradiction exists between Gal. 3:28, "There is no longer Jew nor Greek, slave nor free, male and female, for you are all one in Christ Jesus," and the household code "Wives, be subject to your husbands as is fitting in the Lord. . . . Husbands, love your wives, and do not be harsh with them" (Col. 3:18). The first denies the difference which grounds dominant/subordinate relations, while the second reinforces those same dominant/subordinate relations. We must choose one or the other. When we deny the necessity of choosing between these contradictory texts, we transform Galatians' denial of difference into an affirmation of a romanticized, abstract, and non-relational equality which is not affected when some persons own, control, and use others.

In the same vein, contrast 1 Timothy 2:15, "Yet woman will be saved through childbearing," with Jesus' words in Luke 11:27-28, "As he said this, a woman in the crowd raised her voice and cried, 'Blessed is the womb that bore you, and the breasts that gave you suck!' " But he said, "Blessed rather are those who hear the word of God and keep it!" Women are saved either by the exercise of their reproductive function or by following the path of discipleship laid out by Jesus for men and women alike; these are clearly two very different claims. Again and again in scripture, and in subsequent theological tradition, texts conflict, and we must choose that which accords better with the overall message of the gospel as that gospel is experienced in our individual lives and in communities.

Experience often causes some radical revision in the interpretation of texts. For example, over the last 20 years in my own Roman Catholic church, there has been some very radical revision in the interpreted meaning of Luke 10:38-42, the story of Jesus' refusal to rebuke Mary for not joining Martha in the kitchen. For centuries, the prevailing Catholic interpretation was that Jesus was commending Mary's choice of a life of vowed contemplation (as a priest, brother, or sister) over Martha's choice of a life as a layperson amid the cares of the world.[21] Today the debate over women's roles in contemporary society is so extensive that it is difficult to miss this story's message about the inclusion of women in discipleship. There is also a greater awareness that Jesus rejected John the Baptist's ascetic withdrawal from the world as a model for ministry, and understood withdrawal from the world, as in his temptation in the desert, or his periodic fleeing from the crowds, as moments of preparation for ministry.[22] Jesus went from town to town, and to Jerusalem itself, seeking out the popular masses. He made himself available to the sick, and sent out his disciples to heal and to teach in the towns and villages. Neither Jesus' Jewish society nor the records we have of Jesus' life and teaching placed great value on a life devoted to solitary prayer and contemplation to the exclusion of service to concrete human persons.

As our world and our experience continue to change, there will doubtless be other, new interpretations of the meanings of scriptural texts. Every generation must reinterpret scripture anew, and that reinterpretation includes weighing the value of scriptural texts.

A New Theological Framework for Sexuality

In addition to clarifying a more critical approach to the authority of scripture and theological tradition, Christian sexual ethics needs to rethink its framework for evaluating sexuality. The Christian tradition on sexuality has centered on individual sexual acts, specifically on sexual acts regarded as sinful, and consequently has failed to reflect on the meaning of sexuality itself and its revelatory meaning for humans.

Though ethicists have agreed for years that sexual ethics should be more "relation-centered" and not so "act-centered,"[23] all but a few texts[24] and courses in Christian sexual ethics remain largely structured around acts. Though the treatment of sexual acts—premarital sex, masturbation, homosexuality, contraception, and adultery—has changed a great deal over the past quarter century, even many liberal authors have found it difficult to break from the format of traditional treatment.[25] Even when this format adds a chapter on marital sex which attempts to develop a Christian sexual theology, a chapter on conscience development, and perhaps even a chapter on changing understandings of women and/or sexuality itself,[26] the overall *framework* still suggests that it is the physical structure of the act or the status of those engaged in the act, rather than the qualitative nature of the relationship in which the act occurs, or the motives emerging from that relationship or lack of it, or the consequences of the act on persons, which determine the morality of the act. This approach is responsible in part for the moral blindness of Christian societies regarding practices such as marital rape, for the implication of this approach is that if a licit sexual act (male-female vaginal intercourse) occurs within the properly sanctioned contractual relationship (marriage), there can be no sin. The implication that marital sex is never problematic contributes to a widespread callousness about the quality of marital sex which causes society to ignore the seriousness of not only sexual violence in marriage but also sexual dysfunction.

Additionally problematic is the fact that most of the acts upon which the tradition has focused have been regarded as sinful, for such a focus implicitly teaches sexual moral minimalism, i.e., that virtue in sexuality consists of avoiding these specific sexual acts. This moral minimalism gives no guidance in or opportunities for reflection on sexual virtue as the process of constructing sexual relations, genital and non-genital, which are just, loving, and promotive of individual and social growth.

But even if we could avoid teaching moral minimalism in teaching sexual ethics as structured by sexual sins, the traditional list of sexual sins is woefully inadequate, both in what is included, and in what is excluded. For example, the typical table of contents includes chapters on masturbation, contraception, nonmarital sex, adultery, abortion, and homosexuality. Yet, as many authors point out, both social science research and the general rejection of procreationism among Christians beginning with the 1930 Lambeth Conference have undermined traditional theological objections to both masturbation and homosexuality. Social science research reveals genital self-stimulation beginning in infancy (by eight months) and extending through adolescence in the majority of humans.[27] In addition, there is evidence both that masturbation is relatively absent in infants and children deprived of affectionate touch and personal care,[28] and that persons who have never masturbated are much more likely to have sexual dysfunction problems in sexual relationships.[29] Since most Christian churches have accepted the use of artificial contraception, and most Christians within churches which ban artificial contraception (principally the Roman Catholic) reject that ban, the fact that masturbation is sexual activity without possibility of procreation—the foundational objection in the tradition—is not compelling.

Similarly with homosexuality. The agreement within medical and social science that sexual orientation is not chosen but more commonly discovered[30] absolves homosexual orientation of sinfulness, and calls into question not only the judgment that homosexual activity is deliberately and defiantly chosen activity, but also the unnaturalness of homosexual acts for those with homosexual orientation. Again, for the tradition, unnaturalness was determined almost exclusively on the basis of procreative possibility; but given the general acceptance of deliberately contraceptive heterosexual coitus, to ban homosexual acts on the grounds that they cannot be procreative when non-procreative heterosexual sex is accepted would be unjust discrimination.

But the greatest problem with the traditional list of sexual sins is its brevity. A truly relational perspective on sexual sin would both greatly expand the list and divide it into two categories, individual and social.

In other areas of ethics and moral theology, we recognize two general categories of sin. Just as liberation theology has taught us to recognize both structural violence (the social denial to the poor of basic human needs) and violent individual and group responses to that structural violence,[31] traditional Christian theology posits the existence of original sin, an inescapable predisposition to sin among humans, as well as individual sin, often called actual sin. Many contemporary treatments of original sin suggest that the tendency to commit individual sin may best be understood as the result of the fact that all humans are born into a particular society which is already permeated by sin.[32] Original sin, sometimes called social sin, or the sin of the world, is socialized into us as we learn our world, as we learn to speak a language, to interact with different persons and groups, to accept a specific role in society. Born into a society permeated with racism, sexism, poverty, and violence, we learn varying degrees of complacency toward, and come to accept, these realities; that acceptance, once socialized into us, forms the groundwork for our committing overt acts of sin. In sexuality, too, original sin is present in our world. Patriarchy, misogyny, the related evils of homophobia and heterosexism,[33] and alienation from and disdain for the body and sexuality are forms which original sin takes in the sexual context. They set the scene for the innumerable varieties of overt acts of sexual sin. Our baptism into a church community which is pledged to recognize and resist sin in the world is supposed to free us from bondage to original sin, but baptism's effectiveness depends upon the church community recognizing the specific forms that original sin takes, teaching individual members to resist, and supporting their resistance to that sin.

Our churches have not done a great job at recognizing sexual sin. Parents who disown a child who has gathered the courage to disclose to them his/her homosexual orientation are overtly responding to their learned homophobia. Is the severing of the intimate bond that binds parent and child any less grievous than that of the spouse who commits adultery? If sin is a distancing of the individual from God, do such parents not distance themselves from God, our loving parent? But many of our churches encourage just this form of sexual sin.

It is unconscionable that many forms of sexual violence are omitted from most textual and sermonic treatments of sexual sin, and that some are not even recognized as sinful within the tradition. Fourteen percent of wives in our society are victimized by marital rape,[34] to which our tradition is blind. Between one half and three quarters of working women in our society report sexual harassment in their jobs,[35] but the law has been quicker to recognize both of these as sexual evils than have the churches. Even sexual sins recognized by the Christian tradition are often excluded from many texts in sexual ethics. By ignoring rape, child incest, and child sexual abuse in teaching sexual sin, the implication arises that masturbation and adultery, which are treated, are more serious sins than these sins of sexual violence, as does the implication that these acts of sexual violence are rare, exceptional occurrences. But in our society, between 4% and 5% of young girls are the victims of incest by fathers,[36] between one third and one half of women are victims of attempted or completed rape,[37] and one in nine boys, and one in four girls, are sexually abused.[38]

There can be no doubt that the blindness of sexual ethics texts to sexual violence is rooted in the same original sin that leads to sexual violence itself, namely the patriarchal and misogynist understanding of sex as an inherently dominant/subordinate relation, with women and children assumed to be natural subordinates. Until we enlarge our treatment of sexual sin from individual overt acts to include a critique of social models and institutions which give rise to them, our understanding of sexual sin will remain deficient.

Social Silence on Sexuality as Original Sin

Recognizing socio-sexual forms of sin as original sin also allows us to see society's treatment of sexuality itself as a form of sexual sin. The overwhelming majority of our society is immensely ignorant about sexuality, and this ignorance victimizes many. Many sexual problems, including sexually transmitted diseases, unwanted pregnancy, and sexual dysfunction are often due to ignorance. Is this ignorance sinful? The popular Christian tendency to recognize as sinful only those acts for which individuals are responsible and to see ignorance as removing responsibility for individual actions—the tendency to focus on subjective rather than objective sin—has blinded us to the sinfulness involved in some types of sexual ignorance. Sexual ignorance in our society is not necessary—the information is known. Yet the October 1989 Kinsey Institute survey, released September 5, 1990, on sexuality in the U.S. found that only 20% of the American public could answer correctly 12 of 18 basic sexual questions on topics such as: when females can become pregnant; how AIDS is contracted; normal penis size; the effects of menopause on sexual desire; and who needs gynecological exams or self-exams of testicles.[39] All the information covered in the survey is basic for making informed decisions regarding both personal sexual health and behavior and for decisions on public policy in sexuality. Unnecessary sexual ignorance is *chosen* in our society—by school systems which fear parental opposition more than student ignorance,[40] by churches which see sexual ignorance as evidence of virtue, and by parents, themselves ignorant, who fear that sexual education may lead their children to sexual attitudes and choices different from their parents'. While 60-80% of American adults favor sex education in general,[41] public school administrators indicate that opposition from the community is the greatest obstacle to effective sex education programs.[42] How is this so? While active opposition to sex education in general is limited to a small group of conservative Americans often linked to conservative churches, the majority of parents are concerned about whose values will be taught in sex education programs. Some would prefer no sex education if the values to be taught are not those of the parents. Reflecting this agreement about the need for sex education and the fear of criticism, 75% of large urban school districts in the U.S. do have sex education programs, but only one in ten, for example, includes treatment of fertility, pregnancy, and contraception before the high school level,[43] despite the rising levels of pregnancy among grade school and junior high girls.[44]

Many people disagree that our society is silent about sex. They insist that sex is glorified and depicted in movies, television, billboards, magazines, and newpapers. And it is. Sexual activity is celebrated as the human activity necessary to personal development, the only reliable source of intimacy, as the highest, most satisfying pleasure available (outside illegal drugs). But despite this distorted celebration of sexual activity, society does little to promote the goal of mutual pleasure in sexuality; nor does society promote the goals of bonding and intimacy, which typically are associated only with sex. Just as important, our society fails to help persons understand under what circumstances sexual relationships (and not just sexual activity) can fulfill even broader human needs and desires, such as the desire for identity, community, and purpose. Romantic exaltation of sex is not sexual information—it is a destructive evasion of the need to critically evaluate meaning in sexuality. Such evaluation requires adequate information.

There *is* a social silence around sex—a silence that encourages, among other problems, sexual dysfunction. Sexual dysfunction refers to difficulties people experience in responding to sexual stimulation and experiencing orgasm. Sexual dysfunction affects between a third and a half of all persons to varying degrees.[45] And the majority of all dysfunctions are rooted in ignorance. Anorgasmia, the absence of orgasm, affects about a quarter of all women.[46] Though it has a number of causes, most anorgasmia can be easily cured either by simply explaining to women that orgasm is both natural and normal for women as well as for men, or by additionally describing to women and their sexual partners some common techniques for female arousal.[47] Both anorgasmia and painful intercourse are often the result of ignorance of the process of sexual arousal in females, especially the roles of the clitoris and vaginal lubrication in female arousal.

Male impotence is also tremendously aggravated by ignorance. Most initial male impotence is entirely normal—that is, a result of tiredness, depression, problems within the sexual relationship, or minor health problems. Such impotence is temporary, often lasting only hours or days. But in a society which implies that men should always be ready for sex, lack of erection is a failure of masculinity, and temporary impotence raises anxiety, sometimes in both partners; this anxiety then puts such pressure on the male to achieve erection that impotence may become a repeated occurrence, each incident increasing anxiety.

The most common male sexual dysfunction, premature ejaculation,[48] occasionally affects as many as one half of men, and regularly affects one quarter of them.[49] There is general agreement that one important cause of premature ejaculation is the climate, often characterized by fear and secrecy, in which most adolescent male sexual activity occurs. That is, both the masturbatory experiences of boys and the early coital experiences of many young men occur in a climate which leads young men to learn to ejaculate quickly, for fear of discovery. This haste can become habitual over the years, and makes learning ejaculatory control difficult in later relationships.[50]

Sexual dysfunction is not a minor problem in sexual relationships such as marriage. Shared sexual activity in marriage functions not only as a symbol of love, but can also recreate and deepen love through its affirmation, celebration, and sharing of love.[51] The inability to fully share oneself or to receive the physical gift of the other often strains relationships and can distance the lovers by calling into question the existence of mutual love. It can be the cause of a great deal of suffering, much of which is unnecessary.

Sexual dysfunction is only one part of the unnecessary sexual suffering caused by continued social ignorance of sexuality. Much of our sex education for children is too little, too late. In mistaken attempts to protect the innocence of children from contamination by information about sex, we ensure that the majority of children, who in our society receive no sex information from parents,[52] risk reaching menarche, nocturnal emissions, or other signs of puberty without any understanding of the changes through which their bodies are moving.[53] As of 1990, only 22 states and the District of Columbia mandate any teaching of sexuality in the public schools.[54] However, researchers at the Alan Guttmacher Institute concluded that only three states—New Jersey, New York, and Wisconsin—and the District of Columbia have what can be construed as an adequate program on sex education and AIDS education.[55]

When my colleagues and I have presented grade school sex education programs, there are always one or two girls who cry with relief that their bleeding is "only" menarche, and not some fatal disease they were afraid to mention to anyone. Some, already sexually active, have mistaken ideas about the conditions under which one can become pregnant: for example, that one can only become pregnant from intercourse during menstruation, or never the first time, or not if one's partner withdraws, or not if one douches afterward. There are always a few boys relieved to have nocturnal emission explained to them, some of whom have been punished by ignorant mothers who assumed they had been masturbating in bed. Many young people do not understand the changes in their bodies during puberty, due both to lack of adequate information and to failure to make the information which is provided both clearly relevant and understandable. Those who *are* exposed to sex education in schools often find that it is excessively clinical, not designed to center on the questions and problems children and adolescents have about sex, aimed at whites rather than non-whites, and especially at white females,[56] and presented by teachers who are loath to lead open discussion due both to personal discomfort with sex and to fear of parental backlash if the students take information and questions home. There are small boys whose genital growth is years ahead of the rest of their body, who worry that they will always be out of proportion, or the reverse, boys whose weight and height double, but whose secondary sexual characteristics are late. We allow them to fret, as we do those girls who are very early or especially late to menarche and breast growth. There is hardly an area touching sexuality where our society provides adequate information, and that includes childbirth and all areas of parenting. We often hear of ignorance and fear about pregnancy and childbirth among *teen* mothers, but our society does not include instruction in pregnancy and childbirth in the information we consider necessary for adult life in our society. Most childbirth classes which are available are designed for those already knowledgeable enough to be desirous of specific forms of natural (non-anesthetized) childbirth. The general assumption that childbirth and child-rearing are instinctive in women not only supports the absence of childbirth information in most sex education classes but also disinclines many pregnant women from pursuing the instruction which is available. It is impossible to avoid concluding that in our society sexual information is obtained largely by chance. Children of sexually ignorant or silent parents, in school systems with poor or nonexistent sex education programs, without the health resources of the middle class, will grow up to have sexually ignorant children like themselves.

Is this sin? That depends, in part, on how we understand sin and how we understand sexuality. If sexuality truly is a part of the creation that God pronounced good, if all creation, including sexuality, offers the possibility of mediating God to us, and if shared human touch, genital expressions of love and commitment, and the birthing and rearing of children all can demonstrate the same self-disclosing gift of self which we worship in our God, then brokenness in sexual relations implies some brokenness in our relationship with God—a classical definition of sin.

We cannot assume that where there is sin there will also be an individual sinner, a person who consciously chooses to break with God. We could, of course, call such phenomena as poor socialization around sexuality "evil" and not "sin." We often do this in situations where we recognize disvalue but cannot point to individual sinners. The problem is that this category of disvalue for which there are no identifiable sinners tends to be understood as natural and non-moral. Floods, earthquakes, and epidemics cause suffering, have victims, and are easily characterized as evil. Often, in order to achieve some greater good, we choose to endure or to inflict on another some smaller suffering, but we do not understand ourselves as sinners. The problem with adding deficient sexual socialization to this category of physical or pre-moral evils is that such socialization is neither beyond human control nor is there proportionate reason for enduring it. What greater good does social silence about sexuality achieve? All human activity which causes unnecessary suffering without producing any greater good should be understood as sinful.

Within a critical reflection on contemporary sexual ethics we also need to reject as sinful procreationism, the understanding that the primary or exclusive purpose of sexual activity is procreation. As we shall see in the following chapter, procreationsim has been, despite popular opinion to the contrary, embedded in our society's basic understandings of sexuality; it is not at all an exclusively Catholic phenomenon. Because procreationism focuses moral attention on the ability of a sexual act to procreate, rather than on the dignity and welfare of the actor(s) or the relational context in which the sexual act occurs, cultural procreationism in the West has supported a kind of moral blindness to issues of sexual coercion, coital pain, and particularly conjugal domination and violence.[57]

Sexualizing Theology

In the area of sexuality, the churches have a long-term task of developing a sexual theology, which is considerably more than the theology of sexuality that Norman Pittenger began demanding two decades ago.[58] That task involves a sexualizing of Christian theology itself. We must not only discern God's intentions for human sexuality but we must also integrate our sexual experience into our broader human experience, which is our principal resource for discerning who God is and how God works in our world.

We cannot begin now with sexualizing theology in the churches, for theology is always done out of experience, and the sexual experience of many, if not most, Christians is still not only repressed but incorporates a variety of destructive beliefs and practices. Generalized acceptance of dominant/subordinate relations between men and women in much of the world, for example, results in popular masculinizing of the Godhead, just as negative attitudes toward sexual activity historically resulted in insistence on the virgin birth of Jesus and, in Catholicism, on the perpetual virginity of Mary and her immaculate conception, as well as in widespread social veneration of the hymen.

The initial task in the churches is to concentrate on sexual ethics. The churches need to point out both the contradictions within traditional Christian sexual ethics and the unacceptable messages we convey about our God in the sexual rules and attitudes we attribute to that God. Furthermore, the churches need to help people to draw on their own personal and communal experiences in making choices concerning revelation and sexuality. Only after that task is somewhat advanced can we begin to expect that the Christian community, as a whole, can both continue the social transformation of sexual relationships and theologize from their lived sexual lives.

This is, of course, not the way most of us were taught to understand the interaction between theology and ethics. We learned that theology comes first, and that ethics is deduced from theology. There are two problems with such a deductive approach to ethics: 1) it assumes what has not always been the case in Christianity—that the theology from which ethics is deduced was itself constructed out of reflection of the whole community on their lived experience of God, and 2) it ignores the fact that since ethics is more closely linked to practice than is theology, that ethics is likely to follow changed practice more quickly than does theology. If the Christian community can free itself from captivity to its theological and ethical tradition and experience more egalitarian, intimate marriages, more humane sex roles in society, the validation of sexual pleasure, the ability to choose parenthood for the sake of loving children, and the appreciation—neither oppression nor mere tolerance—of gays and lesbians both for their distinctive individual gifts and for the insights their experience and perspective shed on humankind and God, then the people of God may discover that sexualizing theology radically revises many central Christian doctrines, often in ways that none of us now perceive.

Such a move goes far beyond the need to revive casuistry in order to revitalize ethics, as proposed by Jonsen and Toulmin,[59] for it is not our ability to deal with exceptional cases which is currently at stake in sexuality, but the basic principles and paradigms of the Christian sexual tradition. Jonsen and Toulmin suggest that case studies can multiply the exceptions to inherited moral theological principles, maxims, and paradigms so as to call into question those very principles, maxims, and paradigms. There can be little doubt that since the 1960s American Christians have been engaged in just such casuistry, and academic, ecclesiastical, and popular literature has been filled with case studies which collectively called into question the traditional sexual teachings of the Christian churches. Some of these challenged teachings include sexual complementarity, procreation as a primary purpose of sex, the covenant model of marriage, the two-in-one-flesh image, Christian love as limitless self-sacrifice, and the dualistic vision of human virtue as the victory of the rational soul over the desires of the corrupted body. For Catholic Christians, two additional teachings challenged are the venereal pleasure principle, and the teaching that all sexual sins are grave sins. All of these teachings are now resisted by many American Christians on the basis of reflection on experience. Barring drastic reinterpretation, these teachings will eventually end in the theological dust bin. This is not to say that these teachings were never valuable insights, that they were never revelatory.

It is only to say that, given the socioeconomic and political structures of contemporary life in the Western developed world, such teachings no longer appear to contribute to the justice, health, and well-being of human society. It is becoming clear that within these circumstances the experience of true sexual intimacy offers great insights into God's love, one of which is that divine love is much better imaged by the Trinity than by the biblical covenant between Israel and Yahweh. The covenant is better viewed as a primitive understanding of how God's love operates, a model which was dependent upon human experience with feudal lords and vassals in the ancient Near East. Certainly it makes no sense to explain that marital love is like the love between the members of the Trinity—self-disclosing love between equals whose intimacy overflows onto the whole of creation—and *also* like the exclusive dominant/subordinate covenant of Yahweh and Israel. Within biblical history, the Israelites came to understand that their relationship with Yahweh had outgrown the contractual *quid pro quo* structure of covenant. This is one reason why the bride/groom analogy for the covenant developed: to open covenant to greater possibilities for intimacy. Surely thousands of years later we could do better than covenant to explain our most intimate human relationships.

James Nelson has effectively argued that taking human sexuality seriously will allow us to appreciate the Incarnation in fuller, more meaningful terms, and also to grapple more adequately with the significance of resurrection for human lives.[60] I expect that there is no area of Christian theology which will not be somehow affected. We are coming to understand that *all* of the ways that we respond to God's free gift of love and salvation are responses of our embodied sexual selves—whether they are prayer, community worship, feeding the hungry, or cherishing our children. This developing understanding in turn sheds greater light on Jesus' linkage of the two great commands, to love God and to love our neighbor. The demise, in our thought, of the disembodied, non-sexual, spiritual soul-self (as opposed to a physical, temporal self) and of the exclusive right of the spiritual self to commune with God will give new dignity and worth to all aspects of corporal life, including sexuality.

As Christians transform sexual understanding and practice we may discover that one of our deepest Christian problems is our understanding of self. Jesus' command to love our neighbor as we love ourselves does not shed any new light on how we are to love ourselves, much less on how we are to understand ourselves. It assumes that we already know. But how should we understand the self? To look at texts on Christian marriage today is to find many contradictory treatments of self within the same text, all of them proclaimed as Christian. This is not only a semantic issue. For example, Gallagher, Maloney, Rousseau, and Wilcszak in their *Embodied in Love* make the following claims about marital love: 1) it is giving oneself to the spouse; 2) it is abandoning and emptying oneself; 3) it is sharing oneself with the spouse; and 4) it is developing a mature individual self.[61] These are not merely different phrases for the same thing. They imply radically different, even contradictory things. These authors are not singular in their inability to decide whether the self is positive or negative, whether the self should be obliterated and replaced or developed and cherished, or whether the self should be given away or only disclosed to those we love. When our tradition speaks of self it is not clear whether the self is truly us, or only some false front which makes us seem different and unique from other selves. I believe that ambiguous Christian attitudes towards the body—and the desires that we commonly associate with the body—are one important source for this ambivalence. Ambivalence regarding the self must create some ambivalence in discerning how that self should relate to God and neighbor. Such a regrounding of Christian sexual ethics as is currently under way will require a great deal of creativity as well as courage. Paradigm shifts, unfortunately, are not easy or comfortable, and those who promote them are all too often persecuted.

2. *Ending Procreationism*

One of the most serious enduring obstacles to a sexual ethic which is humane, just, and protects both human and non-human creation is procreationism. Procreationism is the assumption that sex is naturally oriented toward creation of human life. This assumption remains central to most Western cultural understandings of sexual activity. Most Christians assume that procreationism is a Roman Catholic problem. Because artificial contraception has been accepted by one Protestant denomination after another over the decades, since the Anglicans at the Lambeth Conference of 1930 permitted the use of contraceptives in abnormal cases, it is generally assumed that procreationism has been overcome in Protestantism. But procreationism is a much broader and deeper phenomenon than a ban on the use of artificial contraceptives, and it is embedded in Western history and culture in ways of which we are scarcely conscious. There are at least three major areas in which procreationism is apparent in our society.

The first is the common understanding that coitus is *the* sexual act, with all other sexual practices understood as either perversions to be avoided, or foreplay designed to prepare for the "real" sex act. The limitation of "real sex" to penile-vaginal intercourse has no other explanation than the assumption that "real sex" is procreative: penile-vaginal intercourse is the only procreative sexual act. In our society this understanding of penile-vaginal intercourse as the "real thing" is so pervasive as to be taken for granted. Some sex manuals, much of the electronic media, and even many medical institutions and personnel treat penile-vaginal intercourse as the "main event" and describe all else as "foreplay." Many therefore take for granted that when penile-vaginal sex is not possible/advisable, sex is ruled out altogether. Immediately after childbirth or abdominal surgery, during heavy menstrual flow, in the absence of contraceptive protection, during drug therapy which reduces erection, and in many other situations as well, much of our society understands that abstinence is required. The fact that many sexual activities are possible which do not require vaginal penetration by an erect penis is ignored. The general assumption is that such activities are not and cannot be ultimately satisfying in themselves, because they are designed only as preludes to the real thing.

The second problem with procreationism is that it denigrates sexual relationships in which coitus is not possible. From a procreationist perspective, lesbians do not have real or legitimate sex, but "only" foreplay, because real/legitimate sex requires an impregnating penis. Furthermore, this attitude is the foundation of two common pieces of misinformation about gays and lesbians: that the primary gay sexual activity is anal intercourse, and that lesbian sex centers on the use of dildos. In fact, anal intercourse is a distant third after fellatio and mutual masturbation in terms of regular sexual practice among gay men.[1] Dildos are even rarer among lesbians; their use is a distinct minority practice.[2]

This understanding of penile-vaginal intercourse as the only real sex is also a source of a great deal of unnecessary sexual deprivation among the handicapped[3] and the elderly.[4] Persons incapable of coitus—or thought to be incapable of coitus—such as the very elderly, wheelchair patients, amputees, paraplegics, and those left impotent by disease or injury, are often viewed as asexual and treated as such. Among the elderly, some persons give up on sex as not appropriate after female menopause. As erection becomes less full/reliable and traditional positions for intercourse become too demanding for stiff joints and weak muscles, many of the elderly are subtly and not so subtly coerced into unnecessarily giving up sex altogether rather than adapting sexual practice to those activities still possible and pleasurable. This is true for the physically handicapped of any age. The failure to instruct the handicapped in ways to give and receive sexual pleasure not only deprives them, but has contributed to a great deal of unnecessary stress and suffering within their relationships and would-be relationships.

The third area in which procreationism exhibits itself in our society concerns attitudes towards contraception. Especially among the unmarried, procreationism too easily supports an undertanding of children as the "cost" of sex.[5] This understanding encourages sexual activity without contraception as more moral than sex with contraception, even when conception is neither desired nor advisable, and thus encourages irresponsible parenthood. Some unwilling parents, caught in such a situation, feel that the resulting children owe parents for the inconvenience of their rearing.

If coitus is to be a couple's preferred method of making love, it should be so because it conveys greater mutual pleasure and satisfaction, and/or because the couple is consciously trying to conceive. But it should not be assumed that because coitus can be reproductive, it is therefore the most pleasurable, natural, or appropriate act, as procreationism has implied.

None of this sexual deprivation, discrimination, or contraceptive risk is necessary or justifiable. We have a growing body of research that demonstrates that penile-vaginal intercourse is not the only avenue to sexual satisfaction, and may not even be the most effective avenue to sexual satisfaction, especially in women. Women report that masturbation produces stronger orgasms than penile-vaginal intercourse,[6] and lesbian women report higher rates of orgasm than heterosexual women.[7] Furthermore, between 56% and 70% of women cannot reach orgasm from penile-vaginal intercourse alone.[8] They require direct clitoral stimulation either in cunnilingus or through manual manipulation in order to reach orgasm.

Some men report that their most frequent sexual fantasy is not of penile-vaginal intercourse, but of fellatio.[9] Research shows that fellatio is the most common fantasy of male college students, *even during penile-vaginal intercourse.*[10] Among men, the most frequently purchased sexual service in massage parlors (and from many streetwalkers) is fellatio,[11] though coitus is more common with call girls and prostitutes in brothels.

Many different sexual activities have the capacity both to arouse and satisfy sexual desire, and to provide shared pleasure and the intimacy and bonding which can accompany such shared sexual pleasure. For most persons, the major disincentive to engaging in alternative sexual activities is negative attitudes strongly influenced by prevailing cultural procreationism. In an age when a majority of persons needs to seek protection not only from unwanted pregnancy but also from sexually transmitted diseases, "outercourse" (nonpenetrating sexual activities) and other non-coital sexual activities should be promoted.

Another major indication of the continued presence of procreationism in Christian teaching is located in the sexual ethic taught even by those churches which accept artificial contraception—that is, the continued ban on nonmarital sex. Procreationism is the only support for this traditional ban. Traditional Christian sexual ethics, based in both scriptural stories and law on the one hand, and natural law interpretations on the other, predicated that sex was made for the purpose of procreation, and therefore sex belonged in marriage, where the marital union could provide for the needs of children conceived. All sex outside marriage was forbidden as irresponsible in that it either neglected the needs of children or ignored the will of God who both made sex produce children and desired the welfare of those children.

Given both effective contraception and acceptance of other ends for sex than procreation, traditional reasons for limiting sex to marriage are no longer compelling. Theoretically, then, we would have to find other reasons to prohibit sex between unmarried persons, whether that sexual activity was homosexual or heterosexual, solitary sex, as in masturbation, or noncoital sex for the married or unmarried. The continuation by the churches of traditional bans on all nonmarital sex without the construction of new arguments indicates a not-so-covert procreationism.

Separating Sex and Procreation

We need to shift from the traditional inseparability of sex and procreation, which the Roman Catholic Church and a very few others continue to officially teach,[12] to the development of a new sexual ethic distinct from a reproductive ethic. This is not to say that sex and reproduction should be completely severed. Human sexual activity, and not technological intervention, should be the primary method of human reproduction for a number of reasons, as we shall see. But the general direction in which humanity needs to move is toward more pleasurable, spiritually fulfilling, frequent sex, coupled with a reduction in world population. I am not going to fully develop a new reproductive ethic here, but only sketch some preliminary suggestions for a reproductive ethic compatible with the reconstructed sexual ethic on which I will concentrate.

Toward a New Reproductive Ethic

There are tremendous dangers in this area of reproductive ethics. To raise the topic of population stabilization—much less reduction—in a global context is to evoke immediate and forceful critical response. Much of that response arises from the developing world and from subordinated races and classes in the developed world. In the nations of the developing world the history of developed nations'—especially the United States'—involvement in the population issue is well known and resented. That involvement can be divided into three stages according to the dominant motivations invoked in the developed nations: cold war, developmentalism, and environmentalism.[13] It was originally during the 1950s and 1960s that the U.S. began committing funds to poor nations to control fertility, with the object of controlling poverty, lest conditions of increasing poverty further destabilize those nations and make them susceptible to communist propaganda. Since the primary purpose of the population control measures (preventing population explosion, consequent poverty, and communist influence) was external to the individuals in the poor nations, it is not surprising that their dignity, aspirations, and customs were not central to the development of the population programs. The goals of developed nations (thwarting the spread of Communism, which was understood to flourish in poverty) matched well with the goals of many poor governments (lowering birth rates so as to contain social expenditures). These goals were often most efficiently ensured by massive campaigns for inexpensive, permanent means of contraception such as sterilization, often using coercion at the local level, rather than by methods which could be controlled by individuals themselves in response to their specific circumstances.

In the second phase of the developed world's export of population control measures from the late 1960s through the end of the 1970s developmentalism was the rationale given for population control in the poorer nations. Here the eradication rather than the control of poverty was the goal. The process of First World development was thought to be understood, and it was assumed that poorer nations were moving along the same continuum of economic development that the richer nations had moved along, but were only delayed. The perceived need was to move the poorer nations more rapidly along the continuum by attempting to create the conditions which had produced economic progress in the richer nations. The history of the Industrial Revolution showed that both expanding industry through investment and a falling birth rate had been central to the growth of prosperity. So U.S. developmental policy, called developmentalism, focused on huge commercial loans to poor countries for the purpose of industrializing, and on programs to lower the high birth rates characteristic of agricultural nations.[14]

While developmentalism seemed to be more aimed at benefitting the poorer nations themselves, containing Communism continued to be an important motive for U.S. involvement. From the late 1960s until the late 1980s the cold war, while in a new stage, was not over, and the U.S. was still concerned about creating sufficient prosperity in the developing world so as to shield against communist inroads. In addition, developmentalism gave the U.S. economic interests in these nations as well, since U.S. banks, and to a lesser extent the U.S. government itself, were heavily invested in the success of developmentalist policy. Especially in the case of poor nations in Latin America and the Caribbean, the U.S. also hoped that home-grown opportunities and prosperity would over time cut down on immigration pressures on the U.S., and especially on illegal immigration. The consequent failure to focus on the needs and aspirations of the local populations allowed and even encouraged abuse in contraceptive provision, including coercion and lack of informed consent.[15] Many governments of poor nations deliberately used U.S.-funded population control programs to force sterilizations on large portions of the population, regardless of the age or parental status of individuals.[16] In other nations the provision of follow-up medical care for sterilizations and for invasive contraceptives, such as IUDs, was practically nonexistent; in some programs basic sanitary and hygienic protections were absent. Even more common was the use of emergency food distribution, employment, or other life necessities to coerce persons into the programs.

Developmentalism has been largely discredited for a number of reasons. First and foremost, it did not fulfill its purposes. What growth occurred was distributed to the already privileged classes, and in many nations the poor majorities actually became more impoverished during the periods of greatest economic growth.[17] But developmentalism not only failed to alleviate individual poverty for the majority of citizens in the developing world—it also failed to alleviate *national* poverty in the nations of what was called the Third World. Due to external debt, most developing nations are in far worse situations today than they were at the beginning of the developmentalist period, despite the fact that many of them did significantly reduce their birth rates.[18] A basic failure of developmentalist policy was that it ignored the population base and its connection to agriculture, especially the need to make smallholder agriculture more productive as a precondition for industrialization. For these and a number of other reasons, including corruption, graft, and diversion of loan funds to other governmental uses such as military hardware, the huge loans that poor countries floated to finance industrialization did not have the desired effect.[19] Because the loans did not produce economic growth, nations were not able to pay them off. Today terrifically high external debt burdens are the number one economic drag on poor nations—the legacy of developmentalism.[20]

The newest First World rationale for birth limitation programs in the developing world is environmental concern.[21] The environment is now cited as a basic reason for birth limitation programs not only in some population journals,[22] but even in medical literature.[23] From the point of view of many peoples of the developing world, First World interests in birth control in the poor world have been self-serving,[24] and this latest cause for First World interest is no exception. The First World position gets argued like this to developing nations like Brazil: "The earth has reached the level of population that it can afford. We in the developed world have just about reached a replacement-only birth rate, but yours is much higher. As your population expands, you progressively destroy the Amazon jungle, which provides a major part of the earth's oxygen and contains a significant proportion of all the plant and animal species on the face of the earth.[25] Every new factory or electric plant you build spews more carbon dioxide, sulfur, and other polluting chemicals into an atmosphere that has already reached its limit. You do not have the right to endanger the survival of the entire planet by irresponsibly expanding your present levels of pollution in order to accommodate either a larger population or a higher standard of living."

But from the Brazilian point of view, the same argument sounds like this: "We of the First World have already completed the cycle of industrialization which made us rich, but in so doing we have produced tremendous environmental ills. We have wiped out the majority of our forests, wetlands, jungles and rain forests, as well as many species of plants and animals. We have endangered the oceans and the very atmosphere, which now are so fragile that they cannot stand more abuse. Present levels of pollution cannot be exceeded without danger to the whole planet. We of the First World produce 80% of that pollution, and despite the fact that we only have 20% of the world's population, and you 80%, you will just have to make do with your present rate of producing 20% of the earth's pollution.[26] Your process of industrialization will be much slower and more expensive than ours; the planet cannot afford for you to achieve prosperity at the cost of the planet, as we did. Your jungles and wetlands, rain forests, plant and animal diversity are essential for the well-being of the earth as we know it, and for all human life. Your poor billions in poverty will just have to stay poor longer. It's a shame that you can't be as comfortable as we, but then we got ours before the piper had to be paid."

To put it bluntly, the insistence that ecological responsibility demands population reduction (not to mention slower and more costly industrialization) from the developing nations is interpreted as an attempt of the earth's North to invoke the common good in what is really an attempt to preserve its privileges and options at the expense of the basic survival needs of the South.

Given this history, to even raise the topic of population control in many parts of the world is to be associated with this record of abuse and insensitivity. There is great fear that economic and power realities are such in many developing nations that any legitimation of population control measures will inevitably lead to the kind of massive and systematic abuses of contraception, sterilization, and abortion, described by Hartman,[27] as perpetrated by governments in poor nations who accept help from the population establishment (USAID, First World foundations, and the centers they fund) as a condition for securing other necessary or desired funding or favor from First World nations.[28] Many women's groups in both poor nations and rich nations insist that we must continue to proclaim and defend the primary right of individuals within their own communities to control fertility. Any erosion of that primary right—any legitimation of education, persuasion, or incentives (even excluding coercion)—endangers human dignity. Susan Power Bratton's discussion of positive and negative incentives which have been used/proposed for population limitation in poor nations points out that while many positive as well as negative incentives promote injustice, in that the burdens of differential resource allotment often fall on the innocent, negative incentives to limit population have the added problem of contravening basic human dignity and rights, such as privacy and individual integrity.[29]

Population Control: Necessary Despite the Dangers

Nevertheless, and without either minimizing or ignoring the very real dangers which exist in reducing overpopulation, we must insist, with Bratton and many others,[30] that overpopulation is a real and serious problem about which something must be done. The earth is overpopulated because present levels of population cannot be sustained alongside any process toward just distribution of the resources of the earth. The North is right that the common good demands that injury to the environment be reduced rather than increased, but is wrong that the burden of that reduction should be allowed to exacerbate present unjust patterns of distribution. The South is right to insist on more just distribution, but it cannot legitimately ignore the need to protect the environment on which we all depend. These are the two criteria—justice and sustainability—which must be kept side by side.

When we consider these two criteria, we see that not only must rates of population expansion decrease, but in many parts of the world population levels—absolute numbers—must decrease. Consider the U.S. We have tremendous problems *now* in our country with levels of air, water, and land pollution. The ongoing pace of development leads us to cut down more forests, fill in more wetlands, develop cities in deserts, build apartment complexes and power plants on prime farmland, plow up grasslands, and bring up ground water to irrigate arid plains. Together these activities are causing a terrible loss of land and water: falling water tables, soil erosion, and loss of topsoil.[31] But there is more. The industrial and energy production which sustains our lifestyle causes destruction of forests and lakes due to acid rains; devastating oil spills in oceans and bays; holes in the ozone layer, which protects plant, animal, and human life from destructive solar rays; the rise in carbon dioxide levels in the atmosphere (greenhouse effect); toxic chemical pollution of land and water throughout the nation; and the rapid increase of nuclear waste for which we have not yet found safe disposal.[32]

The fall of communist regimes in eastern Europe has revealed to the world a much worse ecological situation than had been suspected. Devastation from acid rain, from intensive industrialization totally devoid of pollution controls, extends not only to forests and lakes but to the human populations as well. When the air and water are so toxic that in some places rain eats through car paint in a year and melts the features off new sandstone monuments in a decade, it is not difficult to understand why there are above-normal rates of emphysema, birth defects, and lung, skin, and other cancers in the human population in heavy industrial centers. Moreover, it has been made clear in the process of reunifying Germany that for a number of reasons reunification will not rectify some major problems. The former West has more than enough industrial capacity to supply the former East. Though the government is subsidizing many projects and groups in the East, and many corporations have bought Eastern facilities, Germany does not need to recreate its efficient and more or less environmentally responsible production facilities in the East.[33] The government has closed toxic waste dumps in the East, but has not addressed their clean-up.[34] Companies which have bought the outdated plants in the East have often preferred to close them rather than invest in new production processes and undertake the delicate work of monitoring and reclaiming the environment from its devastated shape. But for a united Germany to accept ongoing high rates of unemployment in the East violates the ethical requirement that governments secure some approximation of equal distribution of resources for its citizens, and risks political instability as the cost of popular discontent. The fact that Germany neither needs Eastern production nor can easily afford to redress the ecological damage already done in the East allows a situation in which extreme poverty, bolstered by the Eastern populations' psychological need for productive work, may well produce decisions to use parts of the East as a low-risk production site for dangerous industries, and/or as a toxic dumping ground. We see this pattern in poor areas of the globe—where the need for income is so acute that poor nations—and poor neighborhoods in rich nations—agree to become dumping grounds for toxic wastes of various sorts.[35]

But it is not only in eastern Europe that we have combinations of ecological and population problems. Try to drive the German *autobahns* on weekday afternoons, or during vacation periods in the summer. It can routinely take two hours to move 50 kilometers around Frankfurt, and that is without accidents. The volume of traffic waiting on the entrance ramps can be so great as to bring *autobahn* traffic to virtual standstills. This in the nation with perhaps the best-developed highway system in the world, and one of the best (perhaps second only to France) passenger rail systems in the world. It is important to understand that the frightening anti-immigrant sentiment breaking into violence all over Germany, and also in other western European nations, over the last few years is due not only to the pressures of diversity in historically homogeneous populations, but also to perceptions of overcrowding. Though the size of the West German citizenry has actually been decreasing slightly from a 1981 high of 61 million, and is expected to stabilize at 52 million sometime within the next decade, the expansion of drivers on the road, *autobahn* truck traffic, and the appropriation of farm and unimproved land for development continues apace, as in the U.S.

The West German constitution promulgated after World War II understood citizenship in very traditional terms—as more or less limited to Germans—even though it was extremely liberal in offering asylum to virtually all groups, and generously supported asylum seekers. But not only are the Turkish immigrant worker population and the African and Romanian Gypsy immigrants not, for the most part, eligible for eventual citizenship, but growing anti-immigrant sentiment has revived violent sentiment against Jews, and increased support for ending the constitutional right of return of Germans and those of German descent from other nations, such as the former Soviet Union. Most of the anti-immigrant violence has been aimed at those who are understood as racially different.[36] But racism is not the sole, and perhaps not the principal, cause of anti-immigrant sentiment. Contemporary waves of immigrants from other nations to Germany take place in a no-growth economy, not in the high-growth period of economic rebuilding after World War II. There are simply lower profits and fewer jobs to go around. In addition to economic pressure, there is also simple space pressure. To live in Germany is to understand the historic pressures on the largest group of European people, who are confined to a space significantly smaller than France or Spain. Germans do not have any of the American sense of wide-open, unpopulated spaces left in their country. This is certainly not to excuse either historic German expansion attempts, such as Hitler's demand for *lebensraum* in the East, or current violence against foreigners in Germany. It is only to suggest that population pressures do influence conditions for social justice and cooperation.

Another perspective on the problem is provided by a look at an area of social life in the U.S. which is commonly agreed to exhibit unjust distribution of resources: health care. The richest nation on earth spends billions of dollars on expensive organ transplants every year, while in its capital, Washington, D.C., the infant mortality rate is in a class with some of the poorest nations of the world. At its most basic level, the U.S. problem with health care has been that it eats up larger and larger shares of the national wealth every year, despite the terribly unjust pattern of distribution. The pervading sense of hopefulness mixed with suspicion concerning the Clinton-proposed health care system arises from an often unarticulated understanding that while justice demands more equity between the health care given the rich and the poor, the rich cannot be, and perhaps should not be, forced to surrender significant access to organ transplants, experimental drugs and surgeries, plastic/cosmetic surgery or other expensive therapies that escalate costs. The only way to move toward equity seems to entail providing for the poor the entire spectrum of health care provided for the rich—at eventually ruinous expense to all the other aspects of the national budget, including environment.[37]

If we have not been able to find a just and sustainable solution which is acceptable to all parties within the U.S. health care system, then the possibilities for a global solution to the need for just and sustainable lifestyles seem infinitesimally small.

How can we imagine providing equitable distribution of *all* resources over the global population? Providing resources at the rate the world's rich consume them would violate sustainability, even if it were possible in the short term. But getting the rich to agree to any standard significantly below what they now receive seems equally doubtful.

It is important to understand that the overpopulation argument is significantly different now than it was in the 1960s and 1970s. Then the basic question was what was the largest world population which could be fed. Whenever alarms went up about increasing hunger due to overpopulation, the answer from many was always that the earth did produce and could continue to produce enough to eat, that *distribution* was the problem.[38] Most of those who discouraged population control measures based on the adequacy of the earth's resources emphasized the promise of technology. Julian Simon, author of *The Ultimate Resource*, which understood increased population as a good, wrote: "So the major constraint upon the human capacity to enjoy unlimited minerals, energy, and other raw materials at acceptable prices is knowledge. And the source of knowledge is the human mind. Ultimately, then, the key constraint is human imagination acting together with educated skills. This is why an increase of human beings, along with causing an additional consumption of resources, constitutes a crucial addition to the stock of natural resources."[39] And Jerrie DeHoogh and his colleagues in the Netherlands reported from their research that "there are many technological methods by which food production in the world can be increased. On the basis of a detailed inventory of soil characteristics, rainfall, temperature, and sunshine . . . it is calculated that—depending upon natural restrictions to the growth of agricultural crops—the earth is capable of producing 25 times the present amount of food. A great deal of agriculturally suitable land is not yet used; but above all production per hectare could be considerably increased. According to these data, there ought to be sufficient food both now and in the future; the world food supply is thus not primarily threatened by the finiteness of the earth."[40]

But it is not enough to look to technology to ensure sufficient food for the future. Over the long haul it is not enough simply to eat. Families who have been in refugee camps, for example, are clear that having enough to eat is a necessary condition for life to be human, but it is not at all a sufficient condition for human life. Nor are food, clothing, and shelter enough. Human life demands that we live in a community, and that we all have work—human activity which contributes to our own personhood and through which we contribute to our community and our world. Human dignity demands that our communities approximate justice in the distribution of resources and activities. We cannot feed, house, clothe, and provide basic health care and work to the six billion persons who will soon inhabit this world without devastating the planet to the point that it cannot recover as a human habitat. John Cobb and Herman Daly remind us that "in the past 36 years (1950–1986) population has doubled (from 2.5 billion to 5.0 billion). Over the same period gross world product and fossil fuel consumption have each roughly quadrupled."[41] One major reason that we cannot care for six billion people without this fundamental injury to the earth is that, as we have come to understand, the production of food, clothing, shelter, health care, and work requires energy, and our methods of energy production are, for the most part, toxic.[42] Most of our energy comes from fossil fuels—from burning wood, coal, oil, and natural gas. Most of these are non-renewable, like coal, oil, and natural gas, and therefore reliance on them violates a commitment to sustainability. But all fossil fuels, including wood or animal dung, produce dangers to the air quality, especially in the volume necessary for the global population.

Nuclear power has the terrible problem of waste disposal—that is, the absence of any safe method of waste disposal—as well as the potential for catastrophic accidents, as Chernobyl symbolizes. Nuclear accidents must be put within the proper context for comparison, however. If construction of nuclear plants were as safe as the best of the current plans for nuclear plants, the death and injury ratio from accidents would compare well with the continuous damages from pollution by coal-fired plants, for example. However, the fact is that many plants are plagued by problems rooted in inadequate plans, poor construction, and many other pitfalls. The Chernobyl disaster was an example of plans which were unsafe to begin with. Unless there is some solution to the waste disposal problem in nuclear plants, we need not even debate the comparative safety of conventional and nuclear energy plants.

Other sources of energy, such as hydroelectric power, wind power, and solar power, offer promise for the future, but have not as yet been developed to the point that they could provide the massive amounts of energy required to support the earth's soon-to-be six billion human inhabitants. In fact, many analysts think it impossible for them to ever provide the amounts of energy necessary to sustain the numbers of persons at the level of energy consumption now characteristic of densely populated areas of the First World. Even if they can do so in the future, the fact that their development has not been made cost-effective over the last few decades means that their availability for the global task is not near.

Some persons would say: "Well, if these methods of energy production can in the future produce enough for all of us without reducing the world's population, then there is no real reason to reduce the population." This is irresponsible thinking. We have no real sign of political will in the nations of the earth to develop sustainable, non-toxic energy production methods. The nations of the Middle East, supported by other oil-producing nations of the world, supported by the automotive industry and all the suppliers of the automotive industry (tires, batteries, highways, etc.), and supported by the coal and natural gas industries and all the nations in which those industries are powerful, have a strong self-interest in continuing the exploitation of fossil fuels.[43] In the U.S. we have not even been able to raise the gas price enough to make it pay to drill our own oil rather than import. The political will to make gas cost enough that there is incentive to develop non-fossil fuel energy alternatives is totally absent, as the spring 1993 opposition in Congress to President Clinton's proposed energy tax has made clear.[44]

For this reason we must make what progress we c
taneously on all fronts. The process of building political
changes in energy policy is no less slow and gradual than th
building support for further slowing population growth, with a
the cultural change which that entails. We cannot afford to insist
on one or the other. We in the developed world must begin to
build the political will to 1) cut consumption of fossil fuels (and
all resources), 2) eliminate waste in energy (and all resource) production and delivery, and 3) develop energy alternatives, while
we simultaneously 4) teach new cultural approaches to reproduction
which support birth reduction in all sectors of our populations. The
same agenda cannot be justly suggested to the developing world.
While they, too, should concern themselves with elimination of
waste in energy production and delivery, and with new cultural
approaches to birth reduction toward a stable, sustainable population, they should not be expected to reduce already very low per
capita energy use rates, nor should they be expected to heavily
invest in developing energy alternatives, though they have the
responsibility to use what local energy alternatives are known and
available.

A New Reproductive Ethic

The need to move toward reducing the world's population
not only requires that we better distinguish sex and reproduction
in our thinking, but that we rethink reproduction altogether—
what it means, how valuable it is, and what criteria make it
responsible and human. Insistence on distinguishing sex and reproduction does not entail a shift to technologically controlled,
non-sexual reproduction of humans. Such a shift would further
undermine individual human agency in reproduction, which is already an acute cause of alienation for women throughout the
world. Such a shift would further empower the elites who control
the technology at the expense of the individual women and men
who need it. Human reproduction should continue to rely primarily on sexual intercourse—intercourse which should take place

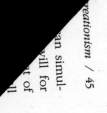

ure

reationism / 45

aships grounded in mutual sexual pleas-

n of sex and reproduction calls for a shift
than a technological shift. It requires re-
derstanding that sex is normally procrea-
l circumstances require contraception, to
n as normally contraceptive, so that only
usly selected circumstances justify procreative openness.

In developing criteria for determining when procreative openness is justified, we need to balance a number of physical, cultural, demographic, and personal factors. In some cultures population has historically been somewhat controlled through cultural customs regarding when couples marry. In some rural areas a man did not marry until he had land, which often meant among the lower classes that he could not marry until he inherited land at his father's death, by which time he might be middle-aged.[45] In other cultures, especially in parts of Asia, the age at which women married was raised until the late 1920s or early 1930s, thus significantly shortening the childbearing years.[46]

A just reproductive ethic will not utilize criteria which penalize the poor, or put undue stress on one gender or class. On the other hand, there is no justification for dismissing culture altogether in a reproductive ethic, as it is crucial to individual understandings of identity and worth. Thus in cultures in which women are valued exclusively as mothers, one needs to be very careful not to so limit childbearing as to undermine both the social status and self-esteem of women. In the same way, impregnation as a sign of virility in men can also be very important in societies in which male pride and achievement are severely limited by poverty and class.

One general guideline is to be cautious. Changes cannot be introduced too quickly. For example, a just reproductive ethic will attempt to maximize the health of women by ensuring that women are not expected to bear children either at too early or too late an age, or too close together. But the shift from a specific culture's present insistence that girls marry at menarche should be gradual. It would be wrong to impose, for example, for reasons of population control, a ban on marriage for women before age 25, especially in a culture in which women are valued only as mothers, for we know that the risk of infertility increases with age. No one segment of the population should bear the entire burden of the shift in the reproductive ethic. This has been a basic problem with population control abuses in many nations. Women (and occasionally men) who have been sterilized without real consent—and sometimes without even their knowledge—have become demoralized, unmarriageable, or are divorced by spouses who want children, in economies largely devoid of real possibilities for women to be self-supporting.

The Goal: One Person, One Child

We need a reproductive ethic that aims at individuals deciding to replace themselves only. If reproductive pairs voluntarily limit themselves to two children or less (one apiece) then those pairs with one child and all the childless adults would together contribute to reducing the global population. This general aim would need to be adjusted where necessary to provide for demographic balance. Places with very high current birth rates (e.g., Kenya, whose birth rate is 4.2, compared to 1.9 in the U.S.) would need to approach such a standard gradually, lest rapid reductions cause a situation in which a much smaller productive population inherits the care of a non-productive elderly population many times its size. Many parts of the world are struggling with what may become devastating demographic imbalance due to the ravages of AIDS; demographic analysis is badly needed already in parts of Africa hardest hit. Unfortunately, those societies most in need of such information have inadequate resources for treating AIDS victims, for gathering information about the demographic results of the disease, and for planning to deal with those results.[47]

In moving toward a just and sustainable reproductive ethic of replacement, a great deal of supportive cultural and economic transformation becomes necessary. For example, in many cultures to have only one or two children is still, despite greatly reduced infant mortality rates, extremely risky. For in cultures where sons represent the only old-age assistance available, it could be suicidal for a poor couple to have only one son, or only daughters. One son, even if he lives to adulthood, might not have the resources necessary to feed two extra mouths; daughters may not have enough control over family resources to take on support of parents. The statistics on infant mortality and childhood death are so terrible for some nations that even birthing two sons is no real assurance of having one survive to care for aged parents.[48] While a long-term goal might be a system of governmental old-age assistance, population control programs in the short term must concentrate on provision of sufficient food and medical care to ensure that first and second children survive childhood.

Allied to supportive changes in old-age assistance is cultural change in terms of sex roles. Increased economic opportunities for women improve women's ability to contribute to care of parents, and to care for children in the event of paternal death or abandonment. Broadening the basis of female worth from its present narrow base in motherhood in many cultures requires first of all reducing women's dependence upon both husbands and later children, especially sons, and providing alternative means for women to contribute to both families and society. Men's dependence upon impregnation as proof of manhood can be similarly decreased through creation of other avenues of achievement.

It is sometimes argued that stressing voluntariness in population control and convincing persons to have fewer children by improving survival rates of children and modifying sex roles entails an extended period of high rates of population increase. That is, some argue that until the new roles are in place and the population clearly recognizes that more children are surviving, they will continue to have many children, but more of those children will be surviving. This seems to be the risk. Regardless of the risk, most of the organizations at the base, certainly most women's organizations in poor nations, insist on emphasizing voluntariness. But extended periods of high population increases are not necessary. A well-organized local program can demonstrate on a village-by-village, neighborhood-by-neighborhood basis drastically lowered infant mortality rates within five years. Programs in

Bangladesh, Colombia, and other nations have been able to reach over 80% of a local population, offering three services: 1) universal inoculations for children, 2) a daily powdered milk or other protein supplement program for protein-deficient children and pregnant and nursing mothers, and 3) parent training and supervision in rehydration methods. Such programs normally more than halve the death rate of children under five within five years. In many communities such demonstrations are sufficient to convince many, though not, of course, all of the couples.

Changes should be not only as gradual as possible, but as voluntary as possible. "Voluntary" is a very slippery word. In general it makes little sense to say that a social change is voluntary or involuntary. In most of our decisions we are both free and coerced. That is, there are aspects of our situation which press us in one direction or another, at the same time that we have the freedom to ultimately resist those pressures. Resistance can be easy or costly, depending upon the strength of the pressure exerted on us. For example, economic pressures (the need for children to provide for one's old age) and social pressure (greater social status and power for mothers of sons) can reinforce each other in favor of a third or fourth child. Yet these pressures are sometimes outweighed in a family by desire for a government job for which sterilization after two children is a prerequisite. Is this a free decision? Yes and no.

The entire concept of voluntariness really only lends itself to comparison: a social change can be more or less voluntary, but never completely voluntary or involuntary. The common line that we often draw between persuasion and coercion is really not too clear. Is a Mexican man who is taunted at the local bar for not being a real man because his wife was seen emerging from the local clinic with contraceptives being persuaded or coerced into refusing to use contraception? Similarly, is a local government in Indonesia engaged in persuasion or coercion when it offers free school books only to the first child of a family? Usually the answer depends upon circumstances: how many times the other men at the bar have taunted him, what other acceptable proofs of manhood he has provided, or whether the economic circumstances allow the family to send subsequent children to school with or without books. Whether we desire to do the encouraged action for its own sake is usually only one of the aspects relevant to our final decision; social pressures, individual circumstances, and anticipated consequences contribute the remainder of the aspects relevant to this decision.

Attempting to ensure that change is as voluntary as possible entails more than one process. First of all it entails seeing that a society's reproductive policy emerges from as democratic and representative a process as possible. All groups in the society should be heard and their perspectives included, so far as possible. Differences should never be settled solely or repeatedly at the expense of any one group. But maximizing voluntariness also means that at an individual level the disincentives used should never cut off choice altogether. It is wrong to enforce a one-child policy by legally forcing abortion of second pregnancies. Nor should enforcement of reproductive policy punish the innocent—such as the loss of housing altogether for families who exceed the ideal number of children. Disincentives which require sacrifice from families who decide to exceed the recommended number of children are acceptable, so long as the sacrifices required: 1) do not include the sacrifice of basic rights or the fulfillment of basic human needs; 2) principally fall on those who made the decision to exceed the norm; and 3) do not encourage parental or social rejection of the "excess" children.[49]

Incentives and disincentives must be specific to particular societies, and even to specific classes within the society. In general, no one incentive or disincentive will be both just and effective across all social groups. Tax incentives in developed nations are a useful way of persuading middle- and working-class parents about family size and other aspects of family life. Tax incentives are less effective for the poor and the rich, for the poor are not affected in that they either don't pay taxes or don't have enough income to protect, and the rich are insulated by their wealth from the pinch of higher taxes. Population policy will need to be very nuanced, and be integrated into many different areas of social regulation in order to spread the incentive and the burden fairly.

3. *More Critical Approaches to Scripture and Natural Law*

Reconstructing sexual ethics within a Western religious framework requires rethinking the resources available for ethics and how they are used. As mentioned in Chapter One, contemporary science and social science must be primary sources regarding human sexual function. Attention to contemporary science is especially necessary in the present because the repressive silence about sex which has prevailed in the U.S. has created an extensive sexual ignorance regarding over half a century of extensive scientific discoveries in the field of sexuality.

At the same time, science/social science can only offer partial information regarding human sexuality. They are neither the most important sources for interpreting the meaning/value of specific sexual attitudes, behaviors or relationships, nor is any specific science privileged in understanding the extent to which change in these sexual attitudes, behaviors, or relationships can or should change. The truths in science are factual truths, truths about what is or what was, not truths about what should be or what would be best. While some of the most basic facts about sexuality may involve the effects of hormones on the fetal brain, about which science can inform us, the most important truths about sexuality for us as a society are much broader. The most important truths about sexuality are about the meaning and value of sexuality and sexual acts. They are truths which include criteria for choosing some sexual acts, or relationships, or attitudes, over others. This is one of the reasons why so many sex education programs are ineffective today. While many of our young people are never exposed to information about sexuality in any systematic way, many of those who are exposed fail to take in the material to which they are exposed.

There are a variety of reasons for this failure to internalize sexual information. One of the most common is that the sex education program failed to present the factual information within a framework of values; without that value framework, the information has little meaning. This kind of meaninglessness is what young people indicate when they say something is "boring." It is boring because there are no clues as to what the information really means—that is, how it relates to the goals and ambitions, the activities, emotions, and relationships of the individual. After decades of vocal objections to sex education programs on the part of conservative Christian religious groups who understand sex, including information about it, as sinful, many school boards have stripped down their sexual education programs to strictly "academic" shape, which is exhausted by teaching reproductive biology and perhaps sexually transmitted diseases. They hope in this way to avoid criticism, since they teach nothing about sexual attitudes or practice, but only basic biology and health. But the cost of their only partially successful attempt to escape criticism is the claim of irrelevance by their audience.

Other school boards have responded to their vocal anti-sex education critics with a more complete capitulation. That is, they have designed sexual education programs which are effectively anti-sexual in that they teach negative attitudes toward sex. Such programs teach biological reproduction (the "facts of life," as they are called) and then go on to stress the risk of sexually transmitted diseases and pregnancy, which are presented as the rationale for a section of the curriculum which urges students to "Say No to Sex." This curricular program gives students techniques for and often role-playing practice in resisting peer pressure to engage in sex and in clarifying their own desire to postpone sex. Such programs often use films and printed materials, and even bring in persons to share their own experiences with both teen pregnancy and STDs.

All of the information conveyed in such programs is valuable and necessary, but it is also all negative. While from many educators' point of view the message is about postponing sex, a message which most parents and teachers support, from the students' point of view the message is that sex is bad. Though such programs attempt to include information about meaning and value, their tendency is to attribute maturity, honesty, and courage to anti-sex attitudes, and irresponsibility, serious risk, promiscuity, and a need for instant gratification to pro-sex attitudes.

Contemporary youth will not, for the most part, accept such a message; it runs counter to their dominant cultural experience. Youth see themselves faced with a desperate search for the sexual partner who will not only provide them with companionship and shared sexual pleasure, but will be bonded to them in exclusive, intimate relationship that fulfills all their bodily, emotional, and relational needs. The example of their parents, the stories in movies, on TV, and in books—all implicitly give them this romanticized view of sex. Everyone must seek a sexual relationship or be adrift and alone, unhappy, burdened with gifts that cannot be shared and needs that cannot be met. Adolescents learn to see sex not only as attractive because pleasurable, but as a human good, and therefore reject the negative message of sex education programs about sex. They cannot agree that sex is not valuable and offers little but ephemeral pleasure in return for major risks. Frequently, they are so suspicious and unbelieving of the negative message about sexuality in school sexuality programs that they tune out the sexual information itself, which could be of some benefit.

We need to formulate a sexual education program which includes a great deal more information about sex, but which presents it within the framework of an honest message about meaning in sexuality. That message must acknowledge the power of sexual activity, which can be either an important but not sufficient avenue for fulfilling basic human needs and aspirations or a tool with which to control, exploit or destroy human well-being, self-esteem, and self-reliance. The sex education message must *also* acknowledge the participation of sexuality in every aspect of the individual person and of human activity. Sexuality is foundational in human beings; sexuality is not limited to genital activity, and celibacy does not make people asexual. Sexuality affects the structure of our brains,[1] the way that we relate to persons,[2] the way we understand our world and attempt to structure our lives, our occupations,[3] our choices around sexual activity,[4] our personality traits,[5] and our social status.[6] It is morally tragic as well as socially disastrous that such a major constitutive part of human personhood is ignored, repressed, denied, or misunderstood in our society.

Moral Resources in the Christian Sexual Tradition

Traditional Christian sexual ethics has understood its basic resources for discerning the meaning in sexuality as scripture (for Protestants) and natural law buttressed by scripture (for Roman Catholics). One of the most obvious reasons for the inadequacy of Christian sexual ethics, as done in the churches today, is that recourse to both of these sources is seriously flawed. In this chapter, I will first briefly outline the case as developed by many others over the last few decades for how it is that scripture provides no clear, simple moral guidance in sexual ethics, and I will suggest how scripture can be used to support a responsible, human sexual ethic. I will then suggest how a radical historicization of natural law tradition can ground a responsible sexual ethic. Finally, I will use the institution of marriage, supported by both scripture and natural law interpretations, as an example of the consequences of inadequate method.

There are two basic kinds of objections to prevailing scriptural and natural law approaches to sexual ethics. One concerns consequences—what are the theological and ethical consequences of this use, and how well do they accord with Christian understandings of foundational Christian beliefs? The second kind of objection looks not to consequences, but rather critically examines the method itself, whether it is a scriptural or natural law approach, or a mixed approach. While the two kinds of objections are certainly related, it is important to develop them separately so as to maximize the force and clarity of the objections.

Scripture

The Protestant Christian tradition looked to scripture for its ethical norms as a way of avoiding the corruption which had crept into Christian practice, and therefore into Christian tradition. Scripture was understood at the time of the Reformation to historically precede the advent of corruption associated with the papacy and/or the establishment of Christianity as the official religion of the Roman Empire. Though there is variation between Protestant denominations, and not all have followed so strictly Martin Luther's insistence on *"sola scriptura,"* there is no question that for Protestants scripture is popularly understood as the primary source of normative divine revelation. Even for Methodists the four Wesleyan sources of revelation—scripture, tradition, reason, and experience—are often reduced to the Bible.

While a case can be made for scripture as a primary source of revelation, it is impossible to defend a *"sola scriptura"* position, however we may sympathize with the intentions and situation of Martin Luther in the early sixteenth century. For scriptural scholarship has made clear, as Elisabeth Schüssler Fiorenza has frequently explained, that the Bible is not a book but a bookshelf.[7] Those books, and frequently sections of books, were written by a variety of authors in varied historical periods, with various—and often conflicting—religious, political, and social intentions. Those writings are not so much history, in the sense of what objectively happened, as they are reflections on and interpretations of what happened, from particular self-interested perspectives, often written hundreds of years after the events which they treat. For this reason, no verse, story, chapter, or book of scripture can be treated as self-explanatory, literal truth.

Episcopal Bishop John Shelby Spong, in an excellent chapter on using scripture in ethics ("The Case Against Literalism") in his

book *Living in Sin? A Bishop Rethinks Human Sexuality,*[8] argues
that in order for scripture to shed any light at all the reader must
ask questions such as: Why was the passage written? What interests did it serve within the author's socio-historical situation? To
what is the passage opposed? What are underlying assumptions of
the author? For the fact is that in scripture we have many incon-
sistencies, contradictions, and outright untruths, even regarding
the most central of Christian beliefs. Not only do different parts of
the Bible differ on such issues as the Resurrection, Ascension, and
Pentecost, but New Testament writers disagreed even regarding
the divinity of Jesus. Mark presents Jesus as divine from his baptism by John as an adult; Matthew and Luke present Jesus as
divine by birth; and John projects the divinity of Jesus Christ back
to infinity within the uncreated Word of God; while Paul, the
earliest of the New Testament writers, does not define at all how
Jesus is divine. As Spong asks, how can we possibly expect scripture to present us with universal sexual norms valid for all time
when scripture presents such a variety of views about the divinity
of Jesus Christ?

Accepting the historicity of scripture—that it emerges from a
historical process, from specific individuals in specific situations
and communities with specific interests and needs—sheds a radically different light on the traditional sexual norms the churches
have lifted from scripture. Those norms of course prohibit all sexual activity outside of marriage, understanding marriage as the
legal, sexual, and domestic union of a male and a female for
purposes of reproduction, with a male role of headship and material provision, and a female role of child-bearer, child-rearer, and
responsibility for the domicile. This union was understood to be
both exclusive and more or less permanent. That is, Jesus was
understood to overrule earlier practices of divorce and polygamy
among the patriarchs. However, insistence on monogamy did not
seem to create a single scriptural standard on marital fidelity and
divorce; husbands were not held to the same rigorous standards
as wives. Differing versions of the Gospels left open whether divorce could still be permitted by exception in the case of an

adulterous wife, though there is no reciprocal openness in the case of adulterous husbands.[9]

Historicizing this scriptural tradition on sexuality makes clear how this set of norms served the interests of the communities involved. The reproductive emphasis resulting from excluding all nonmarital forms of sex and orienting marriage to reproduction served the obvious interests of a small people who were first nomadic and then settlers among foreigners: it maximized birth rates. Other pieces of Israelite sexual practice, such as Levirate marriage, confirm this important function. The prohibition on female sexual activity outside marriage served not only to ensure men's recognition of and responsibility for their offspring. It also allowed fathers to charge husbands a bride price, which made fathers willing to raise daughters who would otherwise not contribute to their family, and gave husbands virgin wives in exchange for that bride price. Further, the taboo on all nonmarital forms of sex served to differentiate the Israelites from their neighbors, many of whom practiced heterosexual and/or homosexual cultic acts. This differentiation, cultivated in many other areas of life as well, served to prevent the assimilation of the Israelites and ensure their survival as a distinct people.

Within Christianity itself, the Jewish sexual ethic prevailed for a number of reasons. First, as far as we can tell from the New Testament evidence, sexuality was not a central aspect of Jesus' reforms of Judaism. There is virtually nothing in the Gospels themselves regarding sexual activity. The closest is perhaps Jesus' refusal to stone the woman caught in adultery, and it is never clear in that story whether Jesus' intended to make any statement about adultery at all; the major point clearly concerns not judging others.[10] The one aspect of Jesus' teaching which concerned sexuality more broadly construed involved the role of women. It seems very clear today with contemporary sensitivity to issues of sex roles that Jesus legitimated very nontraditional roles for women among his followers. This is clear not only in such stories as Luke's account of Jesus with Mary and Martha,[11] but even more clearly in the fact that women travelled with Jesus' band,[12] were acknowledged in all the Gospels as the first witnesses of the

Resurrection, and were, according to the Epistles, accepted in the earliest church as prophets, missionaries, deacons,[13] and, according to Paul, even apostles (Junia).[14] These nontraditional roles for women in the earliest Church are supported both by surviving traditions within local churches which trace their origins to the missionary work of women such as Mary Magdalene, and by many of the early extracanonical Christian writings. But these roles were more or less repressed after the first century, and we have no evidence as to whether or how more or less restrictive roles for women influenced Christian attitudes toward and regulation of sexual activity.

This is not all that surprising. After all, scholars like Elisabeth Schüssler Fiorenza point out that greater freedom for women in Christianity was always opposed in some quarters, especially within the more Jewish communities.[15] In addition, the period of openness was relatively short, certainly less than 100 years. Moreover, this period of greater freedom for women corresponded more or less exactly to the time when the early church was most urgently focused on missionary activity, since it believed that the second coming of Christ was imminent. Just as Paul argued during this period that the shortness of time until the second coming should incline Christians to put off decisions about marrying and founding families so as to concentrate on announcing the Good News to others so they could prepare for the second coming,[16] so it must have seemed to those early Christians that reconstructing norms for sexual behavior had no high priority, given the shortness of time for this world. By the time that the church had accepted that the second coming might be considerably in the distance, the church had already conformed itself to surrounding patriarchal understandings of women's roles, which reaffirmed the patriarchal sexual norms the church had inherited from Judaism. Thus when the Council of Jerusalem in the Acts of the Apostles names, through James, the three rules of conduct which should replace the entire Jewish law which had hithertofore been required of Gentile converts, one of those rules is a ban on unchastity.[17] That ban itself, by its very vagueness, assumes that everyone knows and understands patriarchal sexual norms.

In order to successfully argue for scripture as a primary source of revelation today, then, regardless of the specific issue involved, it is not only necessary to surrender the commonly accepted view of scripture as literally true. It is also necessary to understand that the revelation in some parts of scripture is not contained in the text itself, but in the interaction between the text and the critical examination of the reader. For example, Schüssler Fiorenza writes that scripture sometimes reveals through silence. By this she means that when we want to know how the early Christian community lived, and we take this concern to scripture, we will notice that there is a general silence about the lives of women in the Christian community. It is by reflecting on those odd silences, on the information Schüssler Fiorenza gleans from the greetings and farewells attached to the Epistles, from careful rereading of those New Testament passages which do mention women, on the surprising prominence of women's leadership in those early Christian writings which were excluded from the canon of the New Testament,[18] and from similar indirect sources, that we can piece together, or reconstruct, the actual life of the early Christian community which included both men and women.

This kind of approach to scripture, of course, has many problems. It requires a more or less specialized background in scripture scholarship. One of the basic reasons that Protestants turned to scripture was that it was understood to be clear and accessible to everyone, not dependent upon any special expertise, such as the Catholic church claimed for the magisterium in particular and for the clergy in general. Moreover, such dependence upon specialized scriptural expertise conflicts with popular Protestant, especially low-church Protestant, suspicion and rejection of casuistry, or any situational considerations in morality. That "old time religion" of which so many are fond is distinguished by insistence on the simplicity and absoluteness of its moral code.[19] For example, if the destruction of Sodom and Gomorrah follows the threatening demand of a gang of men in the town for homosexual access to two visitors, and Lot, who protects the visitors, is saved by God from that destruction, then for most of the Christian community the moral of the story is that God hates and punishes homosexuals. The fact that the sex demanded was gang rape does not affect the interpretation of the story's moral at all; it only serves to suggest that homosexuals use coercion to obtain sex. This approach not only serves to confirm already-held misconceptions and prejudices about homosexuality, but it has the virtue—a very real virtue for teaching and evangelization—of being easy to understand and convey within a homophobic culture. Thus the conditions necessary for retaining scripture as a primary source of revelation more or less directly conflict with the ideological assumptions derived from the Reformation regarding the individual Christian as capable of independently being able to discern revelation directly from scripture.

In addition to examining traditional methodological foundations of Christian sexual ethics, another method of criticism is to focus on the consequences of those ethics, and their compatibility with other aspects of Christian teaching and with the experience of those living within the Christian community. The consequences of basing sexual ethics upon scripture include, as could be expected from the earlier treatment of scripture: 1) inconsistency, depending upon which scriptural text was referenced and 2) patriarchalism, in that both the Old Testament and those portions of the New Testament which deal explicitly with sexuality arose out of patriarchal societies. Both scripture's inconsistency and its patriarchalism are problematic in terms of contemporary theologies of God, which tend to lean heavily on God as a just and loving creator.[20] Marie Fortune pointed out in her treatment of sexual violence as sin that one consequence of accepting the patriarchal understandings of sexuality is that God appears to have created women and children to be victims.[21] Old Testament stories present women as booty in war, as sexually used and enslaved, as property sold from father to husband, as liable to being divorced and cast off by husbands without cause. The Old Testament also includes laws on rape which understood a woman's rape as injury to her owner rather than to her, and a law on incest which prohibited a man from sexual congress with any female relative by blood or marriage who belonged to another man, but failed to ban incest with his own daughter or son. Such stories and laws, when presented as the commands of God, create an image of Yahweh as complicit in victimization, as indifferent to the suffering of women and children. The Old Testament analogy of Yahweh as groom to Israel the bride further identifies Yahweh with males. Those aspects of the Christian tradition which understand Yahweh as inherently compassionate, unable to turn aside from the suffering of the Hebrews in Egypt, as a father who always cares for his children, who will not offer stones when the children cry for bread, and the divine son as the innocent who risks and accepts suffering and death as the cost of loving others, are implicitly called into question in a patriarchal sexual ethic. But not only is divine compassion called into question, but also divine justice. Can it be a just God who mandates that women's salvation comes through motherhood,[22] and then makes motherhood for some women a biological impossibility beyond women's control? Can it be just to hold all persons accountable for their lives and actions, and then to deprive half the human race of the independence which would allow them to exercise responsibility for their actions?

Is it possible to reconcile either of the creation stories in Genesis—the first in which man and woman are created simultaneously and given joint command over the rest of creation,[23] or the second in which a generic (androgynous) human is divided into male and female[24]—with the patriarchal stories in which women are property of men? How can the values of the creation stories be reconciled with stories of fathers whose fidelity to Yahweh is praised because they are willing to kill their sons and daughters, as in the stories of Abraham[25] and Jephthah?[26]

Thus there is simply no way to avoid accepting the claim that scripture always requires interpretation, and that the interpretation requires not only information about the author's historico-social location, but also the use of normative criteria external to scripture. As Schüssler Fiorenza writes:

> The historical theological insight that the New Testament is not only a source of revelatory truth but also a resource for patriarchal subordination and domination demands a new paradigm for biblical hermeneutics and theology. . . . I would

therefore suggest that the revelatory canon for theological evaluation of biblical androcentric traditions and their subsequent interpretations cannot be derived from the Bible itself, but can only be formulated in and through women's struggle for liberation from all patriarchal oppression.[27]

We cannot use one part of scripture to help us decide which of two conflicting scriptural texts is more true or revelatory, for that only raises questions about how we selected the original text as normative. To the extent that we can discern the movement and activity of the Holy Spirit within the struggle for liberation, our individual and communal experience of the struggle for liberation is the best source of criteria for guiding scriptural selection and interpretation.

Natural Law

Historically, invocation of natural law occurs within Roman Catholicism (and to a limited extent within Anglicanism) and within the framework of American civil religion with its rationalist, deist roots. Natural law is understood as the unwritten law embedded in all of creation, a law that reasoning humans can discern from observation of creation. For Protestantism as a whole, the claim that human reason can discern the creator's intentions has been rejected in the understanding that human reason was so corrupted by the fall that only God's grace allows humans to comprehend any part of the divine will. Roman Catholics have insisted that the Fall only forfeited humans their supernatural gifts, and not those gifts natural to human beings, such as reason, which retains the capacity, at least in principle, to discern the good. In fact, though these are the historic theological stances of Protestants and Catholics, political/historical factors since the Reformation have muddied the situation a great deal.

Within the American scene, the dominant Protestantism has been the standard carrier for not only the Enlightenment, with its insistence on the power of reason understood in terms of scientific reason, but also for liberal democracy, with its insistence on the rights of the individual to make decisions for him/herself. The theological insistence on the unreliability of reason and the human need for grace does not seem to have moderated in any way the political insistence of American Protestants regarding their right and duty to discern the divine will for their nation. Many commentators would suggest that the connecting link between these two somewhat conflicting stances is the understanding of the Bible as the sole source of revelation. So long as Protestant Americans saw themselves as operating out of a biblical framework—such as working out the new covenant in the new American Canaan—they did not feel they were too dependent upon a corrupted and therefore unreliable human reason.

For American Roman Catholics, on the other hand, the theological insistence on the capacity of reason to discern the good was subordinated to the historical reality of membership in a monarchical church undergoing a strong shift to centralize power in response to a hostile modern world.[28] Nativism in the American context only added local stress to the already-present tendencies toward sectarianism and the relegation of decision-making to clerical elites. It is only since Vatican II, which coincided in the U.S. with the rise of the Roman Catholic population to economic and educational success, even prominence, that U.S. Catholics have come to be as individualist and independent as Protestant Americans. At the present time, in terms of sexual attitudes, the most discernible difference is the slightly greater reliance of Protestants in general to base their sexual attitudes on biblical texts. For most lay Catholics, the sexual grounding of their own tradition in natural law is largely unknown, and to the extent it is known it is understood so vaguely as to be indistinguishable from the rationalist/deistic natural law approaches of the Founding Fathers.

It seems to me that natural law offers a much more useful base for a sexual ethic than scripture. But both historical uses of natural law—by Roman Catholics and deists—are grossly inadequate. In the following section I want to suggest reasons for, and methods of, reconstituting a natural law approach.

In Chapter One, I alluded to some of the many inadequacies in inherited natural law interpretations. Among Catholics during the debate over contraception in the 1960s and early 1970s, it was often charged that the strong tendency to physicalism—to solely biological understandings of human nature—in Catholic natural law tradition was a severe weakness. That is, since the official church teaching looked only to human biology in determining divine will for human sexuality, it concluded that sex was naturally oriented to procreation, and condemned as immoral any human attempt to separate the procreative aspect from the use of the sexual faculties.

The revisionists who protested against physicalism were certainly correct that the human person is much more than his or her biological body, and that human rationality and the psychic structures that govern the use of rationality would seem to be at least as important as reproductive biology for understanding the divine will for humans. But it should be pointed out that the physicalism of the Christian sexual tradition was not only too narrow an approach to the human person, but was based on inadequate biology as well. In particular, the failure to understand female biology led to major errors in the understanding of human nature. Catholic natural law approaches to sexuality were, for the most part, in place by the end of the Middle Ages and reflected the development of science at that time. The female body was understood as genetically sterile—able to contribute only nurture and not form to new life. This task of providing sustenance to new life was understood as the purpose of female life, and females were also understood as lacking in rationality compared to the male, because sensibility and not rationality were necessary for childbearing and rearing. Furthermore, due to lack of knowledge of evolution, there was no awareness of the major evolutionary shift in human sexuality and in the sexuality of the great apes from which *homo sapiens* developed. That shift was a shift away from female estrus. Unlike other animals whose females are sexually available only during their fertile periods, in humans and apes sexual interest and activity became possible throughout the entire menstrual cycle, and not just when procreation is likely. Since there was no awareness of this evolutionary shift, there could be no attempt to understand the significance of this change *away from* sex oriented exclusively to procreation.

In a similar manner, the failure to examine embodied female sexuality combined with the tradition's fear and suspicion of sexual pleasure led to the tradition's ignoring the existence and significance of the female clitoris. A contemporary physicalist approach to natural law on sexuality must take into account that the female clitoris has no function save sexual pleasure—it has no reproductive, urological, or other function in the body. But the clitoris is the organ most sensitive to sexual pleasure. Within the twentieth century some commentators have suggested that the role of the clitoris is to provide pleasure to women as a reward for sex, as a way of ensuring the willingness of women to reproduce the species. But contemporary science has demonstrated that this attempt to link the sexual pleasure function of the clitoris to procreation is a failure. As stated above in other contexts, between 56 and 70 percent of women do not receive sufficient clitoral stimulation in coitus to reach the sexual satisfaction of orgasm;[29] the majority require direct stimulation of the clitoris. That is, the procreative act does not itself stimulate pleasure sufficient to act as reinforcement for engaging in sex for the majority of women. If the placement of the clitoris in the female body reflects the divine will, then God wills that sex is not just oriented to procreation, but is at least as, if not more, oriented to pleasure as to procreation.

This critique of physicalism as inadequately applied in the natural law tradition has been superseded by an even more radical methodological critique which rejects physicalism altogether. I want to develop two forms of the argument for rejecting physicalism. The first is the one originally developed in the late 1960s in the debate over contraception in the U.S. Catholic church.

The Human Person Is More Than Biology

The predominant argument of the revisionists was that it simply was not sufficient to deal with human biology as a way of understanding the sexual orientation of human nature.[30] While it is true that at a biological level sex is oriented to procreation as at least one of the ends of sexuality, this does not justify the principle that there can be no legitimate separation of procreation from coitus. For the human person is much more than a biological mechanism. Part of human biology is a psychic apparatus, a mind which not only thinks but feels. And the nature of humans in community includes not only the ability to reproduce themselves, but also to rear those human reproductions within intimate communities. Rearing demands of nurturers identification with offspring, loyalty to offspring, love, and willingness to sacrifice in the interests of offspring. There are, of course, limits to love, loyalty, identification, and sacrifice in every person—what we might call psychic limits. But these limits are never absolute, even within individuals, for they depend upon the circumstances in which the individual is immersed, the stage of personal development which the individual has achieved, and the level of support available from others. Those individuals whose caregivers extended identification, love, loyalty, and sacrifice to them in the past, and who continue to have networks of intimacy and support, will be able to maximize the limits on their own ability to parent. The intimacy and bonding which committed, mutually pleasurable sex can create may be conducive to the continuation of the individual's ability to extend himself/herself in love and loyalty to existing children.

In addition to psychic limits in our ability to parent, there are also limits to the social resources available to every caregiver. Individual reflection may make clear to individuals that they have reached their psychic limit, or the limits of their economic resources, or both, such that it would be unreasonable to procreate any more.

But that same individual is very probably in need of the grace—the intimacy and bonding, the affirmation of self, and the bodily pleasure[31]—which can be derived from sexual activity, and which is one important foundation for the individual's ability to nurture children well. Thus successful rearing, which seems to be a crucial aspect of procreation, sometimes indicates the cessation of procreation, and a continuation of sexual activity.

The second argument for rejecting physicalism arises, ironically enough, from sociobiology. The physicalist tendency in Catholic natural law theory shares some important aspects with sociobiology. Both tend to look not for new directions in which human nature may be moving, but rather to define human nature with reference to animal biology. The approaches differ as to *why* the connection with animals is stressed. Sociobiology assumes an evolutionary theory which historically roots human nature in animal nature, while Catholic natural law tradition classically associated the spiritual aspects of human nature with God and the angels, but the material bodily aspects of human nature with animals. The problem of Catholic Christianity with physicalism or with sociobiologist explanations of human nature which are biologically determined is that they undermine the moral demands of Christianity.

Much of Catholic moral theology, influenced as it has been by natural law thought, tends to see individual self-interest and the common good as related, though not identical.[32] Much of Protestant moral thought, especially the Lutheran influences, have tended to see individual self-interest as opposed to both the good of another and the common good, and thus have often leaned toward identifying "love of neighbor" with sacrificing one's own self-interest.[33] Sociobiology is not focused on the moral question, but does understand that the biological impetus of all organisms is to "multiply and fill the earth" with themselves. This holds true for macro-organisms such as humans, as well as for micro-organisms such as cells. Sometimes this multiplication acts contrary to the common good, as when a cancer cell opportunistically multiplies and eventually kills the macro-organism. Sometimes this multiplication supports the common good, as when the injection of small amounts of toxins triggers the production of antitoxins throughout the body. So it is with macro-organisms from a sociobiological point of view.

Thus the male langur monkey, native to India and Sri Lanka, who challenges and defeats the male leader of a female harem, systematically sets about killing all the suckling infants over a period of hours or days in order to maximize chances for the birth and survival of his own offspring.[34] Without the sucklings, the females of the harem will come into heat sooner, and the offspring the new leader begets of them will not have to compete for resources with the offspring of the previous leader. While such behavior is common in species that exist in herds of a dominant male and his harem (such as wild horses and some lions), the langurs are distinct in that the new leaders do not, in addition to killing the sucklings, batter pregnant females into aborting. When confronted with a new harem leader, pregnant langurs display a remarkable "false" estrus which allows them to copulate with the new leader, after which he accepts the offspring they carry as his own.[35] Moving from animals to humans, sociobiologists point out that in human beings there are remnants of such motivation, and so point to the higher rate of child abuse among stepparents than natural parents, and to the many folktales which warn of stepparents.[36]

Sociobiologists are most insistent upon the biological basis of human sexual behavior. Sociological data show that human males are much more likely than females to have multiple sexual partners. Many interpret this as an effective strategy for maximizing the number of male genetic offspring by scattering their seed as widely as possible. The lesser promiscuity of females is understood to be dictated by the fact that since women can only produce one pregnancy every nine months, regardless of excess sexual activity, their best chances of maximizing their progeny lie with concentrating on the survival and quality of the offspring, and not on maximizing sexual partners.[37]

The tendency among much of early sociobiology to overstress the biological influence on human behavior was a clear reaction to the reigning social scientific stress in the 1960s and 1970s on a relatively plastic human nature endlessly open to social conditioning. Because of its attempt to stress a biological influence which was in tension with the changes in human relations and institutions proposed in the 1960s and 1970s, sociobiology was quickly seized as a scientific prop for many moral and social conservatives resisting the demands of the women's movement for social change in the direction of gender justice. But sociobiological theory does not support the continuation of patriarchal social structures. Sociobiology is based in scientific theory regarding evolution, and recognizes that human nature has become, through the process of evolution, less and less biologically determined. Deliberately chosen childlessness in postmodern society, for example, cannot be explained with reference to biological drives in organisms.

Neither is Christianity compatible with any form of biological determinism, or any heavy stress on biological influence on human behavior. The basic moral teachings of Christianity regarding God's love and justice toward humans, and the resulting command of "love of neighbor," correspond in the sociobiological model of human nature not to the biological drives but to the sociocultural influences which have over time lessened the grip of biology on human behavior. Biology cannot explain why in a time of scarce resources one human community might endanger its survival by sharing its few resources with another human community ravaged by even worse disaster. Our conclusion must be that there is a certain degree of plasticity in human nature and behavior. When some communities were able to achieve a level of surplus which enabled them to recognize other imperatives than just survival, there developed new norms which, for example, allowed non-productive members—the aged, the severely injured, the defective newborns—to live, commanded hospitality for strangers rather than appropriation of their goods, and accorded social status to aesthetic contributions to the community even when they entailed no survival benefits for the community. We call such developments the beginnings of civilization.

Biologically, evolution occurs through two processes, natural selection of one possibility over other existing possibilities, or genetic mutation which proves adaptive within the process of natural selection. But the human race is not only somewhat biologically plastic, but also somewhat behaviorally plastic. Behavior depends upon a variety of variables: biology (genetics), unconscious drives, behaviors learned in the human socialization process, the ability to reason, the prior development of a self-conscious self, and the specific disadvantages and benefits in specific situations.

Because there are so many variables, no one variable determines behavior. And in theological terms there is no reason to privilege the biological/genetic influence over the ability to reason, over the socialization process (which includes moral and religious socialization), or over the consciously created self. All of these have been elements of human nature, along with the biological/genetic component, since *homo sapiens* developed within God's creation.

These two very different arguments against physicalism seem to me to together demolish physicalism's privileging of biology as defining God's will for human persons.

The Basic Problem with Natural Law: History

Catholic natural law approaches to ethics have been largely ahistorical. Within the modern period the Roman Catholic church first tended to identify all change with sin.[38] Under John XXIII Church teaching shifted to a kind of Teilhardian optimism, within which change in the world tended to be regarded as moving toward greater justice and peace.[39] Since Paul VI, and especially since John Paul II, the Vatican perspective on change in the world has become much more critical.[40]

The modern period did force the church in the twentieth century to accept evolutionary approaches to the origins of humanity.[41] But the Catholic church has never really changed its philosophical understanding of the human person and human nature to include historicity. While the Catholic magisterium now understands that political and economic institutions and systems change, and that humans developed from apes, its approach to human nature is still static. Physicalism is, of course, a major reason for this static quality in some areas of teaching, as evolutionary change in human biology is so slow as to be irrelevant in recorded human history. Thus the results of privileging biology in the interpretation of human nature will have static results.

The language—in fact the very name—of natural law theory inclines to the static. Nature has been understood in the West as that which is given, complete and fixed in itself. Even much of the popular environmentalism prevalent today understands nature as static apart from the activity of human persons which is assumed to defile and destroy it. Similarly, many natural law thinkers have not dealt at any length with evolution because they seem to have assumed that, though the world as we know it is the product of evolution, the process of evolution ended after reaching its goal—the development of *homo sapiens*. Though this static understanding of creation—of nature—historically enabled human beings to discern the divine will inherent in creation, it is not at all necessary. As Bernard Lonergan wrote:

> Any deepening or enriching of our apprehension of man [sic] possesses religious significance and relevance. But the new conceptual apparatus does make available such a deepening and enriching. Without denying human nature, it adds the quite distinctive categories of man [sic] as a historical being. Without repudiating the analysis of man [sic] into body and soul, it adds the richer and more concrete apprehension of man [sic] as incarnate subject.[42]

If the essential form of humans, animals, or the ecosystem as a whole has significantly changed since creation, then humans can no longer work from absolute abstract principles, but must begin with concrete particularity, which includes the historically new.[43] Change in human history/nature has sometimes been viewed as contrary to the divine will, and therefore sinful, and sometimes as in accord with God's will, in which case God is the author of the change, and the direction and goal of the change represents the divine will. Accepting divine authorship of the evolutionary process requires facing the problem of how to go about discerning in creation God's wishes in a specific situation. For if human nature is in constant process of change, and the direction of that change is away from biological determinism and toward both greater freedom and greater responsibility to care for creation, then the moral expectations of humans are in flux, and will become more demanding over time. Clearly, for example, human societies must accept more responsibility for resource conservation and environmental protection than in 1500 CE, both because humans have more capacity for intervention and because human societies have squandered and endangered aspects of creation. But how do we decide how much responsibility is appropriate for humans to exercise, and how it is best exercised? Some degree of ambiguity is inescapable.

If we understand the nature of the human person as both integrated and embedded in a radically historical social situation, then natural law morality will be also historicized, and can no longer take the form of a code, or any longer direct humans to specific acts which are then understand as willed by God.[44] Instead, discernment will be oriented toward the complex and difficult task of understanding human nature in the present moment and situation, and *also* oriented to 1) assessing the direction of change, 2) deciding if that direction is in accord with the central and enduring insights of Christian revelation, and 3) affirming or opposing the direction of change based on that assessment. For if the present represents not creation as God made it, but that original creation as modified many times over by human interactions with the dynamic character which God placed within the nature of creation, then acting in accord with the present state of creation is no guarantee of acting in accord with God's will.

In our contemporary situation it is appropriate to return to the traditional teaching that natural law imperatives intersect with positive law and take three forms or levels of explicitness. Thomas Aquinas gives the example of property, in which the primary level of natural law reveals that God did not distribute property, but made creation to meet the needs of all humans. The secondary and derivative sociocultural level reveals that an efficient system of meeting social needs is distribution of property to individuals; the third and most differentiated level of natural law on property is that reflected in positive law, which regulates the distribution and transfer of property within a specific society's private property system. The argument is that while the primary level is absolute and unchangeable, the secondary level is open to modification over time but is relatively stable, but the third level of positive law regulation is frequently changed for the purpose of allowing more just distribution of property. [45]

Today, taking historicity seriously in natural law approaches to sexuality, we might say that the primary level of natural law reveals that human nature is social, the secondary and social systemic level recognizes kinship as the basic form of social affiliation, and the third and most culturally determined level includes the varied forms and definitions of family and kinship which have prevailed in positive law and custom among different peoples and historical periods. It is two very different things to maintain that the family as modelled on Adam and Eve and their children is God's mandated form for sustaining human sociality, and to maintain that human beings are social creatures and only become fully human in community.

Once we admit the radical historicity of our world—the ongoing dynamism of all its parts, as well as of the whole—the discernment required of humans before action must be separated into two processes instead of one. Instead of discerning from the structures of the existing reality the will of God, we must first discern from human history up to and including existing reality the social, economic, political, biological, and environmental structures and trends in order to understand the processes at work in our world. This process of discernment has been called "reading the signs of the times." Then, in a second step, we turn to the discernment of value. For this second step we examine past history, our own experience, the experience of our own community and that of other communities in order to discern what is most valuable, what satisfies the basic needs and aspirations of all persons, what best respects our deepest understanding of the evolutionary potential embedded in creation. At a basic level, we must decide how we can act within the existing reality in ways that foster life—fullness of life for humans and the ecosystem now and in the future. For this fullness of life is that communion to which God has called all creation. It is by recognizing in our own experience the partial realizations of fullness of life and their absences that we come to recognize the presence of the Holy Spirit that Jesus promised to send to us. In the same way, for the first apostles and disciples it was by finding in Jesus' self and teachings the fullness of life to which the Hebrew Scriptures had pointed them that they recognized the Messiah.

In such an approach, neither nature as originally created nor nature as currently examined is normative. What is discerned is not so much nature only, but nature in history, and what is learned from discernment is not so much which specific acts to do or avoid, but what of the common good is endangered and should be supported by individuals as well as the society. Discernment at this level can lead to a variety of different responses for individual action, and many of these may well be different ways of moving society in the same direction.

The Case of Marriage and Family

It is not necessary to turn either to the distant Christian past or to conservative evangelical or fundamentalist Christians to find examples of patriarchy in Christian treatment of marriage and family. Many analysts understand both marriage and family as essentially patriarchal institutions in both their origins and their present structures. The sociologist Jessie Bernard, for example, argued extensively that U.S. marriage works for the benefit of men at the expense of women, and that this is true not only in terms of objective measures of education, career advancement, social status, and economic security, but also in terms of mental health. She demonstrates that while proportionately more married women report themselves as "happy" than do single women, married women actually describe themselves as considerably more phobic, passive, and depressed than do single women. At the same time, married women suffer from worse mental health than do married men, experiencing higher rates of psychological anxiety, feelings of inadequacy in marriage, negative or ambivalent self-perceptions, and expectations of impending nervous breakdown.[46] Married women have, according to Bernard, accepted the adjustment version of women's mental health advocated by doctors and psychologists for many decades: women must be happy if they have adjusted to their social role—even if doing so makes them depressed, anxious, and fearful.

Christian ethicist Mary Hobgood presents married sexuality in Western culture as defined by heterosexism, monogamy, and organized around child-rearing.[47] Hobgood argues that one of the major supports for traditional marriage is that it is vital to capitalism. Capitalists benefit from the unpaid labor of wives who reproduce and rear the workforce, and take care of all the personal and household maintenance tasks of the workers, thus allowing employers to set hours of work and pay scales which would be otherwise impossible.

Most of the religious defenses of traditional marriage have focused on children's need for stable homes. This is not surprising, since for most of the Christian tradition, as we have seen, the primary purpose of both marriage and sexual activity has been procreation. The social need for children to be materially supported and cared for in relatively stable situations was sufficient in most Western cultures to restrict sexual activity to marriage or to situations in which marriage could result from pregnancy. Of course, there were always other factors which supported this restriction of sexual activity to marriage in the West in premodern times. Demographer S. Ryan Johansson,[48] examining the seventeenth-, eighteenth-, and nineteenth-century European family, reminds us of the much later sexual maturation of both men and women, of high rates of venereal disease for which there were no effective treatments (much less cures), of high rates of infant mortality and of 1 – 2% maternal mortality, of the unpleasantness and ineffectiveness of available contraception, and of the burden that each pregnancy put on the comparatively fragile health of women.[49] All of these factors, as well as the cultural dominance of the Christian prohibition on nonmarital sex, discouraged persons in earlier ages from having sex outside the culturally and religiously approved context for child-rearing, which was marriage.

While the demands of child-rearing have clearly influenced the division of labor between men and women, it is not accurate to say that the needs of children were most influential in determining the structure of marriage and family. The economy has that honor. Since the beginning of the modern period the changes in both the shape of the economy and the structure of the family have changed too rapidly, and in too many linked ways, for there to be any doubt about the power of the economy to dictate changes in the family. Beverly Harrison's "The Effect of Industrialization on the Role of Women," for example, recaps how the Industrial Revolution moved production out of the home where it had occupied both spouses and older children, and into factories where men worked.[50] Over time the greater and greater productivity of factories led to the banning of child labor, one of the last of the elements in the social construction of "childhood" as we think of it today. Between the late eighteenth and late nineteenth centuries the social construction of childhood as a time of innocence and nurture, which historian Philippe Aries describes as beginning in the thirteenth century,[51] combined with the exclusion of most women from economic production to produce the child-centered family, in which the chief role of woman was the care and nurturance of children. Today it is still true that the requirements of child-rearing dictate much of the thinking about marriage.

While much of the concern today about high rates of unwed teen pregnancy involves the inability of teens to materially provide for children, it is also widely recognized that the immaturity of many teens renders them incapable of both providing the nurturance and care that children require and maintaining stable adult-child relationships. The fact that much of the modern focus in marriage has been on the needs of children has drastically affected contemporary understandings of the role of women. Because women's role in the family has been understood for two centuries now in terms of child-rearing, the tendency to focus on the needs of children when considering proposed shifts in women's role or the structure of marriage has severely disadvantaged women.

It is clear that the modern Western emphasis on freedom and liberty as the human condition, the general shape of contract theories of governments, and the resultant focus on human rights have affected men and women differently. There is a strong tendency for the rights of (male) humans to be defined individually, in terms of autonomy, and separately from their relationships, which is not true for women. A pivotal issue in the UN meetings in Vienna in June 1993 on universal human rights was whether universal human rights apply to women. On the face of it, the issue is absurd. If women are human, then human rights inhere in women as well as men. But historically the question of whether women have human rights is relevant and critical. For the role—and therefore the rights—of women have historically been defined in terms of women not as ends in themselves, not as autonomous, as men are, but as instruments, as necessary for the well-being of both children and men. This instrumental understanding has changed little. Women are still subjected to arguments as to why generally accepted rights—such as control over one's body—must be modified with regard to women. Persons and organizations who demand that women need permission of their husbands to be sterilized or aborted, or in some cultures to be issued contraceptive means, do nothing to ensure that men need permission of wives to be sterilized, much less that men who do not have the consent of their wives to sex are charged with legal violation of the wife's right to bodily autonomy. Persons and organizations who oppose the employment of women and advocate various forms of discrimination against working women on the grounds that children need full-time mothers in the home never advocate any modifications in the work roles of men to accommodate the needs of their families. In comparison to women, men and to some extent children are considered ends in themselves, while women are only means. For this reason, until recently all attempts to reform the structure of the family, whether they emanated from the right or the left, tended to focus on changing the role of women. The Catholic church throughout the twentieth century has insisted on a return to the "traditional" female role—women not working outside the home, subject to the headship of men, with men controlling women's property.[52] The attempt of the New Religious Right to persuade women to return to this traditional role sometimes took on a new look—the housewife who greets her husband at the door wrapped in Saran wrap à la Marabel Morgan—but was, at the core, the same submissive, supportive, instrumental role.[53] From the left, on the other hand, though the proposal was different, it too presumed that the problem in marriage was the role of women. Women were, according to Marx and Engels, to be liberated by a revolution which would both abolish private property and restore women as income earning producers, not merely consumers and home maintenance workers.[54] The unpaid, low-status, traditional women's work was to be restructured, socialized, and paid. However, in the eastern European restructuring of marriage and family under Communism, only women's role changed.[55] The problem of marriage was "the Woman problem." It was not considered necessary to rethink the roles of men or children in the family, even though the initial assumption of the left was that marriage was a kind of slavery for women.[56] Is it really possible to abolish any kind of slavery without affecting the lives and roles of slaveowners? Historically, of course, socialist/communist societies never succeeded in socializing traditional female work, but did insist on women's participation in the paid workforce, where internal discrimination was less prevalent than in capitalist systems. But women in the workforce in these nations, like women in capitalist nations, continued to carry the almost exclusive burden of housework and childcare in addition to paid work.[57]

Many of the changes going on in the American family today are traceable to changes in the economy. The fact that the average wage, adjusted for inflation, has been consistently weaker in purchasing power since the late 1960s has been a major factor in the huge increase of married women working.

In rethinking the structure of the family today, some things are clear, and others are still obscure. We should have clarity that:

1) Marriage and the family are historically conditioned institutions which can and should be restructured with a concern for justice understood as treating the needs/desires of women on an equal par with those of men and children;

2) Marriage and the family are conditioned by race, class, and other sociocultural factors as well: the role of married women, for example, varies a great deal within the U.S. depending upon whether the family is, for example, upper-middle-class white professional, rural black tenant farmers, or in-

ner-city on ADC (whether black, white or Hispanic). Such sociological factors influence every aspect of marriage and family.

3) The greater involvement of women in reproduction does not legitimate infringing upon women's bodyright. (In Chapter 6 I will make a case for bodyright as foundational for the development of selfhood, including moral responsibility in the self.) Women will have something more than men to say about human reproduction because divine providence, operating in biological creation/evolution, gave women more involvement in and responsibility for reproduction. This is an excuse neither for excluding men from those decisions about reproduction which are appropriate to their level of participation and responsibility, nor for usurping from women and giving to men control over women's bodies in the name of reproductive equality (because men *can't* bear children but should be equally involved).

4) Roles in the family are not biologically dictated. Because women nurse babies does not mean they are meant to be food preparers and servers. Because men have more upper body strength does not mean they are disciplinarians. No one marital or family pattern is normative, and all others defective in some way.[58] Families do not need to include children. Families need not include blood kin. Families need not be based on marriage. Families can be collections, of persons who are committed to the physical, moral, spiritual, social, and intellectual development of other members of the collective unit in an ongoing way.

5) Marriage can take many shapes and forms. Institutions such as churches and states should allow various forms of marriage, and should be open to any marital roles/patterns which are non-abusive, just, and socially responsible.

Social acceptance of these points would require changing many of our social practices, from census regulations regarding families and households, through laws governing inheritance, guardianship, taxation, and insurance. That is a huge agenda for change. But there are still a number of areas in which our thinking about sexuality in relation to marriage and family is still in major flux. Is there a purpose and content to marriage once it is no longer about the ownership and control of women and children, once both entering and remaining within marriage are fully voluntary? Is there a purpose for couples to marry apart from producing and rearing children? Do the monogamy and the sexual fidelity which have been traditional (at least for women) in the West serve any purpose in sexually egalitarian marriage? In the present post-modern world monogamous marriage understood in terms of an intimate interpersonal relationship meets a variety of human needs which have been met historically, and in other cultures even in the present, in other ways. This should not be understood as an argument that this is the form that marriage should take now or in the future, or that there is anything in human nature, or human sexuality itself which dictates any specific form of sexual interaction or relationship. We live in a world in which culture changes slowly. Most of us will look to satisfy our individual needs and desires for touch, affection, intimacy, and bonding within the marital kind of relationship we have been socialized to accept. For this reason most societies do well to reform general structures such as marriage and family in the direction of justice and tolerance.

4. Sexual Pleasure as Grace and Gift

Contemporary Christians in our society are increasingly distinguished from earlier Christians not only by cresting doubts about procreationism, dealt with in Chapter Two, but also by their intuitions/convictions about the goodness of sex itself. Christian tradition has understood sex on a moral spectrum which has seldom extended further than evil incarnate on the right to morally suspect on the left. Roman Catholicism has taught for some centuries that in sexuality there is "no small matter," meaning that all sexual sins are serious sins. While we may and should deplore the negative assessment of sexuality in the tradition, there is one positive note: Christianity has understood sexuality as powerful. One of the problems within the cultural shift away from the traditional Christian understanding of sexuality which has been occurring in secular culture is that the power of sexuality is denied along with the demons long understood as animating sexuality. Sexuality is treated lightly, in terms of privacy, of recreational activity, as a body function with no more meaning or importance than other body functions.

But sexuality *is* powerful. There are complex connections between personal sexual identity and the expression and satisfaction of certain basic physiological and psychological needs and desires. Recognition of the power of sexuality in our lives and world is essential for understanding sexuality as a positive force, as a source of transforming grace.

Within the traditional negative focus on sexuality in Christianity there is a tendency to identify the source of evil in sex with sexual pleasure. Augustine and Aquinas agreed that had it not been for human sin, coitus would be governed by reason, not desire, and that humans would engage in coitus with the same deliberation and intent as they now sow seed in their fields.[1] Augustine taught that intercourse was, even in marriage, at least venially sinful because it was virtually impossible to have intercourse without pleasure.[2] Note that this conclusion, and the previous example of the sower, presume male perspectives on sex. Male perspective on sex is virtually exclusive in Christian sexual theology. Women are not sexual sowers, and pleasure in sex is by no means inevitable for women.[3]

Comedians today make great fun of the teaching socialized into too many of us that "if it feels good, it must be bad." That this is the stuff of humor reveals that we as a society are aware of our ambiguous attitudes about pleasure. We are uneasy about our tendency to assume that pain and discomfort signal virtue, and pleasure vice. We know we have been conditioned to associate pleasure, especially sexual pleasure, with hedonism. Given our socialization to sexual repression and the glorification of pain, hedonism, often taught as the sole alternative to repressive asceticism, appears almost irresistible. And yet rationally we know that egocentric hedonism is neither responsible nor mature, that it runs contrary to the interests of human community. So many Christians feel trapped between egocentric hedonism and masochistic understandings of goodness, and ambivalent about both of them.

Sexual Pleasure: Not Irresistible

Within the Christian sexual tradition there are two different explanations for the low esteem in which sexual pleasure is held. St. Augustine is often used to exemplify an understanding of sexual pleasure which was predominant in the early church. He saw sexual pleasure as dangerous because it is virtually irresistible. St. Jerome agreed, and one of his strongest arguments for virginity was that only those who have never experienced sexual pleasure can be free of its dangerous tentacles. Pleasure which is irresistible causes a loss of control over our activity, makes us irresponsible, and, therefore, causes us to neglect our moral duties. Sexual pleasure lures us into a focus on our own individual satisfaction, and therefore tempts us to be selfish, to ignore or abuse others. For many of the leaders of the Christian church in the first few centuries, the good Christian was one who avoided sex so far as possible, and, when forced to fulfill marital obligations to one's spouse, performed those sexual duties with as little pleasure as possible.

The second explanation for the low status of sexual pleasure in the Christian tradition is often attributed to St. Thomas Aquinas, who maintained that sexual pleasure is something that humans have in common with animals. It is part of our lower animal nature, and not part of the higher rational nature which links us to the Almighty and which is characteristically human. For animals sexual pleasure is a good, said Thomas, but for humans it has a kind of intermediate status. It is not evil, for it is part of our God-given nature. But it is not a truly human good.[4] For that reason sexual pleasure was not understood as a proper end or goal for human activity. Sexual pleasure is not wrong, but it should be oriented to more human (i.e., rational, higher) ends in order to be justified. Within sexuality, Thomas understood sexual pleasure as an indirect benefit of pursuing higher ends, such as procreation.

Though forms of both these arguments have influenced our society, the Augustinian understanding of sexual pleasure as an evil which robs humans of control of their actions and causes them to ignore the rights and needs of others has tended to prevail in American Christian culture. Our society has taught us that sexual pleasure is evil because it is irresistible. It overwhelms both human reason and the human will. Under the influence of sexual pleasure reason no longer functions to distinguish good from evil, and the will no longer chooses the good.

Because sexual pleasure has been so understood, sexuality became a taboo subject. Sex education came to be seen as encouraging "carnal thoughts," which themselves could be sexually pleasurable and thus lead to the overpowering of reason and will.[5] Generations of young adults were taught that the simplest of sexual pleasures, such as holding hands in the theater, should be carefully regulated, if not avoided, lest lust come to dominate a relationship.

The understanding of sexual pleasure as irresistible not only mandated sexual avoidance, but also provided very convenient excuses for irresponsible behavior in sexual situations. Men and women have used and continue to use the irresistibility of sexual pleasure as the primary excuse for out-of-wedlock pregnancies. Both unmarried men and women continue to report to surveyers that female virtue theoretically demands sexual abstinence, and that virtuous women do not plan for immoral sex by procuring a diaphragm, or condom, or pill prescription. But sometimes on dates even virtuous women are overwhelmed by sexual desire, and their willpower crumbles. (Men are not expected under the prevailing double standard to be capable of resisting, or required to resist, sexual desire.) But women's lapse is understood as a much lesser moral lapse than planning for premarital sex would be, for at least her *intentions* were pure, even if her will wasn't strong. Of course, the cost of these pure intentions is a high risk of unwed pregnancy. In the U.S. the percentage of children born to unwed mothers rose from 10% to 21% between 1970 and 1985.[6]

Another situation in which we encounter the argument for sexual pleasure as irresistible is male excuses for either forcing sex on women or excluding women from pleasure in sex. Women who ask male lovers to slow down, to extend both foreplay and intercourse, and to vary both positions and techniques so as to allow women to become aroused and reach orgasm frequently hear, "Can't do it, old girl. That's not the way the plumbing works. When the little man is ready, he's ready, and nothing I can do will stop him. You have to catch up as best you can." Thus any number of deficiencies in male technique, including premature ejaculation, get blamed on the demands of male biology.

The same excuse is frequently used by sexual harassers: "Sorry, I just couldn't control myself. You are so attractive I just had to touch you/take you out/have you." And of course, this argument is central to most rape defenses: the rapist was caught in the throes of male sexual desire which, once aroused, is uncontrollable. Responsibility should be placed on her who first aroused his desire. This is why 100-lb. women who were raped and assaulted by 200-lb. men can be the real culprits: they wore shorts, or smiled, or bent over, or failed to lower the shade the last half inch, or accepted a date with him. Social attitudes are beginning to change around the use of this argument in rape—but very slowly.

This argument that sexual pleasure is irresistible simply is not true. Humans frequently resist sexual pleasure, men as well as women. Cohabiting couples who find themselves kissing will frequently make the decision to postpone lovemaking now, though they are together and already aroused, and to wait until later when there would be more time, and less chance of interruption. Longtime lovers scoff at the idea that sexual pleasure can't be resisted, because resisting immediate sexual pleasure is essential to being a good lover, especially for males. The inability to postpone immediate sexual gratification constitutes an impediment to concern for the pleasure of the partner. Lack of sexual control is characteristic of premature ejaculators, and correlates with low levels of sexual technique and often with low-intensity orgasm. It is *control* of sexual pleasure—knowing when and how to postpone sexual gratification, using techniques to build arousal in self and partner—which intensifies sexual pleasure for oneself and one's partner.

And yet we really don't want to say that what men need to do more of in sex is exercise greater control. Need for control is a prison we have built around men in our society. Men need to be liberated from the oppressive compulsion to be in control of themselves, others, and all situations. Yet men, and women, too, need to accept responsibility for controlling sexual desire. Are there different kinds of sexual control?

A few years ago a young couple preparing to marry after some years of living together met with my husband and me as part of our church's marriage preparation program. In the course of the discussion of things they would like to change in their relationship, the woman said very hesitantly that she'd like it if he'd lose control in sex more often. The man was flabbergasted, and exclaimed, "What do you mean? You've always told me what a good lover I am!" She tried to explain that he did everything right—he touched her in all the right places, in all the right ways, he made sure she was ready before moving to the next step, he asked her for suggestions, and he always took her with him in orgasm. "But you're too perfect—like a machine! I feel like I'm dying and being born, flying and crashing, but I can't feel you doing any of that with me, because you're too in-control. I can't feel you enjoying it. To me, your trip looks like a head trip, not a whole body trip. And I end up feeling like a musical instrument used by you, the musician."

What this women was saying of her lover some men say of themselves. They come to feel oppressed by the internalized voice that says they must remain in control, and feel themselves as if in a control booth watching the lovers from a distance. This oppressive control is a characteristic sexual danger which resides in the male role. How can the masculine sex role stereotype both defend male sexual desire as irresistible *and* demand that men remain in complete control of sex? The two are actually not so contradictory as they seem. In fact, the defense of male sexual desire as irresistible often emerges from a recognition that no human beings can be in complete control of their emotions and desires all the time, in all situations. The kind of rigid control of feelings, the lack of need for any other persons, which is demanded of men in general is recognized as not possible. The excuse that male sexual desire cannot be controlled is often an attempt by men, and even by sympathetic women, to cut some sexual slack for men in a role which allows little slack, to allow them to vent some of the pent-up pressure in a sexual outlet. For too many males the concept of uncontrollable male sexual desire is the only alternative to sex as a kind of performance, a test of expertise, without spontaneity or intimacy. Without this alternative sex is merely another area of stress and testing where one's masculinity is on the line.[7]

Sex should not be a source of anxiety for men, but neither should it be an avenue for venting men's frustrations by abusing women. Rather sex should be one way of *lessening* the anxiety men experience in other areas of life. If this is to happen, we need to ensure that in demanding that men accept responsibility for their sexual activity we do not invoke the traditional model of opposition between sexual desire and human will. For when we understand virtue—responsibility—as the triumph of the will over the sinful desires of the body, we embrace an understanding of self-control which is, in fact, repressive. Our very language betrays this model: we say, "Yes, we can control our sexual desire," as if our sexual desire were something apart from us. This model of self we inherited is not that of the embodied self; we have been taught in too many ways to see the desires of our bodies as enemies of our "real" selves.

This inherited model of sexual control is dangerous. It is the root of what makes women fear men as dangerous; it is responsible for a great deal of men's pain. The center of male socialization is repression—the repression of feelings, emotions, wishes, desires. But repression is not necessary to ensure "control" of sexual desire. Sexual desire is not a raging river in flood about to overpower us. It is not beyond reason. This is somewhat easier for women to accept than men, for as James Nelson points out, women do not have the experience of being unable to prevent an erection when on public display,[8] or being unable to prevent ejaculation past a certain point of stimulation. Such experiences easily lead men to see sexual desire as neither controlled nor controllable, when in fact they remain in ultimate control of what they do with an erection, and of the circumstances which bring them to an ejaculatory point of no return.

Neither men nor women should see sexual desire, or any other bodily desire, as an enemy to be feared and controlled. We need to understand our sexual desires as one set of messages to ourselves about how we are. All of us need to learn to hear the messages circulating in our bodies, to interpret them correctly, and to cooperate with them. Repression—denial of the body messages—is dangerous, even fatal. Denial of some specific body messages—of chronic pain, of tiredness, of changes in our body's rhythms—is frequently responsible, especially in men, for unnecessary deaths due to late discovery of conditions such as cancer and hypertension, which are treatable when discovered early. We need to listen to our body messages so that we act to meet our needs—whether they are for rest, for physical closeness, for release of muscle tension, for interpersonal intimacy, or many others.[9] Many of the impulses we call sexual desires are really about different bodily needs, but are interpreted as sexual because they are so often satisfied only sexually.

Sex can release muscle tension and allow us to relax, it can warm us by raising blood circulation, it can include the stroking of our skin which releases endorphins, it can provide stimulation and excitement to remedy boredom, and it can restore emotional intimacy which banishes loneliness. Many of these sexual desires could be satisfied nonsexually, by a hot tub, a 30-minute workout, a massage, a long conversation with a close friend, or cuddling with a young child. And not every desire needs to be satisfied every time we feel it. We walk down a street past a bakery, and our mouths water at the plate of eclairs. Next door, in the museum lobby we stop to look at a display of primitive erotica, and our mouths go dry. If we stay long enough to become involved in sexual fantasy, we may feel more signs of arousal. But we do not need to do battle with ourselves to prevent our arousal from compelling us to throw the next passerby to the ground and ravish him, any more than we need to blindfold ourselves in order to pass the eclair.

When the desire for an eclair, or for sex, becomès truly compulsive is when the sex or the eclair has come to represent something else for us, something more than what they are in themselves. For example, the eating disorders which are so common among young women in the U.S. seem to include not only identifications of food with the normal appetites of the self for self-esteem, body pleasure, and nurture, but also feelings of unworthiness and the need for redemption which demand the repression of the bodyself through the punishment of starvation and purging.[10]

That something else is some desire we have repressed and refused to recognize. Many persons, especially men, have internalized so much body repression that sex is virtually their only experience of being touched, stroked, held, or kissed. It is no wonder that so many women often accuse men of being sex addicts, or of interpreting any touch as sexual. If your sexual partner is virtually the only person allowed to touch you, and if all of your emotional needs must be met in sex, you will soon experience every touch as sexual, and come to need a great deal of sex. Such attitudes toward sex are not limited to men, of course, but since women are normally allowed to feel and display a much broader range of emotions than men, and are not expected to control anyone, even themselves, most women's problems with repression lie in different areas.

Sexual Pleasure as Premoral Good

One of the major tasks of Christian morality in the present age is to claim sexual pleasure as a good. We could argue that sexual pleasure is a good using traditional models of argumentation. For example, we could say that sexual pleasure is good because it is a deliberately created part of God's creation. Such an introduction to both sexual pleasure and sexuality *in toto* is common in the Christian churches, which then proceed to the many restrictive rules which must be followed in order to control this "good" portion of creation. It simply is not enough to say that sex is good because God created it. God is just as responsible for creating the AIDS virus, Hurricane Andrew, sub-Saharan African drought, and piranhas as God is for human sexuality. It simply is not self-evident that all parts of creation have the same capacity to represent and mediate God to us, which is what endows them with goodness.

However, we could further argue that discernment of human biology (in the female at least) proves that God intended that sexual activity be at least sometimes primarily for pleasure. As we saw in Chapter Three, physicalist approaches to natural law based in contemporary biology, rather than in medieval misunderstandings of science, would provide evidence for sexual pleasure as divine intention. If theologians of the ancient and medieval world had included women among them, or if biological and sexual knowledge of the times had included women's body knowledge, the use of natural law thought would have led either to a greater moral approval of sexual pleasure, or to the abandonment of natural law thinking long before the reformers.

But sexual pleasure can be argued as good for a much simpler, more commonsensical reason. It feels good. Like a hot tub for aching muscles, cool water on a hot day, a shot of morphine after waking up from surgery, and the taste of ice cream on the tongue, sexual pleasure makes us feel good. We like it. Pleasure itself is a good. It is a premoral good. To say that pleasure, or in this case sexual pleasure, is a premoral good does not mean that it leads to moral good, but that it is ordinarily a good, and should be understood as one aspect of the general social good. However, there are always some specific situations in which a premoral good may be outweighed by a conflicting premoral good within the process of moral discernment.[11]

Of course, in any specific case the enjoyment of one good may require the sacrifice of another good. And so I often sacrifice the sexual pleasure I might have had by making love with my husband on a weekday morning in order that I get to my class on time, my husband gets to work on time, and the kids get to school on time. All of these are goods also. The fact that we sacrificed the sexual pleasure we might have had in order to secure other pleasures (the satisfaction of meeting responsibilities and trusts, the economic security of employment, etc.) does not make that sexual pleasure bad. Nor does the fact that sexual pleasure is here sacrificed make it less important or valuable. At other times, I decide that sharing sexual pleasure with my husband has been neglected, and is now more important than staying late to finish up a project, or even cooking dinner for the family. Both of these will then give way to sexual pleasure.

It sounds very simple—and simple-minded—to say that sexual pleasure is good because it feels good. It will be objected that some people derive their pleasure from killing or maiming, from abusing children or inspiring fear. Some even derive *sexual* pleasure from such activities. This is true. But while the stimulus for their pleasure is evil, this does not mean that the pleasure itself is evil. We *need* pleasure; we need *body* pleasure. It is no accident that persons who live with great and constant body pain so often become physically distorted, and sometimes even grotesque. This is true not only of human bodies, but of human spirits. Pain and suffering can distort our humanity. We need to limit as much as possible the pain to which we are prey, and to maximize our experience of body pleasure. While no one kind of body pleasure is necessary, we need to create so far as is possible a life and a lifestyle which satisfies human needs for pleasure. For some of us, that will be a lifestyle of rugged outdoor exercise, clean air, and the beauty of nature. For another it may be hot tubs, frequent sex, central heating, art museums, and professional massage. For yet another it may be cuddling sweet-smelling babies, frequent hugs and pats from friends, and cultivating clothes and bedclothes which pamper the skin. But one of the influences which determine our lifestyle should be the messages from our body about what is pleasurable.

We have inherited great moral fear about such "catering to our bodies." Look at the warnings about masturbation. In addition to the condemnations of masturbation as sinful because non-procreative, a misuse of the sexual faculties which should be oriented to producing new life, a major objection to masturbation is that it is very literally self-centered. It involves a turning to oneself for the satisfaction of one's desires, rather than a healthy turning outward to another person who is different and could broaden and complement one.[12]

Traditional condemnations of masturbation as serious sin have not been abandoned upon recognition that infants begin self-stimulation of the genitals soon after birth. Only the satisfaction of their drive for oral gratification precedes this drive for genital gratification. And many infants of one to two years successfully stimulate themselves to orgasm (without, of course, the semen the boys will not have for many years). This self-stimulation of the genitals does not end in infancy, but accelerates at puberty. By the age of 20 at least 92% of males report masturbating, and about two-thirds of females.[13]

The fact that the vast majority of humans masturbate, even the fact that infants long before "the age of reason" masturbate, does not constitute proof that masturbation is a moral good. However, it does tell against the claim that masturbation is invariably sinful, even if it does not point to its being a moral good. The more important evidence is that research shows that the practice of masturbation does not prevent men and women from seeking out sexual partners. In fact, among women, it has become clear that women who have masturbated are more likely to experience general sexual pleasure and, in particular, orgasm in partnered sex than are women who have not masturbated.[14] Rather than finding that solitary sex is an obstacle to shared sex, research suggests that solitary sex is helpful to women in later partnered sex in a variety of ways. The practice of masturbation provides three specific kinds of beneficent knowledge: 1) physical knowledge of her body (its genitalia), 2) knowledge of the process of sexual arousal and fulfillment, and 3) knowledge of her own pattern of arousal.[15]

These three are distinct. Most women who have not masturbated cannot describe the female vulva. Many are so socialized not to think about "down there" that they cannot answer questions about the relative locations of the urethral opening, the vagina, and the anus. They are not aware of having two sets of labia, and are even ignorant of the location and function of the clitoris. Beginning with bathing and toilet training as toddlers, they have been taught not to explore their bodies, that eventually they will give themselves to a man who will explore their bodies and, if they are lucky, convey an appreciation of their bodies to them. Lack of knowledge of one's body makes ownership of and responsibility for that body immeasurably more difficult. For example, ignorance of one's genitalia handicaps a woman in seeking medical help for abnormal changes in her genitalia, as well as in taking responsibility for treatment of medical conditions involving genitalia and the reproductive tract. If women do not know the structure of their genitalia, they are very unlikely to have a language for speaking of its various parts. Without language there is no communication. Learning to leave responsibility for one's body to others—to sexual partners, doctors, and nurses, for example—makes it easier to abdicate to others responsibility for one's life and society.

Similarly, knowledge of the stages of sexual arousal and fulfillment is important. And such knowledge is not innate. Women, and occasionally even men, who have been either protected from sexual information, or socialized to fear and hate sex, can be extremely uncomfortable with the unfamiliar and intense sensations of sexual pleasure. Comfort with the sensations of sexual pleasure is essential for fully experiencing pleasure, especially orgasm.

But the most common problem with women who have not masturbated is that in entering partnered sex they have no idea of their own personal pattern of sexual arousal. They do not know what gives them sexual pleasure, or what causes discomfort. Because they are not familiar enough with their body to know what touch is arousing, they cannot convey that information to a partner. Furthermore, their ignorance of their own response pattern deprives them of a basic framework for anticipating what touch will best arouse and pleasure their partner.

It is important to note that these characteristics associated with a lack of masturbatory experience have moral significance. A lesser degree of ownership of one's body, a lessened sense of being in charge and responsible for one's body, and consequently for one's life, and inability to anticipate how to pleasure one's partner or communicate to one's partner how to pleasure oneself should not be encouraged, but rather recognized as moral deficits.

Disgusting, many respond. Why should we teach women to pleasure themselves when the essence of Christianity is to live an other-centered life? Why isn't it sufficient to teach each of the partners to concentrate on loving the other as well as possible? Why tempt anyone toward selfishness or self-centeredness by inviting them to pursue personal pleasure? This way lies hedonism!

When presented with such questions, many groups balk. Undergraduate students immediately respond by dividing into two sides claiming to be "Christian" and "non-Christian." The "Christians" inevitably adopt the perspective that love of neighbor requires a certain blindness to the interests of the self, and that to focus on the self to any degree is to be overwhelmed by greed, lust, and other sins. The "non-Christians" believe that in order to defend the possibility that pleasure can be moral, that the good of one person can also simultaneously be the good of another person, that they must renounce Christianity.

But sex is perhaps one of the best life arenas for demonstrating that self and other are not naturally hostile. Their relationship is much more complex, much more influenced by the specific situation. In sex it becomes apparent that the interests of the self and the interests of the partner are largely linked. At a very basic level, if I do not know what pleasures me, I have fewer clues as to how to pleasure my partner. But also, within sexual activity it becomes clear that exercising my ability to arouse and please the partner excites me. It makes me feel successful, powerful, confident, and able to love well. Those feelings drive me to further pleasure the partner, and that pleasure drives the partner to share his pleasure with me by arousing and pleasuring me. It is very, very seldom that sex can be extremely satisfying for one partner and not satisfying for the other. Often the person reporting such solitary pleasure in shared sex has actually settled for much less than the optimum pleasure out of ignorance of what is possible. In rapes by strangers, for example, where one might imagine that the rapist experiences great pleasure despite the lack of pleasure in the victim, rapists most often report that their pleasure in the sex itself was not great, certainly not as pleasurable as their non-coercive sex. These rapists report that their deepest pleasure came not from the sex, but from their control of the victim, from her fear, or obedience, or pain. Supporting such reports is evidence that rape situations have a much higher than normal incidence of both erectile dysfunction and premature ejaculation.[16]

Our society has much too much fear of hedonism and not enough understanding of it. Hedonism is a way of life in which one consistently chooses the pleasure immediately before one. All humans are born into hedonism. All human infants pursue pleasure single-mindedly. Freud called this the pleasure principle behind human behavior, and insisted that hedonism is natural for young children. But the pleasure principle does not continue to dominate our lives. Even as young children the pleasure principle comes to be challenged by our discovery of the reality principle: that is, we learn to connect behaviors with their consequences. Not only do we learn that when we reach out to grab the pretty flames we get burned, but we also learn that indulging our desire to knock all the dishes off the table will bring punishment, and restraining such desires will bring a reward. Humans thus learn, beginning in childhood, to use and develop their rationality in the process of limiting the pleasure principle to accord with the reality principle. This development of rationality is also the development of the ego, the adult self, which uses reason to replace, a little at a time, the superego as source of moral guidance. At the same time the ego struggles to bring to consciousness, piece by piece, parts of the powerful but unconscious id, so that unconscious desires and associations lose their power to determine behavior as they are exposed to rational consciousness and can be balanced against other desires and associations.[17] This process lasts all throughout our lives. In theological terms, we call this same process the development of conscience.[18]

This means that from a psychological perspective humans are always to some extent hedonists. Even mature adults are, and should be, motivated by the desire to maximize pleasure and minimize pain. Their maturity consists not in giving up pleasure motivation, but in their ability to discipline their pursuit of pleasure, and to include a maximal number of others with them in that pursuit. Many Christians object at this point that this may be Freudianism, but it is not Christianity. Christians are not supposed to be motivated either by pleasure or by pain avoidance. Christians are supposed to be motivated by concern for others. But are these two really separable?

Freud insists that the mature adult who is able to love others and to sacrifice his or her own desires in the interests of loved ones has not rejected basic human hedonism in favor of love of neighbor, but has rather learned both to utilize reason in disciplining hedonism, and to take pleasure in the pleasure of others. That is, for the truly other-directed person love of neighbor is built upon, is an extension of, love of self. This is, of course, in accord with the specific form of the love comand, to love your neighbor as yourself.[19]

From this perspective, persons who desire to be exemplary Christians, true lovers of their neighbors, should not strive to deny pleasure or inflict suffering on the self, but should rather strive to find ways to relate to and connect with the neighbor. For if we are connected to our neighbor, if we become accustomed to feeling, even in a very diminished form, their pain and their joy, then we will be willing to accept some sacrifice of our pleasure for the sake of increasing their pleasure. For in that exchange we are protected from absolute loss of pleasure by the fact that we feel their increase of pleasure with them. The parent who sacrifices a lung or a kidney to save the life of her child not only accepts the physical pain of the surgical process itself, but also the loss of bodily integrity and the higher risk of death entailed in possessing only one such organ. And yet the parent who loves the child may experience this sacrifice as minimal to nonexistent, because the joy of having the loved child alive and healthy is so overwhelming. Jesus' teaching about the reign of God takes up this same theme—that the sacrifices entailed in discipleship to the reign can be major sacrifices—the loss of one's family, even the loss of one's life—and yet the disciple will count them as nothing because the joy to be found in discipleship, in loving the neighbor as oneself, is so great.[20]

All humans are always trying to maximize their pleasure and minimize the pain in their lives, but most humans shift from the absolute hedonism of infancy to a modified hedonism as we learn that to minimize some of the worst pains we have to postpone some of our pleasures. Most adults literally could not survive as absolute hedonists—it is no accident that absolute hedonism has historically been the province of the grossly wealthy and powerful, whose basic needs are provided by others, leaving them free to pursue immediate gratification. Such adults may have the freedom to live as children. But most of us, faced with the situation of the ant and the grasshopper, are forced to imitate the ant in practicing delayed gratification.

In philosophical terms, it should be clear that I am advocating a form of moral utilitarianism. "Utilitarianism is the doctine that the rightness of actions is to be judged by their consequences," writes J. J. C. Smart.[21] Within contemporary debates over utiliarianism, there are many different conflicts. One conflict within utilitarianism from its historical beginnings with Bentham concerns the split between hedonistic and ideal utilitarianism. Smart classes Bentham as a hedonistic act utilitarian, and G. E. Moore as an ideal rule utilitarian, with J. S. Mill somewhere in between hedonism and idealism in his utilitarianism.[22] Most of the pop academic treatment of utilitarianism, not to mention the Christian pastoral treatment, has viewed all utilitarianism in terms of hedonistic act utilitarianism: as if all utilitarianism demands that each act be chosen only on the basis of its pleasurableness to those affected. It is no wonder that Christians, and many others with a commitment to community and its common good, have rejected utilitarianism. On the other hand, an ideal utilitarian like Moore holds that pleasurableness is not even a necessary condition of goodness, which is then open to the ascetic, body-denying repression of Christian history.

In the debate about the place of pleasure in a sexual ethic, I want to take a middle position which is much closer to those of both Aquinas and J. S. Mill than to either Bentham or Moore. That is, pleasure is a necessary but not sufficient condition for goodness. Pleasure is a term that covers a great number of distinctly different sensations. The pleasure that I felt in making love with my husband to celebrate our twenty-fifth anniversary was distinctly different from my pleasure in discovering that my efforts in constructing and utilizing a compost bin for our garbage had actually produced usable humus. My pleasure in the humus is also drastically different from the "pleasure" I expect to feel when we finally wake and bury my uncle long stolen from his family by Alzheimer's disease. I agree with Mill and Aquinas that there are higher and lower pleasures, though I am not in agreement with either's method of classifying those. Higher pleasures, it seems to me, have benevolent consequences for others. I think this is a part of what Aquinas meant when he says that a pleasure is measured by its end, and that the ultimate end is God.[23]

But, it seems to me, sexual pleasures are not, according to this understanding, lower pleasures. A particular act of sexual pleasure that conveys to a wounded loved one respect, admiration, comfort—unconditional love—may free that person, and the relationship itself, to heroic acts of love for the wider community. On the other hand, it is possible that the individual who uses reason to examine his/her conscience and make his/her peace with God may feel a rational, moral pleasure which only serves to confirm the individual in a state of solitary self-justification.

It seems clear to me that we are learning that touching and cuddling babies—and all God's human children—makes them better able to both give and accept love, and thus makes them better able to participate in the reign of God that Jesus announced. I have argued that body pleasure is a good in that it communicates to us our own goodness. That sense of self-goodness is essential if we are to understand ourselves as beloved by God, and thus able to communicate God's love to others.

This goodness of body pleasure, of sexual pleasure among other kinds of body pleasure, does not mean that the absence of pleasure is necessarily evil. I do want to argue, however, that the deliberate deprivation of body pleasure requires justification. For example, as we attempt to structure a world in which the resources of the world are shared justly, we should be willing to live simply for the sake of justice. However, to the extent that simplicity entails a lessening of pleasure for persons, pleasure should be lessened only to the degree necessary for justice, and not from any understanding of the goodness of material deprivation itself. So with sexual pleasure. The willingness to postpone pleasure in sex when one knows a partner is tired is a good, but postponing sexual pleasure in general is not good.

What does this imply for celibacy? There is no major problem with temporary celibacy, as in the abstinence that most parents desire for their young teens. For it is clear even to many teens that the pleasure deprivation in celibacy is compensated for in the freedom from a great deal of pain: the pain of unwanted pregnancy or STDs, as well as the pains inflicted in sexual relationship by inability to respond to the needs of the other due to immaturity and unformed character.

Permanent celibacy, as any other form of pleasure deprivation, should be chosen only with the understanding that the individual accepts this deprivation as instrumental in procuring some greater pleasure, *and* has developed appropriate alternative avenues for satisfying the physical, emotional, and symbolic human desires normally satisfied by sex in this culture.

While the repression of body pleasure which has linked celibacy and spirituality is well grounded in the Christian tradition, the reaction against this religious inheritance in the West has increasingly given rise in the last few centuries to a justification for hedonism. The individualism of Western culture, and especially of American culture, makes hedonism a real threat. Freud's reality principle may limit the pleasure principle so that we moderate our drive to pleasure based on our recognition of threats of punishment or promises of reward, but life in our society does not necessarily bind us to persons and groups around us so that we are able to feel their pain and their joy. And when we do not feel their pain and their pleasure we will not be willing to sacrifice any of our own pleasure in order to alleviate their pain or increase their pleasure.

But what has gone wrong here is not the pursuit of pleasure, but the lack of human connection within society due to modern urban society's mobility and anonymity. This lack of connection—the lack of feeling another person as one's neighbor—is not remedied in any way by asceticism in general or by any specific form of self-denial. Understandings of love as selfless and opposed to the self-interest assumed to motivate sex are not the answer to social atomism. The lack of connection in society—the lack of community—has already diminished the self by diminishing its relations; practices of self-denial can *accelerate* that diminishment. We need to understand that selfishness is not the result of an enlarged self, but rather of a starved one, a self starved for connection, for mutuality, for community, for love.

Possibility of Abuse

To say that the most basic purpose of sex is pleasure upsets many who fear that the adoption of such a position would lead to a great deal of abuse. What is to prevent people from simply following through on every sexual impulse, without learning delayed gratification? People ask, Isn't this the problem with our society, the reason for the high rates of teen pregnancy, abortion, venereal disease, and even AIDS—that sex is understood as an appropriate avenue for pursuing pleasure, with no concern for moral restrictions?

A great deal of sexual activity today is both irresponsible and even exploitative. But many centuries of Christian denial that pleasure is the primary end of sex have not increased the level of responsibility in sexual behavior. For the churches to continue to frown on sexual pleasure in defiance of the experience and intuitions of the vast majority is to continue to undermine the authority of the churches on all issues, and specifically on issues of sexual responsibility. Especially among the young, the church's credibility on sex would be dramatically increased if the church began its sexual teaching by insisting that God deliberately made sex both good and pleasurable. To do this would validate a great deal of individual Christian experience, and encourage Christians to use their lives as experiential bases for further reflection on ethical responsibility in sex.

This is not to deny that there will be many who will seize upon the validation of sexual pleasure to justify various forms of sexual abuse. However, I think that the use of *mutual* sexual pleasure as the primary end of sex narrows the number and kind of abuses which can be justified much more than do present church teachings. Under present Church teachings on sex in marriage, for example, there is no need for consent, since the spouse's body belongs not to him/her, but to the other. Not only is there no need for pleasure, but even pain is not excluded.

Painful intercourse does not prevent conception. Nor does it prevent the satisfaction of the marital duty. There is nothing in traditional Christian teaching on marital sex which indicates the serious problem that sexual dysfunction can have on marital relationships. If mutual sexual pleasure were at the center of the church's teaching on sex and marriage, then we would not have the widespread blindness to, and therefore tolerance of, marital rape, domestic battery, and sexual dysfunction in marriage. All of these clearly prevent sexual pleasure from being mutual.

What abuses could we expect to see? Uncommitted, recreational sex, frequently under the influence of alcohol and other drugs. Exactly what we have among youth and the not-so-young in the U.S. now. But at least we of the churches would have an agreed-upon starting point for discussing sexual responsibility with young people. The present situation is preferable only for those persons who are interested in condemning rather than dialoguing with the young, and who are more concerned about the "purity" of the Church than the welfare of humans.

Sexual Pleasure as Safe and Beneficial

Sexual pleasure is as natural an end for sex as is procreation, and, unlike procreation, sexual pleasure does not necessarily threaten either the biosphere or the health and welfare of human communities and their individual members. Sexual pleasure itself contains no dangers, and masturbation is likewise safe. Indiscriminate and unprotected sexual sharing, on the other hand, can be both unhealthy and even deadly, due to the epidemic proportions of a variety of sexually transmitted diseases, of which AIDS is only the most deadly.

Sexual pleasure itself, with responsible initial precautions, is not only safe for self, but also for others and for the biosphere. It is also tremendously beneficial, both individually and socially. Many of us are so conditioned to hear "pleasure," especially "sexual pleasure," with negative emotions that we have not examined the many ways in which pleasure, in particular sexual pleasure, is beneficial for us, both as material organisms and as conscious, relational beings embedded in community. If our society, and especially our churches, are to successfully combat the identification of sexual pleasure with hedonism, it is important that we examine what we mean by sexual pleasure.

Sexual pleasure is a term which covers a great many experiences. It can include involuntary physical pleasures which, depending on circumstances, can be emotionally painful—like a young boy's erection when called to the blackboard, or orgasm in a rape victim. Sexual pleasure is always physical—all pleasure, like all feeling, is experienced in our physical body. But some pleasures are more physical than others in that they engage more of the body, more of the senses. To resolve a mental puzzle gives us pleasure that is physically experienced in the rush of energy felt at the moment of discovery. The pleasure which comes from remembering a recent night of lovemaking involves more of our physical body, for the physical process of arousal may even begin, with genital engorgement, myotonia, and increases in pulse and respiration. Actual involvement in sexual activity can multiply the physical sensations as our senses of touch, taste, smell, hearing, and seeing are all stimulated, our imaginations become immersed in remembering and projecting sexual pleasure, and our bodies begin the physiological processes involved in arousal. For some persons, and perhaps for all persons at some times, some of these avenues of physical stimulation may be blocked.

Victims of sexual violence often experience very disturbing blockages of imagination and memory which prevent pleasure, sometimes despite all the physiological signs which normally accompany sexual pleasure. But not all blockages are so dramatic. There have been a number of popular surveys over the last decade that report large numbers of women preferring to be kissed and held more than coitus or other activities culminating in orgasm/ejaculation. Many of these women do not see themselves as rejecting sex (the dominant male interpretation) so much as preferring one kind of sexual pleasure over another. If by this they mean that sometimes they would rather cuddle and kiss, and perhaps take a nap together, and other times they prefer the passion and satisfaction of orgasm, but that there are more of the first than the second, that is one thing. This would be a not uncommon pattern, for example, among the elderly, or among some physically handicapped persons, for whom coitus can be very physically demanding. But if these women are presenting kissing/cuddling as a separate activity from, and an alternative activity from, coitus or other sexual activity including orgasm/ejaculation, then something is wrong, for that is not the response of persons who are active partners in mutually satisfying sex.

The Power of Pleasure

There is no question that sex can be powerfully pleasurable. Indeed, virtually all of the power of sex is dependent upon the pleasure involved in sex. Human beings are moved by pleasure. Thomas Aquinas was right—as was Freud—that the pursuit of pleasure and the avoidance of pain are the prime motivators of human behavior.[24] We are attracted to sexual activity because we learn that it is pleasurable, and because what few sexual instincts humans have as compared to animals seem to be oriented to pleasure.

Sex is pleasurable in many different ways. Mere bodily touch is pleasurable. Another person's touch on our skin normally releases chemical compounds called endorphins, which function as pain-killing anesthetics. The effect of endorphins, of course, can be overridden by fear or severely painful stimuli associated with violent or threatening touch. But human touch is normally pleasurable. We actually seem to *need* the pleasure of touch. Infants denied physical touch do not thrive. They do not grow, do not eat or sleep well. They do not develop normally intellectually and emotionally.[25] Older humans seem to need human touch as well. Elderly persons who are touched affectionately often retain their health and their alertness much longer, and complain of pain less than those deprived of touch.[26] The therapeutic aspect of touch is one reason for the popularity of massage. Warm, firm handstrokes smoothing one's skin and loosening muscle tightness can be more than momentarily pleasurable. So pleasurable is massage that it sometimes requires restraint not to lean into the hands providing such pleasure and/or relief, and not to express those feelings audibly. Persons who have not been severely scarred either by lack of physical affection or by touch that violates their integrity can use memories of how pleasurable touch was affirming, supportive, and even healing to understand what we mean when we speak of the therapeutic potential of touch.

Touch can be interpreted in a variety of ways. Sometimes we interpret a person's touch as sexually arousing. Our sexual response in such cases is a response not only to the touch itself, but to our interpretation of the touch, for the same degree of pressure to the same point on our bodies by another person might not be interpreted as sexual. This ambiguity of touch, and the importance of individual interpretation, is common for touch directed at nongenital areas of our bodies. Genital touch is, in our society, the only touch which is virtually always both intended and interpreted as sexual outside the medical context. And yet even here interpretation is critically important, for genital touch from one person may be sexually arousing, while the same type of genital touch by another person may feel repulsive, threatening, or perhaps even boring, even though both genital touches are clearly interpreted by the person touched as sexual touches.

We experience body pleasure, including the type of body pleasure we call sexual pleasure, not only from other people's touch. Our own touch, combined with the power of our imaginations, can stimulate us to sexual arousal, even orgasm. This self-touching aimed at sexual arousal and pleasure, which is called masturbation, is practiced in humans from early infancy, as noted above.

While Christianity long taught masturbation as sinful, today many Christians are rethinking the grounds for that prohibition. For example, we no longer believe that masturbation entails "wasting" embryonic human persons, as Christians in some previous periods believed.[27] Nor do we understand the story of Onan in Genesis 38 to support such an understanding of wasting seed. Onan died not because he wasted his seed on the ground, but because, out of greed, he failed to fulfill Yahweh's will that he raise up a son to carry on his brother's name and lineage.

The most prominent reason for the prohibition on masturbation in the Christian tradition has been the understanding that the sexual faculties are oriented to procreation and must be used only in a manner open to that end. Approval of contraception by the vast majority of Christians in the twentieth century has caused the argument against masturbation to focus more on objections to sexual pleasure, and especially to solitary sexual pleasure. A basic problem in masturbation was that the end of the act was sexual pleasure, and sexual pleasure was understood as, at best, an acceptable consequence of sexual activity aimed at some truly human good such as procreation. The more dominant position understood sexual pleasure as itself evil.

Out of these objections to masturbation came charges that masturbation encouraged *ipsation,* an inward turning that cuts individuals off from others. That is, the pursuit of solitary sexual pleasure was understood to teach individuals to look to themselves for the satisfaction of their needs and drives, instead of orienting individuals toward other persons. If the gospel is understood to discourage narcissism and hedonism and, instead, to demand of Christians an outward orientation to others, masturbation will seem contrary to the gospel imperative.

As we have seen, there is a certain compelling logic to this argument until one turns to examine it more deeply. When we do, however, we learn that it fails to correspond to reality. Virtually all males masturbate as youths, yet virtually all shift to partnered sex by adulthood.[28] Very low levels of adolescent masturbation are more linked to low levels of sexual interest, and thus to low incidence of partnered sex, than to high levels of partnered sex.[29] While many fewer women masturbate as adolescents, those who do are more likely to be sexually successful within partnered sex because of greater self-knowledge.[30] The turn to solitary sex in adolescence actually seems to facilitate and not to impede learning to turn to others for the meeting of physical and sexual desires and needs.

Pleasure in the Sexual Response Cycle

This conclusion regarding the relation of masturbation to partnered sex gives us some insight into the overarching argument of this chapter: that sexual pleasure is a premoral good. So accustomed have we become to arguments that sexual pleasure is morally evil, or an animal pleasure unworthy of humans, that when we attempt to justify sex as a good in itself we overlook sexual pleasure as the primary reason for acknowledging the goodness of sex, and seek to justify sex with reference to some of the other, more indirect ends of sex. The most common of these, of course, was procreation, but it is now being displaced by many Christians in favor of other, more relational ends, especially intimacy and bonding. That these alternative ends are non-sexual makes them more easily accepted in a society trained to moral suspicions of sex.

This shift to justifying sex by pointing to the nonsexual goods of intimacy and/or bonding between the partners fails to examine sexual pleasure adequately, and therefore fails to see that both intimacy and bonding within sex are normally dependent upon mutual sexual pleasure. Because this attempt to bypass consideration of sexual pleasure turns to intimacy and bonding as ends of sex, the justification for sexual activity extends only to partnered sex. There is seldom any recognition that intimacy with one's own body is possible; there is even less recognition that a good is at stake.

In dealing with sexual pleasure as the first and foundational end of sexual activity, then, we need to keep in mind not only partnered sex, but also the solitary sexual activity of masturbation. Only when we recognize the sexual pleasure in masturbation as a premoral good, and masturbation itself as acceptable moral behavior aimed at that good, will we be able to justify sexual activity in itself, and not for its ability to produce some other nonsexual good.

The physical process of sexual response is basically the same in all sexual activity, and that physical process is important, not incidental, for the moral and spiritual meaning of sexual activity. Within the cycle of sexual response, there are at least three types of physical pleasure possible; each is associated with one of the three different stages of the sexual response cycle: arousal,[31] orgasm, and resolution. The first is the pleasure of arousal itself—of sexual touching and stroking and being touched and stroked, the pleasure of anticipating the next move in sexual exploration.

Sexual arousal anticipates other, more intense levels of sexual pleasure. It excites and provokes a hunger for sexual satisfaction. Arousal produces both vasocongestion, the engorgement with blood of tissues around the genitals, and myotonia, or muscle tension, throughout the body. Heart and respiration rates increase as well.

Sexual arousal can involve all our physical senses and our imagination as well. In fact, the role of the imagination is by far the most dominant one. It is with good reason that many have commented that the human imagination is the most powerful engine of arousal in the human body. Under some circumstances sexual arousal can take on additional emotional and spiritual dimensions, depending upon the level of symbolism to which the individual is tuned. For example, undressing can be mutually exciting for both partners, a source of physical sexual stimulation which also involves the imagination and the memory. But undressing can have additional meaning when the partners' mutual commitment allows each to interpret the other's undressing as an unmasking of not only the body, but of his/her whole life and consciousness. In such circumstances the act of undressing becomes an act of trust, a promise of intimacy, and a commitment to reveal the inner self as well.

The physical pleasure of orgasm is distinct from that of arousal. While pleasure builds during arousal, it peaks with orgasm. In orgasm there is no anticipation of the next moment of pleasure; rather there is a more or less total surrender to the sensations of the moment. Particularly for males, because of the close connection between ejaculation and orgasm, there is an identifiable point at which the male becomes conscious of imminent, unstoppable explosion: once semen is pumped into the urethra, there is no possibility of delaying ejaculation and thus orgasm. Female response is more varied in a number of ways. Females do not experience this degree of lack of control over their response—orgasm in females can be prevented at virtually any stage in the approach by ceasing stimulation. Furthermore, females lack the refractory period of males, the period of recovery after orgasm (ejaculation) which is necessary before the response cycle can be repeated. With the proper stimulation females have almost unlimited capacity for orgasm.

Yet while many females demonstrate a capacity for multiple orgasms in a very short period, many other females do not achieve orgasm at all, and some do not achieve even relatively low levels of arousal from sexual activity. Thus while we can speak of sex as powerfully pleasurable, we must remember that such terms refer to the capacity of sex to be pleasurable, and not to any universal bestowal of sexual pleasure on those involved in sex. Even apart from outright sexual violence, sex can be not only devoid of pleasure but actually painful, especially for women. This subject will be dealt with in greater depth later.

Orgasm is impossible to describe adequately. Descriptions of contractions in the vaginal walls, or spasms in the urethra, are not extremely helpful. Orgasm is often described in terms of cessation—cessation of thought, of communication, of control over one's limbs and voice, even of consciousness itself. It is sometimes described as a little death, a losing oneself. We speak of coming back into ourselves after orgasm, as if we have been gone from our bodies. It is certainly paradoxical that we both prize the extreme pleasure of orgasm, and yet describe it as the loss of all those things which ordinarily give us value and worth, those aspects which make us who we are.

Many people refuse to probe the question of how or why orgasm is perceived as pleasurable. They just enjoy the sensations, or at most share with their partner the images which the sensations bring to mind. And orgasm can function as a time out, an escape from ordinary time. But orgasm, like other stages in the sexual response cycle, can denote more than a positive, pleasurable physical experience. It can also function as an experience of divine reality. Gallagher et al., authors of *Embodied in Love,* after being explicit that the meaning of sexual intercourse resides in the ecstatic experience of orgasm, go on to write: "Thus intercourse does not merely express or symbolize love, express or symbolize intimacy with God. It *is* love. It is trinitarian intimacy, our intimacy with the three divine persons."[32] That is what many of the references to sex as experiences of heaven mean to convey. It is this spiritual or religious sense that persons try to capture in more secular language about the merger of two human hearts, or the ultimate experience of human freedom. Orgasm, like all sexual pleasure, envelops a variety of levels of meaning, and therefore a variety of levels of value.

One way orgasm is sometimes understood is as a foretaste of death, an experience of losing oneself, of losing control of everything.[33] There is a sense in which, for both men and women, achieving orgasm has both voluntary and involuntary aspects. Willing orgasm is not sufficient—the body needs sufficient stimulation. But orgasm also often demands a kind of conscious, deliberate letting go of control over oneself and one's reactions, a willingness to immerse oneself in the sensation. The pleasure which washes over us when we surrender to the experience and let go of control reinforces the lesson that it is OK, even good, to let go of control, to open oneself up to other people and experiences, to let down our protective barriers, our self-consciousness. When sex is not segregated from the rest of our lives, the pleasure of orgasm can reach far beyond the moment of intense pleasure itself, and change, a little at a time, the way we relate to our partner, and even to the larger society and world. It can encourage us to trust more, to be willing to risk more, to reach out to others more. When our sexual experience is segregated from the rest of our lives, the pleasure of orgasm may only produce desire to experience orgasm more often, as a kind of escape.

A third kind of physical pleasure in sex involves the resolution phase of the sexual response cycle. After orgasm we are physically relaxed, sometimes to the point of feeling boneless, like a puddle of melted wax. Tension and stress are reduced, if not temporarily eliminated. Beyond this immediate feeling of physical well-being and relaxation which occurs in resolution, there can be divergent experiences. For example, some couples may reach orgasm, separate, dress, and part. Sometimes a partner may reach orgasm, pull away, roll over and sleep, or take off for the shower, leaving the partner in bed.

Other couples find resolution a very important and pleasurable part of lovemaking, an extended time to hold each other close and drift off to sleep still entwined, or to cuddle and verbally share. Some couples discuss their feelings, profess their love, praise and thank each other, suggest variations for the next time, or draw on the tenderness and affection generated by physical intimacy to deal with some obstacle or problem in their relationship. That is, one of the pleasures which can be enjoyed during resolution is a strong sense of emotional as well as physical intimacy. The physical intimacy produced in arousal and orgasm can be prolonged and enjoyed during resolution, and can often aid in generating or restoring a sense of emotional intimacy as well. The contentment of the resolution phase, then, can be a contentment of both body and soul.

But the pleasure of intimacy in the resolution phase is usually dependent upon the couple having reached orgasm. Failure of either or both to reach orgasm after high levels of arousal is frustrating in both a physical and an emotional sense,[34] though in a long-term, frequently sexually satisfying relationship, an occasional failure on the part of one or both to reach orgasm may not seriously impair the sense of intimacy generated by sexual arousal and physical closeness.

The achievement of emotional intimacy originating in sexual intimacy is also dependent upon and perhaps proportional to the level of openness on the part of each partner to attachment to the other. Emotional intimacy is more likely to be generated if two persons are making love to express an already-acknowledged attraction and commitment to each other, but such attraction and commitment can be created in part through sharing the sexual response cycle, *if* both partners are at least open to the possibility. Openness to attachment to the other can be indicated in a variety of ways. In our society the most effective indication may well be the degree of willingness to be vulnerable to the other. This willingness to be vulnerable often takes the form of personal disclosure, which can either precede sexual intimacy or be provoked by it. Sometimes other forms of willingness to be vulnerable are more primary.

In many, but not by any means all, women (and more in the past than currently), the very willingness to share sex demonstrates this willingness to be vulnerable to the partner. For in sex, especially with men, most women feel very vulnerable. The very language we use to describe women in sex recognizes this vulnerability. Women in sex are commonly described as "open," "penetrated," "probed," "plowed," not to mention "under," "laid," "had," and "taken." The old rock song title "Will You Still Love Me Tomorrow?" reflects many a woman's fear that she is being courted to be sexually used and emotionally abandoned.

In our society no girl grows to adulthood without knowing at some level that she is vulnerable, and that her vulnerability is inherently sexual. Research suggests that one in three or four girls is sexually molested as a child,[35] and one in four adult women will be the victim of rape or attempted rape in her lifetime.[36] One in seven women is raped by her spouse,[37] and 10 – 21% of women are beaten by their sexual partner.[38] While females are still often left in a great deal of ignorance about sexuality in general and specifically about the precise nature and degree of sexual risk, girls are warned from the time they are very young that they, much more than young boys, are vulnerable to sexual hurt in the dark, in strange places, when alone, or with strange males. In recent years young women are increasingly warned to choose partners/spouses carefully, in the knowledge that many seemingly normal male sexual partners abuse women.

Virtually any deliberate injury done to a woman will be committed not only by the other sex, but will also be directed at her sexually, neither of which is true for men. Many wives experience their first conjugal battery during pregnancy or immediately after childbirth.[39] The verbal abuse which precedes or accompanies such blows tends to be sexual—accusing her of infidelity or wantonness, or of not being sexually adequate.[40] In a society where women face such risk, virtually all women who agree to sex with men demonstrate in that agreement an acceptance of vulnerability.

While lesbian sex does not raise for women the physical threat of abuse that heterosexual sex does,[41] the fact that women's sexual attitudes are formed under social conditions of mandatory heterosexism means that for many lesbians as well, willingness to participate in sex often expresses a great deal of personal vulnerability. This may be one reason why both heterosexual women and lesbians are much more likely to restrict sexual partners to those they love, or at least feel some concern for, than are either heterosexual or gay males.[42]

Of course, not all women who demonstrate vulnerability through willingness to participate in sex do so out of a desire for either physical pleasure or intimacy. For some, agreement to sex is part of a death wish, an attempt to further punish or degrade herself. This is a common female response to a history of child sexual abuse, especially incest.[43] Other women may accept the risk of vulnerability in sex out of desperate need for material support (whether monogamously in marriage or through some form of prostitution). Some women have been taught to use sex as a source of power, and may "surrender," and make themselves physically vulnerable to another in the expectation of thereby gaining some degree of power over the other. In these patterns there is physical vulnerability, but it is not accompanied by an emotional openness which leads to a mutual self-disclosure oriented to therapeutic intimacy. And, of course, there are also men who share with many women the identification of sex with love or intimacy, and therefore feel themselves vulnerable in sex. For many men who are unaccustomed to feeling vulnerable, their vulnerability in sexual love can feel very disturbing and uncomfortable.

Other Pleasures in Sex

There are other relational pleasures associated with sex as well. Sometimes sex is valued as a way to stave off the pain of loneliness. The lover who has been away on business often returns feeling lonely, deprived of the familiar someone to touch and talk to, to be with and listen to, and immediate sex becomes a reaffirmation of intimate connection. Sometimes loneliness can lead to temporary sexual involvements with relative strangers.

Sex can be both an attractor to initiate relationships, and a support for maintaining relationships which alleviate loneliness over the long term. I not only take pleasure in making love with my husband, but I take pleasure in sleeping next to him even when we have not just made love. The presence of his sleeping body provides a kind of special comfort and security that the body of my son, or my mother—or, I presume, anyone else—in the same bed would not, for I do not know their bodies in the same intimately sexual way, nor have their bodies been for me the source of such tremendous pleasure as has the body of my husband.[44] His body in many ways represents to me our history of intimacy, of companionship, and of sexual pleasure. When he is away I miss him, and feel closest to him in our bed.

Sometimes sex can be satisfying as a distraction, as in times of anxiety and waiting. Sometimes sex can stave off boredom. At other times sex can be an affirmation of life, as when a couple has just experienced a brush with death: a near-fatal accident, the death of a friend or relative, the serious illness of their child. Sometimes sex can be an affirmation of the ongoing life of a relationship, as after there has been some major battle in the relationship which had shaken the couple's faith in the future of the relationship. Then sex can celebrate the reconciliation and reaffirm the commitment to each other.

For some persons sex can also be a way of proving oneself, of proving to self and others one's sexual attractiveness, which is often understood as an important measure of self-worth. Some persons seem to have a strong and more or less constant need to prove their attractiveness, in the sense of measuring it by notches on the bedposts. For others, such a need may be very situational and brief, such as after a rejection by a spouse or lover, when one's ego has been especially battered.

In all of these situations the pleasure of physical sex is important, but it may not be the most powerful pleasure experienced.

Goodness in Sex: Rooted in Pleasure

Sexual pleasure is not morally neutral—it is too powerful to be neutral. Sexual pleasure feels good, from the pleasure of having the surface of our skin touched and stroked to the ecstatic loss of self-consciousness in orgasm. Sexual pleasure not only offers us the happiness of acute well-being and immediate freedom from suffering but, because sexual pleasure also offers possibilities of meeting a number of basic human needs, it can be truly joyful. Sexual pleasure is therefore, as we have said, a premoral good—meaning that it is, in the normal scheme of things, good, before we morally evaluate its role in any particular situation. This premoral goodness is what the author of Genesis meant in the creation story when God pronounced creation good. The author did not mean that everything in creation would always be associated with moral good, but only that creation as a whole was generally oriented in the direction of the good. Just as we say that a particular person is a good person, though we know that that person, like all persons, is not perfect and in some specific situations has sinned, so we say that sexual pleasure is good. This is not to deny that it is open to misuse, misinterpretation, and deliberate abuse.

Sexual pleasure is not only good, but it should be the primary ethical criterion for evaluating sexual activity. Many will object that any of the above-mentioned intentions and results of sex have equal or superior claim to be the ethical criteria for sexual activity. Why not intimacy, or bonding? Why leap over the purposes Christianity has recognized as purposes of sex to focus on one which is antithetical to the Christian tradition?

The reasons for choosing sexual pleasure as the primary ethical criterion for evaluating sexual activity have nothing to do with the fact that the Christian tradition has largely identified it with sin rather than virtue, but rather have to do with the nature of sexuality and its effects. First, except for procreation, all positive functions of sex depend upon sex being pleasurable. Second, pleasure is more easily and immediately recognized than intimacy and bonding, which develop over time and do not necessarily intrude themselves on human consciousness in the same immediate, forceful way that sexual pleasure does. Third, our society is beginning to recognize the many ways in which we have been trained to avoid pleasure, and how destructive and unhealthy such behavior is. Finally, if most of us in this society are honest, the primary purpose for which we turn to sex is pleasure, whether it is the pleasure of passion or the pleasure of emotional intimacy.

Our discomfort with sexual pleasure is one result of the failure of Christianity to affirm self-love, and the tendency to overstress the element of sacrifice in love of neighbor. Christianity has never really taken seriously the real wisdom in Jesus' injunction to love one's neighbor *as oneself*: that love of neighbor must begin with love of self. We cannot love the neighbor well unless we love ourselves well first, for we literally will not know what the needs of the self are and how they are satisfied.

Good sex refutes one of the dominant Christian treatments of love of neighbor, the one most closely connected theologically to Lutheranism,[45] but actually strong in all Christian churches: that love of neighbor is diametrically opposed to concern for self, and that the presence of concern for self inevitably undermines love of neighbor. In good sex, as in the basic message of Jesus about the reign of God, we learn that the overarching interests of individuals march together, and are not opposed to each other, but are mutually satisfied through just, loving union in community under God's reign. The Christian message should not be read as: sacrifice now out of love of neighbor, and reap rewards later in another life. Rather the basic message of both Christianity and sexual sharing should be interpreted as: discover that loving the neighbor, despite the sacrifices involved, can bring about a relationship which satisfies the deepest needs of one's self.[46] In sex, if one partner is consistently acting to pleasure the other person without openness to receiving pleasure him/herself, the pleasure of both persons in the relationship decreases. The active partner can over time become the controlling partner, which both partners can come to resent.[47] Mutuality, then, is a necessary goal in love, without which love can be distorted to oppress both the lover and the loved.

The Importance of Pleasure Being Mutual

Thus sexual activity must not only be pleasurable. Another requirement is that when sexual activity is partnered, sexual pleasure must not be exclusive, but rather mutual. It must extend to both participants. Sexual pleasure can be evil when it is exclusive—when it is derived either through the inflicting/accepting of pain, or through excluding a partner from pleasure either deliberately or accidentally.

Inclusiveness is a basic human value. We need to be included in community—in a specific human community which gives us identity, companions, and a system of values for approaching reality. Inclusiveness became a basic Christian value because both Jesus and the early church after his death reached out to those excluded from the larger society.

If there is a single most important characteristic which distinguished Jesus from the established groups of his own time, it was his inclusiveness. He did not exclude sinners from his company or his concern, as did the Pharisees, whose very name meant "separate ones."[48] Neither did he exclude the physically imperfect, as did the Essenes,[49] or the poor and needy, as did the wealthy Sadducees.[50] His vision of the reign of God was broader than the narrow nationalism of the zealots; it included much more than expelling the Romans and reforming the Temple elites.[51] It included reforming the entire society from the bottom up, toward inclusive care. Jesus did not exclude, but rather championed women and children, who were defenseless property in his society.[52] He did not despise the crippled and sick, shunned as possessed and unclean by public opinion, but he touched and healed them.[53] Even prostitutes and tax collectors, viewed as the most serious of sinners, were welcome at his table.[54] For Jesus, nothing was so grievous a sin against his Father's love as exclusion.

In the same way, the early church became inclusive because it recognized that God gave the gift of faith without regard for status or merit.[55] Because membership in the church so frequently cost individuals their families, friends, and the orienting structures of their former lives, the community became not just inclusive in terms of formal membership, but became a true family—the source of identity, of companions, and of a system of values for interpreting reality. Inclusiveness in the church family, the family for whom God was parent, meant exemption from oppressive use by other community members—by other children of God. One does not exploit brothers and sisters merely as means to one's own end, but respects them as ends in their own right.

According to New Testament sources, Jesus never directly addressed sexual behavior. But Jesus taught about the reign of God which was breaking into the world through Jesus in parables, stories of everyday human activities, as well as through his own actions and activities. In the parables, Jesus made clear that the reign of God is both paradigmatically inclusive, and that it is a thing of joy and celebration. Perhaps the parable image best supported by example in Jesus' own life is table fellowship, for Jesus again and again acted out his parable of the king who sent his servants to invite strangers from the roads to his banquet.[56] Jesus was rebuked not only for keeping company with sinners—with those who should have been excluded—but also for the celebratory nature of his meals. Many scribes and Pharisees criticized his preference for celebratory banquets over the asceticism of John the Baptist, which was thought more appropriate for a holy man who claimed to be the messianic prophet.[57]

At Jesus' most exclusive meal described in the New Testament,[58] the Last Supper, the patent reason for the meal was, of course, celebration of the historic Passover event. But the events of the meal reinforced both themes of inclusiveness and celebration. John's account, which substitutes Jesus' washing of the disciples' feet for the institution of Eucharist, sounds the inclusiveness theme most strongly. Power is not to be used to exclude or control, but to support and enable.[59] The other Gospels' accounts of the institution of Eucharist sound the note of celebration, for Eucharist provides a social ritual of both remembrance and empowerment. The community celebrates the ongoing life of Jesus in the community through the communal meal. As bread and wine sustain the body, making it grow strong and healthy, so the body and blood of Jesus—his life and death—sustain the life of the community of believers. Eucharist becomes a way of experiencing—participating in—the reign of God, which Jesus described as like finding a treasure in a field, like adding leaven to 50 pounds of flour, like the mustard seed growing into a mighty tree, or like crop yields of 30-, 60-, or 100-fold when sevenfold is the Galilean norm.[60] Experiencing the reign of God in communal celebration of Eucharist is (should be) an experience, then, of unexpected joy. It is like other images Jesus gave of the reign of God—of a fishing boat overloaded with fish, of 5000 fed with a few loaves and fishes, of water made into good wine for thirsty wedding guests, or the king's banquet to which beggars and travelers were invited.[61]

We do not have sexual examples of the reign of God from the Gospels. But for many in our society, sexual examples would be more than merely acceptable ways of describing such experiences of God's reign on earth. For many persons, their *primary* experience of inclusive love, of openness to another, of being accepted and enhanced, of being empowered by love to reach out in love to others, is sexual. I can still remember the profound shock I felt at hearing, some twenty years ago, a respected theologian say that her major religious experiences all occurred in bed or on the delivery table. I cannot count the times since that I have heard similar statements from men and women. For many, the primary *experience* of divinity itself, as well as of God's intention for the reign of God, is sexual. There is in sex, as in Eucharist, the potential for participating in divinity.

Many will gasp and object to this comparison, and immediately point out many instances in which it seems sacrilegious to point to sex as experience of God: rape, promiscuity, commercial sex, pornography. But, of course, the same may be said for Eucharist. Some people decide to receive Eucharist to show off new clothes, or to make business contacts, or to protect their reputation in the community. Many receive Eucharist out of habit, without reflection. The Eucharist can be defiled to mock God and church; it can be exploited for political ends. In both sex and Eucharist, inherent power and goodness are at the mercy of human intentions and decisions, which can either minimize or distort them.

Costs of Ignoring Mutuality in Sexual Pleasure

Because of the capacity of sexual satisfaction to image the reign of God so well, to engage in sexual activity without commitment to one's partner's pleasure is to exclude the partner from this experience of God's reign. Repeated exclusion from sexual pleasure does not merely exclude the partner from sexual experience of God's reign. Repeated exclusion makes of this excluded partner a thing, a means to exclusive personal pleasure. Persons treated as sexual means must utilize a great deal of personal energy to resist this understanding of themselves as things/means. Persons treated as means will also have less energy to put into resisting such treatment because the experience from which they have been excluded is a major source of the intimate acceptance, enhancement, and empowerment which rekindle in us personal psychic energy. And these persons excluded from sexual pleasure are not alone in their deprivation. Those who exclude, either deliberately or unconsciously, their partners from sexual pleasure are also deprived. Their pleasure is both diminished and usually distorted, sometimes seriously.

The sexual pleasure of those who use others in sex is diminished by the inability of the user to feel, in addition to his/her own physical pleasure, any of the reflected pleasure of the other. For many lovers, the taking of pleasure in the pleasure of the other is so powerful that if one partner agrees to sex without taking pleasure in it, this is understood by the other as a betrayal, not a favor.[62] Sex under such circumstances is interpreted as demeaning the lovers' experience of sex, and as a rejection of the bond which allows them to take pleasure in each other's pleasure. The "sacrifice" of pleasure by others for us is often not as meaningful to us as their willingness to share pleasure with us.

Failure to include the partner in pleasure can result from insensitivity to the partner as well as from the deliberate intention to deprive the partner of pleasure. Either source can initiate a tendency to understand sex as a material trade. If there is no openness to mutual intimacy with the lover, sexual relationship can only be understood at a material level, whether it is a casual affair or a long-term monogamous relationship. The assumption in such an understanding is that both partners look out for their own pleasure and interest, that their initial and ongoing consent to sex is based on individual perception of self-interest. If one lover cannot detect sexual pleasure in the partner, there must nevertheless be some benefit to the partner, or the partner would not continue to consent. That benefit might be relief of boredom, curiosity, loneliness, financial recompense, or many others. These become alternatives for sexual pleasure as motivator.

Persons who exclude partners from sexual pleasure are usually not willing to see themselves as users/abusers, but instead develop concepts of the "I am not my brother's keeper" variety which justify the absence of concern for the partner. Such concepts are predicated upon the equality of all, an equality which then relieves all of us from responsibility for and connection to others, who are to look after themselves.

The ideologies developed around such concepts exist in many other areas of life. It is this kind of ideology which allows persons in First World nations to morally justify paying debt-strapped Third World nations to accept First World toxic waste, and which prompts U.S. legislators to dismantle support programs for the poor. In all areas of human life these individualist, egalitarian ideologies serve to maintain dysfunctional structures which undermine the health of human communities and their shared environment. They ignore the social nature of human beings, and deny the fact that we are diminished by one another's pain and deprivation, just as we are enhanced by one another's growth and pleasure.

At least equally dangerous is a second distortion of sexual pleasure connected with excluding partners from pleasure: the confusion of sex with dominance. When sex is confused with dominance, sexual pleasure becomes dependent upon the experience of controlling/being controlled. A young heterosexual couple may grow up socialized to understand sex in terms of dominance, and the female's failure to find pleasure in sex may never be known to her lover because in a dominant/subordinate relationship she may not feel she has a right to complain or make suggestions. On the other hand, her own experience of sex as lacking in pleasure may influence her to teach her daughters passive roles in sex, which preclude their own sexual pleasure, and lead them to interpret sexual activity in terms of male dominance.

We live in a society which, as many have noted, confuses, even identifies, sex and dominance, pain and pleasure.[63] This confusion sets the stage for individuals of either sex to use sex as a method of controlling another, and thus using that other for one's own interest. Most of us have been so conditioned to identify sex as a form of male domination of women that we immediately think "men" when we hear "sexual control" or "using persons for one's own ends." In many ways such a response is both understandable and justified. Certainly the tendency to use physical domination to obtain sexual pleasure is virtually exclusively male. But women, too, have learned that sex is powerful and can be used to control others. Women today, like women throughout history, have bargained to exchange sexual access to their bodies for male concessions of various kinds. Oftentimes, the offer of sexual willingness was the only resource socially allowed to women with which they could secure even basic needs. In every other aspect of their lives, often including decisions around marriage, they were powerless. Greater, though still unequal, rights for women vis-à-vis men in our society have not replaced the tendency of some women to use men's pleasure in sex to manipulate men, any more than it has replaced the tendency of some men to obtain sexual pleasure by coercing women.

In some ways none of us has escaped the association of sex and dominance. It has become entwined in our most basic sexual attitudes. For example, what do we find sexy, or potentially arousing? Men and women alike have been socialized to believe that sexual pairing should be heterosexual, that males should be older, larger, and more powerful (socially and economically as well as physically) than females. Any indication of equal or greater female power—a higher female salary, or a comparable female educational level—is in itself an anaphrodisiac which must be compensated for with overwhelming male mastery in other areas if the relationship is to have erotic potential in the eyes of either the partners or observers. Our society has not taught men to feel masculine with a female who is far taller, bigger, older, or richer than they, and few women respond romantically to shorter, smaller, younger, poorer, less powerful men than themselves.

Our society's sexual fascination with dominance is clear in a great many ways. Between one-sixth and one-third of all men and women regularly fantasize coerced or coercive sex not only during masturbation, but also during intercourse with their partners.[64] Studies of rape and rapists have revealed that many rapists are not motivated by sexual desire or arousal, but rather by desire to exert power over another, to visit personal anger on another, or to inflict pain on another.[65] There is a great deal of evidence that date rapists are the only rapists who may be sexually motivated.[66] L. L. Holmstrom and A. W. Burgess suggest that forcible rape always contains three components: power, anger, and sexuality, and conclude that sexuality is rarely the dominant theme.[67] In another study, A. N. Groth, Burgess, and Holmstrom observed that in each case they investigated either power or anger dominated. They concluded that rape, rather than being primarily an expression of sexual desire, is, in fact, the use of sexuality to express issues of anger and power.[68] Rapists have been socialized to identify sexuality as about using others as objects and women as appropriate objects for their power and anger, and so they act out these non-sexual motives genitally.

One of the clearest clues that such rapes are pseudosexual and not truly sexually motivated, is the common complaint by rapists of lack of sexual pleasure in the act of rape itself.[69] The rate of premature ejaculation, erectile dysfunction, and even ejaculatory dysfunction among non-date rape rapists is far above the normal rate. Many such rapists are clear that the real turn-on came not from the sex, but from the control, the exercise of power, or from the fear or pain of the victim.[70]

Most of us have been socialized to be turned on by domination up to a certain point, at which we become uncomfortable and then repulsed, and say, "This is violence, and unacceptable." But there are many examples of domination in sex which we accept as normal, or even necessary for sexual arousal. "Wimp" is a term of contempt used for nondominant males; women are not ridiculed or demeaned for being nondominant, but rather for demonstrating any behavior which could be construed as dominant. Dominant women are called "dykes," "butches," "ball busters," and are sometimes regarded as in need of being "put in their place." Because men are considered natural dominators, to them falls the role of initiating and controlling sex. Thus there comes to be a certain "rightness" to coercive sex which stops short of physical violence, and a resulting readiness on the part of observers and participants to approve coercive sex. Perhaps the best example of this readiness to approve coercion is the array of surveys of students, both college and high school, regarding judgments as to whether sexual coercion in specific situations should be understood as justified or as rape (unjustified).

In a study of students at Washington State University in 1985 and 1986, 5% of the women and 19% of the men did not believe forced sex on a date is rape.[71] In a 1985 study at Cornell, 19% of women reported having intercourse against their will on a date because of "coercion, threats, force, or violence"—but only 2% of these saw themselves as having been raped.[72] Giarrusso and associates report that 39% of male high school students said it is justifiable to force a girl to have sex if she is drunk or stoned.[73]

Charlotte Muhlenhard and S. Andrews report that men consistently rate forcing a woman into sex as more justifiable if she asked him out, went to his apartment or to a party or "parking," if she wore sexy clothes, if she kissed him voluntarily, or if she drank alcohol.[74] Muhlenhard and Felts asked men to read a date scenario in which the female date at a party drank iced tea instead of alcohol, wore a pleated skirt, tie-neck blouse, and penny loafers, did not kiss the date, and said no three times and moved away in response to her date's sexual advances. The college men in the study were asked to evaluate, on a scale of 1 (no willingness) to 9 (completely willing), the female's interest in having sex with the date. The average score that the college men attributed to the female's willingness to have sex was a 4.5![75]

It is this readiness to approve coercive sex which makes it so difficult to convict date rapists or sexual harassers: heavy penalties for behavior that many men and even many women perceive as within the normal limits of male dominance seem unjust. Victims of such dominance are therefore required to force the dominator to use violence against them if the victim's sexual refusal is to be believed.[76] Provoking victimizers to violence, of course, can be very dangerous. Nevertheless, for the majority in our society only evidence of clear physical violence moves dominance across the limit which divides the normal from the forbidden.

At the present time the eroticization of dominance is particularly problematic for those segments of our society attempting to move in the direction of mutuality in sex, both in sex roles and in sexual pleasure. The problem is that there is often some very real conflict between what persons intellectually desire in sex—that which is both just and socially beneficial—and what actually turns them on. Unfortunately, the idea of sexual mutuality, and the image of mutual pleasuring, are not nearly so powerfully erotic for most people as are the idea and image of domination. For this reason it is difficult to overstress the necessity for the feminist project described by Beverly Harrison and Carter Heyward as the eroticization of mutuality.[77]

While this presents some problems for most of us, who are not comfortable admitting, much less strategizing to combat, our internalized eroticization of dominance, there is one segment of our population with an even more severe problem, and their problem constitutes a general social problem. For while most of us are sexually aroused by some degrees of sexual dominance, for some, especially those whose only experience of sexual arousal took place within extreme sexual domination, there may be *no* capacity for arousal without dominance. Furthermore, arousal may result not only from sexual domination, but from domination in general, and even from indiscriminate violence. In fact, there is a large-scale and ongoing debate about whether persons who rely on domination for arousal become desensitized to it and thus require greater and greater degrees of domination (violence) in order to become aroused.[78] This is not, of course, an exclusively contemporary phenomenon. The concept of "bloodlust" has a long history, as does the connection between war and rape. Instead of recoiling from violence in themselves and others, some persons are attracted to it, sexually aroused and energized by it.

Why does this happen? One of the most obvious reasons that such a distortion of sex could appear is that sex is inherently powerful. Not only does sexual activity itself have great power to motivate, energize, and move humans. Human beings are also powerfully affected by the social organization of gender, and by sexual relationships.[79] All power can be used for good or for ill—it is open to distortion. In human history there are two competing understandings of power, one of which is dominance, and the other of which is shared or mutual power. One of the central concepts of the reign of God that Jesus announced was power as servanthood, rather than as domination. He taught his disciples that while pagans lorded it over each other, that among his followers the leaders would be servants, enablers, persons who demonstrated the equality of all as children of God.[80]

This was not a totally new message. The Hebrew Scriptures depict God both in terms of dominance, which led God to jealously protect divine power by punishing human attempts to exercise it,[81] and in terms of power sharing, which we see in the first creation story, or in the reciprocal, but not equal, provisions of the Abrahamic and Mosaic covenants. The movement from the Hebrew Scriptures to the New Testament is away from understandings of God as basically dominant, toward understandings of God as more interested in intimate relationship with humans than in formal obedience. God remains powerful, and is still in the New Testament sometimes characterized in terms of domination. But increasingly God becomes interpreted, especially by Jesus, as desiring from humans love and confidence, and not fear and submission (though both elements are still found in the Jesus of the Gospels).

Recent Christian theology has not appreciatively altered its treatment of divine power. Most Christians today are still not conscious of the tension, or even conflict, within their theology when they confidently assert both that God is love, and that God sent Jesus to suffer and die so that the gates to heaven—that God had closed in anger at the sin of Adam and Eve—would be opened. Because we have not distinguished power from its familiar form (domination), and understand that love to be effective must be powerful, we fail to see the tension between love and domination.

It is clear in the New Testament that Jesus' disciples never did really understand or accept his teaching or examples of servant leadership. Despite the innate attractiveness of this concept of servant leadership, the world, and the churches as well, are still struggling to understand, accept, and embody this concept. It should not surprise us that sex is distorted by understandings of power as dominance, because every other aspect of human life is similarly distorted. The struggle to replace domination with a sharing of power is a long-term struggle. It is today a more crucial struggle than ever before, for human survival in this age demands that we renounce the practice of domination, which effectively requires that we cease worshiping domination in our image of God. We need not accept wholesale the complex theory of René Girard regarding the role of religion in primitive societies: as protecting societies by restraining human fascination with violence by means of the sacrifice of scapegoat victims.[82] But analysis of our historical reality reveals that 1) the Christian tradition has presented God in terms of righteous domination and demands for violence, 2) humans have assigned superiority to the sex understood as dominant, and 3) humans have eroticized the exercise of domination. We will not remove the dangerous, even lethal eroticization of domination until we follow Girard's suggestion: admit our fascination for and worship of violence (the epitome of domination), and stop projecting it onto God. We cannot afford to worship domination any longer, even if, as in our own society, the exercise of domination is so much more subtle than in the past because it is domination not by individuals but by small groups who hide behind systems and institutions. We can no longer afford the damage to the environment which our attempts to master rather than cooperate with nature create. We can no longer afford military domination, either in terms of its cost to our debt-ridden economy increasingly mortgaged to Japan, Western Europe, and the petro-nations, or in terms of the potential ecological damage of military action, whether with nuclear or conventional weapons. Domination of all sorts, including sexual domination, which is often considered the primary historical model of domination, must be eliminated.

Symbolic Power of Sex

As we have seen, sex is not only powerful, but a great deal of the power in sex is symbolic. All real power rests in the capacity to convey, to represent, ultimate meaning. One way in which systems of domination survive is by manipulating symbols to obtain the reluctant consent, if not the real support, of members of the society.[83] Human societies vary a great deal in their treatment of sexuality, but in virtually all the power of sex is expressed and understood symbolically. Because sex has been historically understood as primarily for procreation, it has functioned symbolically to represent life. In symbolism, every concept also includes its negation. Thus sex has functioned to represent life as emerging out of, or victory over, death. It is important that we recall that for almost all of human history, and still today for many of the world's people, life has been and is a precarious, temporary toe-hold carved out of surrounding death. Relatively few lived to adulthood until recently. Life was short and hard, even for the survivors. And humans were constantly aware of the precarious-ness of life, for death from hunger, famine, war, accident, and epidemic threatened constantly. Life was a hand-to-mouth battle for survival, often in competition with others for scarce resources.

Life and death were more closely existentially linked in the past than for us in this society. Many women died trying to birth children, and many men died in hunting and war—both activities which inflict death to protect and preserve one's community. The basic biological strategy was to maximize the birth rate. The larger the number born, the better able the community was to survive the losses due to epidemics, accidents, war, and maternal mortality. The only situation in which this was perhaps not the best survival strategy was hunger from famine. But on the whole, this strategy of maximizing initial numbers so as to maximize sur-vivors worked well. Sex for procreation was life-enhancing for human communities.

As we saw in Chapter Two, we have entered a stage of human development in which community survival must mean lower birth rates. We cannot afford any longer for sex, under-stood in terms of reproduction, to symbolize life in general. We must assign new primary symbolism to sex. Lovers will continue to turn to the emotional intensity of sexual union as an affirma-tion of their continued existence amidst experiences of death or disaster. But we must separate much more carefully two different aspects of life in sex: the generation of life and the sustaining of life.

Christianity in most of its forms has recognized both aspects of life through its sacramental system. The two sacraments most common among Christians are baptism, which is a ritual of birth, and communion (Eucharist), which is a ritual of life maintenance (feeding). In the Catholic church, which recognizes seven sacra-ments, only baptism is about birthing. Five of the sacraments—Eucharist, reconciliation, anointing of the sick, marriage, and confirmation—all involve the channelling of grace into nurturance of individual life (Eucharist, the anointing of the sick), or nurturance of relationships which bind the community together (reconciliation), or support of persons through the stages of development in human life (confirmation, marriage), in addition to connecting individuals and the church community to God.[84]

We must shift from an emphasis on the generation of life to an emphasis on the sustaining of life. Sex has symbolized both; most societies have explicitly emphasized the generation, and subsumed the maintaining of life under generation, as Christianity has done. We must now differentiate the two meanings, and stress sex as symbolic of maintaining life.

How does sex sustain life? Through its ability to bond. There are many, many different ways that human beings bond. Humans bond through shared work, for example, as well as in shared play, or pain, or death. Sexual love is another. Sexual love is more limited than these other methods in that most humans in the history of the world have understood and preferred sex in pairs, not in groups. Therefore sexual love as direct human bond usually binds only pairs and not groups together. On the other hand, sexual love is able to bind humans together strongly, more strongly than other shared activities. Sexual love has the ability to bind humans into living together—into sharing the bulk of their lives, and not just pieces of their lives.

Within Christian history this unitive purpose of sex was never well developed. Most discussions of the unitive aspect began with the second of St. Augustine's three purposes of sex. Augustine maintained that the three purposes of marital sexuality were: procreation, a symbol of unity, and a remedy for concupiscence.[85] Augustine himself never developed the idea of marital sex as a symbol of unity other than to say that the sexual union of spouses symbolized the unity of God and the soul, or Christ and the church. Later twentieth-century theologians tried to build this concept of sex as a symbol of unity into something resembling interpersonal intimacy in the wake of Protestant shifts toward allowing artificial contraception, which was seen as displacing procreation as the primary purpose of marriage. Twentieth-century theologians were too liberal to be comfortable with stressing sex as a remedy for concupiscence, and so turned to sex as symbol of unity, as something which could be related to the interpersonal love relationships couples stressed as their own interest in sex. This is, of course, the direction we need to go, but Rosemary Ruether was certainly right: we need to acknowledge that Augustine himself never understood sex as an expression of a personal love relationship. For him and for a majority of the Christian tradition, sex was either sinfully masturbatory (intent on one's own sexual pleasure) or sinlessly and impersonally instrumental (using the other for pleasure or procreation).[86]

In Augustine's culture it would have been very difficult to make a strong case for a heterosexual relationship based in interpersonal love, due to the low esteem in which women were held.[87] In the cities, as opposed to the countrysides, in the Roman Empire the prevailing sexual mores for men were neither exclusively heterosexual nor exclusively homosexual. Most men were both married and engaged in homosexual affairs, though minorities of men were exclusively gay or straight. The sexuality of women is virtually unknown, since the (male) writers of the period present women as sexual objects and mothers only. In the mid-fourth century, Christianity began to pressure for the regulation of homosexual practices. Gay marriages were outlawed in 342, though the law was often disregarded since there were no penalties attached. Late in the fourth century, there were a number of proposals to outlaw adult men taking the passive role in homosexual sodomy, since that role was understood as appropriate to young boys only, and in 390 the selling of men and boys (but not girls and women) into prostitution was outlawed upon pain of death. Some historians, including Boswell, suggest that Ambrose, bishop of Milan, imposed this law on the emperor as a penance for a massacre by the army in Thessalonica.[88]

During this entire period, literature was filled with a debate over the superiority of homosexual love over heterosexual love. The argument for homosexual love was the classical one: that real love, the love that inspires community, courage, and all the civic virtues, is between men, and women are only for the necessary work of procreation. Thus Boswell quotes the defender of homosexual love in the debate Plutarch recounts in his *Moralia*: "True love has nothing to do with women's quarters, nor will I agree that you have ever felt love for women or girls, any more than flies feel love for milk."[89] The reason that it took so long for Christianity to wear down practices around homosexual sex for married men is that Christians such as Augustine agreed with the defenders of homosexual sex in their evaluation of women. They agreed that women were not capable of being real companions or partners of men. This is why Augustine argued (and Aquinas later agreed[90]) that the Genesis reference to Eve as helpmate must have referred to her as a helpmate in the work of reproduction, for in any other work a man would be more helped by another man.[91] In such a context interpersonal love relationships between men and women were beyond the capacity of imagination.

The single greatest challenge to humanity today is the creation of community, of a sense of relatedness, even interdependence between all groups and individuals. What recent humans had known of community is in the process of final disintegration in the developed world, and is fast crumbling elsewhere under the destructive impact of "modern culture." We are in the process of becoming more radically alone, despite our increasing density. We are learning that escaping from the confines of traditional societies does not make us autonomous only in the sense of free and independent, but also in the sense of being unconnected and lonely. Without being surrounded by extended family and lifetime neighbors who in traditional societies know one intimately and reflect back to one who one is, people increasingly find themselves faced with the need to create other intimate relationships to perform this function. Yet the pursuit of intimacy puts us in conflict with our society's reverence for autonomy.

At the same time that we as individuals suffer the lack of relationship, our larger society is disintegrating from the lack of community which results from large-scale pursuit of autonomy. There is no longer a sense of the whole of which each is a part. We have come to expect greed and corruption, opportunism and dishonesty from our leaders in politics, business, banking, criminal justice, education, government, and even the churches. We become accustomed to expecting that individuals make decisions based on a narrow range of self-interest, rather than on the needs of the entire community, or the needs of those least able to meet their own needs.

Sex is not enough, of course, to create human community. But sexual love is certainly one important part of the necessary process of deliberately setting about to create connections between humans. There are in all relationships, regardless of the degree of intimacy involved, both privileges and obligations, advantages and disadvantages, pleasant and unpleasant aspects. But the intense pleasure which sexual love promises—the ability of sexual love to satisfy many physical, emotional, and spiritual needs of human persons—and its ability to deliver such pleasure immediately are the strongest possible reinforcements for extending ourselves to others in relationship. Humans are willing to risk a great deal for that kind of pleasure, and also to put up with a great deal. Sex—as symbolic of commitment to a sexual relationship—must come to symbolize the ability of persons, whole embodied persons, to experience union. Full union is momentary, but the ability to find ecstatic union with another even briefly allows us to know and reflect on union, to recognize the ability of union to enhance and fulfill us, and thus to recognize the worth of risking disclosing and committing ourselves to another.

The survival of human life today seems to require that persons learn to live together cooperatively. If we cannot live together in twos sustained, at least in part, by shared sexual pleasure, then how can we hope to live together in nonsexual union? In the developed world we are beginning to move in this direction. In the American colonies the average woman had between 12 and 13 pregnancies. In 1970 U.S. women averaged 2.6 births; in 1990 U.S. women averaged 1.8 births.[92] In Kenya women averaged 8.1 births in 1990.[93] Sex in Kenya, or in the American colonies, was and is a much more powerful symbol of generation of life, because it much more often resulted in potential life and birth.

Birth rates are now dropping, even in developing lands, while levels of sexual activity seem to be rising.[94] Sex is increasingly for the purpose of sustaining relationship. In the U.S., sexual activity has clearly been increasing while the birth rate has dropped. The frequency and duration of sexual activity, both coital and noncoital, has been steadily rising at least since Kinsey's initial studies in the late 1940s, and it is strongly suspected that this increase began in the 1920s.[95]

These are, for the most part, good trends—good for human life as a whole. The earth cannot support a larger population; birth rates must drop. But the increase in sexual activity can not only enhance individual life, but can also be useful for human life as a whole. To the extent that we consciously choose to define symbolic power in sex in ways that enhance community, stressing the goodness of human pleasure and the unitive, bonding function of sex, the human community benefits. We can and should choose to emphasize the unitive function of sex, and to ground that union in pleasure. But the unitive function of sex can only be one small part of our search for community. The danger in stressing the role of sexual love in the creation of community is that sexual love may be seized as a substitute for broader community. This is a primary characteristic of the developed world, especially of North America. The privatization of sex, and the many forces urging persons to retreat from the concerns of the public world and instead immerse themselves in the rewards of the private world of sex, marriage, family, friends, leisure, and recreation, are fairly far advanced.

So disintegrated is the sense of community in our society that there is a strong hunger for intimacy, despite a fear of intimacy as a threat to autonomy. Persons lack a sense of being intimately known by and cared for by others; they feel isolated and alienated from others. The historic ethnic communities which grounded our ancestors have given way to extreme mobility, to the breakdown of the extended family, and to the disintegration of ethnic neighborhoods. Sexual intimacy achieved in romantic love—which was never a significant part of traditional community—is now often promoted as the cure for the alienation people feel. It promises to cure loneliness, to allow us to know and be known. It offers us a someone who can reflect back to us who we are.

But sexual intimacy is no panacea for all the ills brought on by the contemporary collapse of community. The achievement of emotional intimacy through sexual relationship is not only complex, but very limited. Though some people will be able to achieve sexual intimacy with more than one person, and perhaps more than one person at a time, for most of us there is simply not enough time in a day or a week to earn a living, take care of domestic and childcare chores, participate in our larger community/culture, and achieve and maintain intimate sexual relationships with a number of different persons. Most of us find it a strain to maintain one truly intimate sexual relationship, and this one relationship cannot possibly carry the strain of providing for all our social needs, of removing the alienation we feel in all the other parts of our lives. If we are feeling alienated on the job from other workers, from the work itself, and from the environment, there is no real cure for that alienation except restructuring the job. No sexual relationship can prevent our feeling alienated in that job, or that alienation from affecting how we feel about ourselves and others.

Nevertheless, we are bombarded on every side with a romanticization of sexual relationship in our culture, a romanticization which offers itself as the only alternative to total experiential alienation. That romanticization of sexual relationship functions to shift human energy away from reforming alienating structures into vain attempts to achieve an intimacy which supposedly will, of itself, banish the feelings of, if not the fact of, alienation. But unless we attack the real causes of alienation the romanticization of sexual intimacy is self-defeating, for the expectations of sexual intimacy become so high that no relationship can satisfy them. So some individuals abandon sexual relationships one after the other in order to search for the perfect partner with which to establish this intimacy. Thus arises the phenomenon of serial monogamy.

While neither sexual intimacy nor the bond it can create will replace the social needs of humans, such as justice and community, they do have a great deal to contribute to the task of creating human community. Sexual intimacy and bonding can contribute to the creation of community in two ways: 1) vision—sexual intimacy and bonding give us insight into what community is, how it meets human needs, and how satisfying it can be; and 2) energy—sexual intimacy and bonding can be a great source of energy for the task of social change toward community.

Vision. Any kind of intimacy with another enlarges our vision.[96] I have a very close friend of over 20 years who lives a thousand miles away. Missy is an architectural restorationist, and from her I have learned to apppreciate cities—buildings, bridges, and monuments—in wholly new ways. Because of my interest in her and her life and work I have learned new perspectives on current political/economic issues around buildings. She has tremendously influenced my political stands and activism on historic preservation, urban development, and low-income housing—issues which, without her influence, would be viewed solely from the very different perspective of my work with Habitat for Humanity, which builds/rehabs buildings for low-income family ownership. Missy has expanded my vision of what needs to be done, of the breadth of appropriate community concerns in housing, and of what interests can march together. The intimacy of close friendship provides this kind of extension of vision.

To an even greater extent my vision has been enlarged by my intimate sexual bond with my husband of 25 years, Frank. Through him I have come to learn of rural immigrant life in the Midwest, of family lifestyles and traditions very different from my own demonstrative, sexually open, irreverent, and often insensitive family. Through my relationship with him as he went through law school and 18 years of practicing corporate law, I have been exposed to lawyers, bankers, politicians, businessmen, and to their debates over trends and issues affecting them. Because I love him, I have been interested in the activities of his life, and through that interest my vision of how government and the economy actually work has been tremendously enlarged. Not all the extensions of vision are pleasant or welcomed at the time, but the result of this process is that my vision of what needs to be changed if we are to move toward community becomes less naive and more informed than before. Thus one important way that intimacy with one person draws us close to others as well is by enlarging our vision of what needs to be done to meet the needs of the entire community.

Energy. Sexual intimacy and bonding are also a source for the energy required for reconstructing community. All forms of intimacy bring us to care for the persons with whom we are intimate, and thus to care about what happens to them. The more intimate we become, the more their welfare becomes ours (not replacing, but only adding to our concern for our individual welfare). Their triumphs become ours, their sufferings ours as well. Thus, if their interests or welfare are unjustly threatened, if they are hurt or otherwise abused by others or other forces, we become angry and active on their behalf. We are often able to marshall energy against that which threatens them even before they are, because they are often distracted by questions as to why they are suffering: Did they bring this on themselves? Is God punishing them? Do they deserve this suffering or threat? Whereas we who are intimate with them more clearly recognize their innocence and therefore the injustice of the situation. (Of course there are times when our intimacy with them may lead us to a very different route: "You really did bring this on yourself, and can't blame God or anyone else. You have been irresponsible, drinking, missing work, overspending, not watching your diet and exercise, etc.")

We may know in a general way that manufacturing jobs have been moving out of the U.S. over the last 20 years as U.S. companies seek out the lowest wage rates in the world, and that where manufacturing jobs have been replaced, they have been replaced, for the most part, with much lower-paying, non-union, often minimum-wage service jobs. But for many of us this knowledge alone does not change our attitudes or move us to action.

Our own economic situation and that of our family, friends and neighbors has not changed appreciatively, which suggests to us that the impact of this trend on "real" families is minimal. But the spouses of workers who lose their job to this pattern of capital flight are much more easily energized by concern.

Jim and Kay are friends we met at church. In 1980 Jim was a 48-year-old skilled foundry worker, a production supervisor, at a time when the heavy metal industry was closing down all over the U.S. In the previous 12 years, he had lost work three times as the foundries he worked in were closed or sold and reopened with non-union labor. In 1980 he was unemployed all year, but kept busy as a volunteer worker in the church where he was a permanent deacon. In 1981 he got a foundry job at an hour's commute, but two years later that plant, too, closed. After 26 months of unemployment (less than half with unemployment benefits), he was offered a job in a nuclear-processing plant. He and his wife of 25 years went round and round about whether any job could be worth the health risks of nuclear radiation on a 53-year-old man with hypertension, who smoked heavily. This job not only involved processing uranium, but in a processing plant notorious for violations of safety regulations. In the previous 15 years, this plant had "lost" 2500 pounds of radioactive material in the form of dust.

Left with no pension or health benefits when earlier employers went out of business, Jim was desperate. He felt the stigma of unemployment again, and he feared for retirement. He could not afford to work at most of the service jobs available to 53-year-old black men with high school educations, like McDonald's. So he has now worked at the processing plant since 1984, first in production, and then, when production was closed, as a supervisor in the toxic cleanup program scheduled to last at least another 10 – 15 years. Who knows if his increasing medical problems are the result of his job, or just aging?

About the same time Kay took a new job as director of a small nonprofit corporation founded by a few church-identified individuals to rehab and administer extremely low-income housing. When she began working with the black low-income clients and the white upper-middle-class board of directors, she felt pulled in two directions. The white professional board members assumed that unemployment indicated some kind of personal instability—alcoholism, drugs, laziness, mental illness—and were reluctant either to rent to or hire applicants whose work histories had gaps representing unemployment. Initially inclined not to annoy the "deep pockets" on which her salary depended, Kay took some time before she challenged their position and insisted that such an attitude served to further handicap persons already suffering from the loss of production and other blue-collar jobs. At the same time, as she saw again and again in the lives of the applicants the same employment patterns she had lived through with Jim, and as she encountered the prejudicial ignorance of board members, her intimate relationship with Jim became not only a window into a major social problem, but a source of tremendous energy for change.

Her passionate commitment to Jim energized her to refute the interpretation of the board, to further analyze the situation, and to finally plunge into local and regional programs for job creation and political action to control capital flight.

We cannot help but care about those with whom we are intimate, and caring about them gives us energy to challenge institutions, social trends, or individuals which threaten or oppress them. As the availability of other forms of intimacy declines under the same pressures which destroy traditional community, sexual intimacy becomes more and more important as a source of both vision and energy. But sexual intimacy by itself is no more able to create community than it is to replace community in fulfilling human needs. Sexual intimacy must be understood in ways that support the development of intimacy of varying degrees in friendships and families, with co-workers and neighbors. We cannot be intimate with everybody, but neither should intimacy be limited to one person, lest it lack the strength necessary to enlarge both our vision and our energy for the task of creating community.

5. *Mutuality in Sexual Pleasure as Normative*

We have said that once we reject procreationism as species sui-
cide, the most salient characteristic of, and chief motivation for,
sex is sexual pleasure. Sexual pleasure is a good because it en-
hances our sense of well-being by satisfying some basic human
needs: for touch, for excitement, for physical release, for companionship. But sexual pleasure can also be a means to the satisfaction of other human needs and desires, through its ability to bind
persons together in intimacy. A Christian sexual ethic should encourage sexual pleasure in sex, emphasizing its social as well as
its individual functions. A Christian sexual ethic should make mutuality in sexual pleasure normative. Any failure to include one's
partner in sexual pleasure is, first, a violation of the Christian
imperative to love one's neighbor, and second, a rejection of the
social function of sex which is dependent upon the mutuality of
pleasure. This chapter proposes that accepting mutual sexual
pleasure as the primary purpose of sexual activity requires respect
and care for the partner and responsibility for avoiding pain and
maximizing pleasure for all affected by that activity, and examines
existing obstacles to the acceptance of mutual sexual pleasure as
the primary norm governing sexual activity.

The derivation of both respect and care for the partner and
responsibility for all affected by one's sexual activity is fairly obvious. If we have a Christian obligation to love all our neighbors as
ourselves, then our choice of actions must be governed by a utilitarian calculus of how to maximize pleasure and minimize pain
for all those neighbors. This will be true in sexuality as in other

areas of human life. As we saw in Chapter Four, mutuality serves to maximize pleasure in sex, in that my own pleasure is intensified by evidence that I am able to pleasure the partner, and a pleasured partner is more likely to be an active partner—active in pleasuring me. The communication of respect and concern between partners within sexual interaction also serves to maximize pleasure in sex, in that it invests each of the physical gestures and actions with additional symbolic meaning. This can be true even within what many persons would call casual sex. If one partner prior to sex inquires as to how the other partner is coping with the long dying process of her parent, and then responds with sincere sympathy to the answer, the other partner may then be able both to interpret the ordinary touches and actions in sexual interaction as expressions by the other of sympathetic care and concern, and to take greater pleasure in them. The level of meaning invested in sexual activity is intensified by the degree of respect and care that exists between the partners, and the greater the meaning, the greater the potential for pleasure.

Since all persons live in societies in which all the actions, including sexual actions, of members of the society impinge on all the other members of the society, minimizing the pain and maximizing the pleasure in sexual choices will require responsibility. This responsibility will take two forms: protecting the entire society from painful consequences of sexual activity, and to the limited but very real extent described in the previous chapter, maximizing the communal benefits derived from personal sexual activity.

Of course, neither all cultures nor all Christians in all cultures would agree. Some cultures understand sexual pleasure as sinful, to be avoided whenever possible, and risked only for purposes of reproduction. Some cultures object to the inclusion of women in sexual pleasure, and some have even devised methods of surgically eliminating sexual pleasure for women, as with clitorectomy and genital infibulation, which sometimes function as female puberty rituals.[1]

While there is no justification for maintaining the superiority of one *culture* over another, still, if we are to make any judgments at all about the welfare of specific persons, we must evaluate some particular cultural *practices* as superior to others. The exclusion of women—or anyone—from sexual pleasure, and the cultural repression of sexual pleasure, are morally inferior to their alternatives.

Cultural variation also exists between groups and societies which *accept* mutual sexual pleasure as normative in sexual activity. There will be variations between classes, churches, and racial/ethnic groups within the same nation in how these two criteria are interpreted. For example, some more traditional Americans maintain that the function of shared sexual pleasure is to bind persons together in intimate stable relationships, while many young persons in America maintain that the function of sexual pleasure is that it helps one to know and appreciate one's body while establishing links with a variety of persons. Both groups value sexual pleasure, believe that it should be shared between partners, and invest it with the power to bond. But the exclusivity and depth of the bond are contested, and the experience of sexual pleasure as an important way of learning to accept and appreciate one's body is only claimed by one side. On the other hand, a person from a very traditional society might well say that the function of sexual pleasure is to keep men anchored in the home, providing for wife and children. All might agree that sexual pleasure helps make bearable the strains and inconveniences of living together.

Acceptance of mutuality in sexual pleasure as an ethical criterion for sexual activity implies mutual consent to sex. While mutual consent to sex is a radical moral criterion in terms of existing sexual practice in our society, it is neither so radical nor so adequate as mutual sexual pleasure. Mutual sexual pleasure demands far deeper changes in sexual practice, and itself implies mutual consent. Mutual consent does not come near ensuring mutual sexual pleasure.

Persons consent to sex for all sort of reasons short of mutual sexual pleasure, some of them terrible. When we pose mutual consent as the primary ethical criterion for sexual activity, we are forced to keep adding criteria to deal with those situations in which formal consent is given but sex is less than freely chosen and truly voluntary. Children may formally consent to sex to gain approval, affection, or material favor. Prostitutes formally consent to sex to support themselves. A secretary may formally consent to sex with her boss, or a student with a teacher. So we add ethical principles which insist that children cannot give real consent, and that sex between superiors and subordinates is illegitimate because the imbalance of power prevents free consent. But there are always other circumstances which illustrate the need for further middle axioms. For example, what about persons who hate and fear sex due to past abuse, but who may nevertheless freely consent to sex out of love or gratitude toward another person who is perceived as desirous of sex? Sexual pleasure which implies consent to sex, and not formal consent only, is the primary requirement for ethical sexual activity. Sex which is not aimed at mutual pleasure is not only incapable of promoting intimacy and bonding, but is actually, especially if repeated, destructive of relationships and self-esteem.

There are some who would deny that mutual sexual pleasure requires mutual consent to sex. There are, they say, persons who enjoy being coerced. My answer is both yes and no. The number of persons who enjoy being coerced is very small. These persons are also conflicted; their "pleasure" is at the same time a kind of self-punishment, a denial of their own worth and dignity. They are the most seriously affected by the religio-cultural confusion between pain and pleasure which, as we saw in Chapter Four, infects Western culture.[2]

On the other hand, there are many persons who seem to take pleasure in the *appearance* of being coerced. One of the reasons that some men do not take seriously women's "NO" to sex is that they have experienced women who want sex, but verbally reject it, hoping to be persuaded, so as to avoid being responsible for their activity.[3] This is not real coercion—but it is extremely dangerous, because it trains men to disregard the expressed wishes of women—many of whom really mean "NO" and are raped nonetheless.

There are many other examples of what appears to be coercion and is not. Many women, and some men, fantasize about being coerced into sex.[4] In their fantasy, they choose the partner, the circumstances, the sexual acts, and the consequences. The fantasized coercion has the virtue of removing from women who have been socialized to shun sex the responsibility—and guilt—for choosing sex, and of relieving men of the burden of having to always initiate and control sex. Such fantasies do not at all indicate any desire to actually be coerced. Similarly with many of the sadomasochistic sexual games couples play—if the partner to be bound freely supplies and dons the padded cuffs and chains, this is not coercion. It is rather another manifestation of our society's eroticization of dominance. (This is not to approve S/M games as totally innocuous. Clearly any physical pain or damage inflicted would tell against mutual pleasure.)

How Restrictive Are These Criteria?

If we are to begin with these two ethical criteria for sexual activity—that sexual activity should be pleasurable, and everyone involved should experience the pleasure—how restrictive would such criteria be? Interestingly enough, to use mutual pleasure as the criteria for ethical sexual activity is to demand enormous transformation of the sexual landscape in our society. If "permissive" treatment of sexuality is that which allows almost any practice, or which fails to demand significant changes in present practice, then these proposed criteria are not permissive at all.

The proposed criteria would require, first of all, taking seriously all those obstacles and circumstances which currently prevent sex from being mutually pleasurable. Those include, among others: genital mutilation (usually of women), fear of pregnancy, fear of AIDS and other STDs, rape and sexual abuse, sexual coercion/harassment, sexual dysfunction, ignorance of sexual biology and technique, and, last but not least, poor sexual communication. The criterion of social responsibility would also weigh in against sexual activity which involves contracting STDs; conception outside stable, ecologically responsible child-rearing situations; or public policies which support sexual ignorance, sexual dysfunction, sexual abuse, or sexual coercion/harassment. The criterion of respect and care for the partner would at least rule out instrumental understandings of partners, including sexual objectification.

Genital Mutilation

So far from universally normative is this criterion of mutual pleasure in sex that there are 85 – 114 million women living today—including half the female population of Egypt[5]—who have been genitally mutilated, most either by clitoridectomy or by the even more severe genital infibulation, in order to remove pleasure from sex for women.[6] Clitoridectomy—excision of the clitoris—has the effect of reducing for most women the possibility of sexual arousal, and removing the capacity for orgasm. Genital infibulation, which includes the removal not only of the clitoral shaft, glans, and hood, but of the labia majora and some of the labia minora as well, not only leaves the female vulva a mass of scar tissue which must be painfully torn open for each act of coitus, but also results in massive tearing of scar tissue in childbirth. The absence of sexual pleasure for women who have been genitally mutilated is not accidental, but is the central purpose of the surgery: the impossibility of sexual pleasure for women removes from women any incentive to infidelity, makes them undemanding sexual partners, and also supposedly increases the pleasure of men by making the vaginal entrance permanently "tight."

Though genital mutilation is not unknown among men, it is much more rare, and seldom interferes with sexual pleasure. For example, the most common male genital mutilation is circumcision, which admittedly is practiced in our society on a scale far beyond its medical advisability.[7] That is, though the medical profession has determined that there are few, rather rare, medical reasons for penile circumcision, the practice is widespread: most newborn males are circumcised in the U.S.

Yet male circumcision does not negatively affect male sexual pleasure. The practice of subincision among the aboriginese of

Australia and New Zealand is an example of male genital mutilation which *can* interfere with sexual pleasure, but it is clear that this is not at all the purpose of subincision.[8] Subincision is the repeated lengthwise lancing of the shaft of the penis to obtain a cleft which resembles the female vulva when the penis is pulled back between the legs. This cleft is ritually opened to produce a flow of blood in male imitation of the menstruation of females, in order to ritually claim for men the female power to give birth. It is clear that the surgery is done to males by males for the purposes of ritually enhancing the sexual power of males. If sometimes the surgery goes badly, and capacity for erection or ejaculation is sacrificed, this is accidental and not the intention. Certainly adoption of mutual pleasure as an ethical criterion for sex would invalidate any medical/surgical procedure either designed to reduce or eliminate sexual pleasure, or likely to effect such results, unless the absence of such procedure threatened the life or general welfare of the individual.

Good Women as Sexually Passive

Women have been and continue to be much more victimized than men by attempts to limit or eliminate their capacity for sexual pleasure. Many cultures, including our own, which have not surgically prevented women's sexual pleasure in great numbers have attempted through socialization to achieve the same result. The standards for acceptable female behavior have seldom if ever legitimated any direct seeking of sexual pleasure, even in marriage. Our society has taught that a crucial difference between ladies and lower-class women is that ladies were not motivated by sexual desire and did not pursue sexual pleasure. Ladies have been regarded by tradition as sexually passive. Sexual pleasure has been thought to be appropriately pursued by men and animals; women who evinced interest in sexual pleasure were considered indiscriminate, and therefore available to any partner. In fact, this separation of good women from wanton women is one of the reasons we continue to have as a society severe problems with rape and other forms of sexual coercion. Men who accept this traditional view of women have been shown more likely to justify rape, and more likely to believe in the more common rape myths, so that women who ask men out, go to men's apartments, voluntarily kiss their dates, or go "parking" are understood by such traditional men as wanton and unrapeable.[9] Women who accept this traditional view of women are more likely to offer token resistance to sex in order to be thought ladies worthy of respect. They thus confirm for such traditional men that force is the way to get a not-so-willing woman turned on.[10]

Sex Roles as Obstacles to Sexual Pleasure

If mutual sexual pleasure is accepted as a moral criterion in sex, a major resocialization of both men and women will be necessary. Both men and women must understand that women as well as men can and should find pleasure in sex, and both men and women must learn techniques for arousing and satisfying themselves and their partners. The sexes must jointly take active responsibility for mutually pleasurable sex, both because justice demands it, and because the more active a participant to sex is, the more sexually satisfied he or she is likely to be.

It is too often the case that as persons in our society come to accept that women should find sex pleasurable, the existing pattern of male domination in sex is not abandoned, but merely enlarged, so that women are in effect pressured to find sex pleasurable, and men are ordered to take responsibility for women's pleasure.[11] Responsibility for women's pleasure as well as their own is an onerous burden for men, and is often the source of a great deal of male anxiety around sex. At the same time, the social shift to validation of women's right to pleasure in sex is often meaningless to women because it occurs within a sexual relationship which is unequal in power. When asked by their partner, "Did you come?" many women do not feel able to say no, to offer suggestions, or make requests, without damaging the partner's ego, which can be uncomfortable and sometimes even dangerous in situations characterized by dominance/submission. Thus women lie, and learn to fake orgasm. About two-thirds of women in our society fake orgasm at least periodically.[12] On the other hand, some women fail to take advantage of sincere invitations from male lovers to share control of sex. They can be motivated by fear of responsibility, feelings of inadequacy, laziness, or distrust. Some men would like nothing better than to have their lover initiate and take a leading role in sex play, either occasionally or regularly. And yet some men who sincerely issue such invitations find themselves overwhelmed by feelings of having lost control, and unable to participate in shared control.

These sex roles can be problematic in homosexual relationships as well. Lesbians, for example, often have trouble beginning a sexual relationship since both partners have been trained as females to wait for a man to make sexual overtures, and, except for relatively few young women exposed to urban lesbian culture, have no models of lesbian interaction.[13] This lack of initiative can be a problem not only for initiating a relationship, but also for achieving regular sex. On the other hand, this lack of models does present a kind of freedom to create relationships as the partners wish, without a great deal of outside cultural pressure. As Mariana Valverde says about lesbian sex: "(T)here are no conveniently traditional roles to fall back upon. There is no missionary position."[14]

Gay men, on the other hand, have been socialized as males to be assertive, even aggressive in initiating sex. Newcomers to gay turf, especially straights who stray in, are often horrified and even terrified at being the target of repeated aggressive physical advances by gays. Neither gay nor straight men have been socialized to be the recipients of sexual initiatives or aggression. Relationships between two assertive-to-aggressive persons can become more competitive than ones in which there is the moderating presence of a submissive person.[15]

Over the last half of the twentieth century two complementary trends in gay and lesbian culture have occurred. The first is that the majority of gay and lesbian couples no longer model heterosexual sex roles within the couple. That is, in a gay couple, there is usually no "female" partner, and in a lesbian couple, neither woman plays a male role. Where such heterosexual-based roleplaying survives among homosexual persons, it is usually among older gays and lesbians.[16] This break with heterosexual imitation has also initiated a break with the pattern of dominance/submission within couples. Many gay and lesbian couples are models of mutuality in terms of sexual activity, shared power and decisionmaking, and cooperative work.

Many observers have noted that while there are significant populations of both homosexual and heterosexual men and women who have put a great deal of time and energy into constructing egalitarian sexual relationships over the last few decades, the results of those efforts seem more differentiated by orientation than by gender. That is, homosexual couples, both gay and lesbian, are generally agreed to have been more successful than heterosexual couples in constructing egalitarian couples, as well as egalitarian groups and subcultures.[17] At the same time, there is continuing concern at what seems to be a much greater difficulty among gay and lesbian couples in preserving the sexual spark within relationships over extended years.[18] Some observers have also noted the increase in (or perhaps an increased openness about) sado-masochist sex play among gays. Though practiced also by some lesbians and heterosexuals, the dangerous practice of "fisting" or "handballing" which became popular in gay communities in the late 1970s has become predominantly a practice of the gay male community.[19] It is possible that S/M sex play is a way of reintroducing into sex the dominance that a couple has excluded from their overall roles. This would make sense in a number of ways. If we have strongly eroticized dominance in our society, then it will be difficult to sustain the erotic quality of egalitarian sexual relationships. Gay and lesbian sexual relationships tend to be more egalitarian and would likely have somewhat more difficulty sustaining eroticism. There may be a number of explanations for the existence of a large-scale sado-masochism industry and a parallel network of nonprofit sadomasochist social organizations, but the connections forged in our culture between pain and pleasure certainly help make egalitarianism a threat to eroticism.[20]

Sexual Ignorance and Sexual Dysfunction

If both men and women are to take responsibility for achieving mutual pleasure in sex, then a great deal of education work must be done in our society. The level of ignorance about sex is tremendous, and often significantly interferes with sexual pleasure. Again, ignorance is more likely to impede the pleasure of women than of men, but men's pleasure is also affected by sexual ignorance.[21] Take, for example, ignorance about female arousal and orgasm. There are many men and women who not only do not know what moves women toward orgasm, but do not even know that orgasm is physically natural and right for women. Two of the most common sexual dysfunctions among women, lack of vaginal lubrication and anorgasmia, are both often the result of such ignorance. The most effective remedy for lack of vaginal lubrication is simply sexual stimulation in extended foreplay. Effective stimulation may be anything from kissing for some women to direct stimulation of the clitoris for others. Vaginal lubrication is the result of vasocongestion in the vaginal walls, which occurs with arousal. Without vaginal lubrication, penile penetration is painful, and if the vaginal walls are sufficiently dry, penile penetration and thrusting can actually tear them. It is no wonder that for many women achieving vaginal lubrication immediately changes sex from painful to pleasurable, and may occasionally end anorgasmia.

Anorgasmia can sometimes also be resolved in women merely by professional or partner assurance that orgasm for women is right and natural, despite what the woman has been socialized to believe. The single most effective cure for anorgasmia is sufficient stimulation. Most men and women simply do not know that the stimulation afforded by penile vaginal intercourse is not sufficient to bring most women to orgasm.

Sexual ignorance not only cripples women's sexual pleasure. Ignorance about the mechanics of impotence cripples many a man's pleasure in sex as well. It simply is not understood that it is normal for all men to have temporary periods of impotence. When very tired, stressed, sick, or anxious, most men have periods when they cannot get or maintain an erection. Unfortunately, male socialization teaches men that masculinity requires that a man be ever ready for sex, always able to sustain an erection. This means that an occasional inability to become erect may be, and often is, interpreted by a man, or by his sexual partner, as cause for serious worry. Anxiety over this otherwise temporary situation often causes ongoing impotence—a vicious circle. [22]

Similarly, the single most common male sexual dysfunction, premature ejaculation, [23] is also the most easily resolved, usually by the affected male and his sexual partner without professional help. But in the absence of knowledge about premature ejaculation many persons fail to recognize or resolve this problem and suffer for years. Premature ejaculation is penile ejaculation which occurs before the man and his partner desire it. It includes ejaculation which occurs in early stages of arousal, before insertion, as well as ejaculation after insertion, but before the couple wanted to cease stimulation. While premature ejaculation diminishes male sexual pleasure in heterosexual sex, it often has a devastating effect on female sexual pleasure, since women's level of arousal usually lags somewhat behind that of their male partner. The sexual frustration caused by premature ejaculation can be an important factor in relationship breakup. [24]

For some couples premature ejaculation negatively affects their feelings and attitudes about sex and each other without their ever recognizing the presence of premature ejaculation—the existing pattern is accepted as normal. In such a situation, the couple is unlikely to seek relief, and some couples continue patterns of premature ejaculation and resulting anorgasmia for 20, 30, and 40 years.

The Semans stop/start method of treating premature ejaculation is simple: the partner manually stimulates the penis until the premature ejaculator feels close to ejaculation, when all stimulation ceases. Excitement is allowed to subside, and then stimulation begins again. The cycle is repeated a number of times. Over time the man learns better ejaculatory control. [25] Improvement is usually clear within days to weeks of practice.

In both impotence and premature ejaculation it is usually clear that partners of the afflicted, whether they are male or female, have some self-interest in curing these male dysfunctions, since their own pleasure depends in part upon penile erection. Partners also have an interest in ending lack of vaginal lubrication and anorgasmia, though these female dysfunctions do not so readily disrupt partners' purely physical enjoyment of sex. While it is possible to achieve sexual satisfaction with a partner who is not finding pleasure in sex, it is almost always a more satisfying experience with a partner who is equally enjoying him/herself. The partner who is enjoying him/herself will be both more responsive and more actively stimulating to the partner. Since most partners take great pride in, and satisfaction from, contributing to the other's pleasure, this pleasure of the other rebounds to one's own pleasure as well.

Fear of Pregnancy

If sex is to be mutually pleasurable, then as a society we need to address the fears that stalk contemporary sexual activity. Fear of pregnancy is an old fear which still haunts sex, especially among the young. A variety of effective contraceptives need to be made available to all men and women, along with counseling as to the most appropriate form in particular circumstances. At the present time race and class factors may seriously affect the provision of contraceptive services, especially to the young. Poor and minority women are much more likely to receive prescriptions for long-term chemical contraceptives such as an IUD or the Norplant patch, about which there are more safety concerns and questions, while white middle-class women are more likely to be considered "mature" and "responsible" enough to use the more temporary and safer barrier methods such as diaphragm or cervical cap. At the same time, the very women who are prescribed the riskier methods are the very women least likely to have ongoing relationships with a personal physician, and most likely to receive medical care on an emergency basis at local hospitals or clinics.

[handwritten margin note: need to make a much better case this claim is to be supported]

Abortion should also be accessible. The Catholic bishops have been ineffective in persuading the majority of Catholics that abortion is illegitimate killing of innocent life which should be banned by law.[26] Though many Americans deplore the fact that there are so many abortions, the majority do not want the legal option foreclosed. At the same time, the provision of contraceptive and childcare support should not be interpreted as unreserved social support for sexually active adolescents.

Sexually Transmitted Diseases

Fear of sexually transmitted diseases is not new, either, but has accelerated tremendously since the beginning of the AIDS epidemic in the early 1980s.[27] Although AIDS is in a class by itself both because it kills, and because it kills all those infected with it, it is by no means the only STD (sexually transmitted disease) which is epidemic. In the U.S., 3 – 5 million people are infected with chlamydia trachomatis each year; affected women risk pelvic inflammatory disease, sterility, ectopic pregnancy, as well as blind newborns. Gonorrhea is contracted by almost a million Americans every year, with many of the same risks as chlamydia, but with additional risks of permanent joint damage and damage to the heart, liver, spinal cord, and brain. In 1988 over 40,000 cases of syphilis were reported in the U.S. Experts believe as many as nine times this many exist. Syphilis is deadly if untreated, leading to heart failure, blindness, ruptured blood vessels, paralysis, and severe mental disturbance.

Herpes affects over 120 million Americans; over 100 million have HSV-1 (called oral herpes, though 20 – 50% of herpes infections of the genitals are with HSV-1, and not with HSV-2, called genital herpes) and 20 – 30 million have HSV-2. Though there are treatments for herpes, there is no cure, and the infection can recur any number of times after the primary infection. Ten to forty percent of those with HSV-1 experience recurrence, as do 30 – 70% of those with HSV-2.

Between 1 and 1.5 million Americans are infected with AIDS. According to present research, they will exhibit the disease after 8 – 11 years of incubation, and most will die within less than 2 years after the onset of the disease. Only 12% have lived beyond 3 years.

If fear of STDs is not to destroy or impede the pleasure of sex, then both individual and social efforts are necessary. The health and safety of society depends upon persons infected with STDs both getting whatever treatment is available and abstaining from sexual activity while infected. It requires that all of us learn both to be comfortable with, and techniques for, disclosing our sexual histories to partners so that they can evaluate the risks they run and the safety measures needed. Our own health and safety will require that we not merely worry about our safety during or after a sexual encounter, but that we evaluate risk and, whenever necessary, protect ourselves—with condoms or a "no, thank you"—*before* sexual encounters take place. To say that sex should be mutually pleasurable should mean not only that an act of intercourse was pleasurable, but that the entire encounter was pleasurable. No one who contracts herpes, much less AIDS, in a sexual encounter will thereafter remember that encounter with pleasure.

Such precautions are not merely necessary for those who engage in casual sex. They are increasingly necessary for everyone. Many more young people are waiting longer to marry than in the past. One of the implications of this delay is that more young people have had other sexual partners before marriage, even if they have restricted sex to exclusive committed relationships. But if I have had two sexual partners, and each of them had two partners before me, and each of those four persons had had two partners, and so on, there are many potential avenues for an STD to reach me, and for me to then pass it to a new spouse. Since some of the new AIDS research indicates that the routinely specified three-month wait to detect AIDS antibodies may be seriously inadequate,[28] preventing STDs or fear of STDs from undermining sexual pleasure may become increasingly difficult.

Making sex more pleasurable by reducing risk and fear of STDs requires that all persons with any previous sexual experience, or whose prospective sexual partner has any previous sexual experience, engage in planning and preparation for sexual activity by:

1) becoming informed as to the symptoms of various STDs;

2) engaging in reciprocal exchange with any potential sexual partner about: how long since last sexual contact; any symptoms of any STD; any high-risk partners;

3) watching carefully for the presence of any symptoms of STDs for at least three months after last sexual contact;

4) getting tested for STDs if any STD symptoms are present, or if previous partners disclosed STD infection, or if previous partners belonged in any high-risk group for STDs. If you have been asymptomatic with an STD in the past, it is advisable to be tested if you have had a new sexual partner since your last test;

5) considering abstaining from sex until all the above precautions are completed;

6) using condoms for at least three months after the date of either partner's last sexual contact with another person.

These precautions are *minimal.* Many very serious STDs are asymptomatic in up to 40% of the infected population. Neither you nor the partner who infected you may have any clue that you have a serious disease, but the damage from the disease can be just as serious as if all the symptoms were present. This is true of both chlamydia and herpes, for example.

In addition, though the length of the *average* incubation period for both genital warts (which are increasingly linked to cancer) and AIDS is three months, it is important to note that genital warts have been known to break out as late as 18 months after contact, and that AIDS antibodies have been shown to develop as long as 36 months after contact. In the case of AIDS, at the point the antibodies become present and can be detected by the ELISA test, the individual may still be *8 – 15 years* from developing the *symptoms* of the AIDS disease.

Furthermore, condoms are not adequate heterosexual protection against many STDs, especially for female-to-male spread, since female vaginal lubricants will wash over the male scrotal area whether or not the male wears a condom. Also, the genital sores of herpes, or genital warts, may be present on the male, but elsewhere than on the penis covered by the condom, or present in the female, but elsewhere than the vagina which the condom blocks the male from contacting. The inadequacy of the condom is also true for the new female condom. The benefit of the female condom is not that it provides any more protection from either pregnancy or STDs—in fact, it is believed to be slightly less effective—but that it can be used by women who are not successful in persuading male partners to use male condoms.

Sex Education as an Avenue for Change

If sex is to be as fully pleasurable as possible, both individual behavior and social policy must change in many ways. This section has attempted to survey some of the more obvious specific changes required for maximizing mutual sexual pleasure. Virtually all of the changes mentioned above depend upon a greatly improved system of sexual education in this society. In the U.S., public policy around sex education actually supports sexual ignorance in a number of areas.

There are three aspects of contemporary sexual education which promote sexual ignorance and which therefore need to be addressed. One is the assumption that the goal of sex education is sexual abstinence among adolescents. Another is the assumption that sex education is primarily cognitive, designed to promote rational, informed decision-making.[29] These two are, of course, related, in that the assumption of most educators is that rational, informed decision-making will lead to sexual abstinence among the young. The third assumption is that sexuality is essentially private.

It is a serious mistake—and severely short-sighted—to aim sex education at discouraging sexual activity among the young.

Yet there is no question that this is, in fact, the aim of existing programs. Marianne H. Whatley writes:

> The curriculum *Values and Choices* (Search Institute, 1986) recently came under attack in one Wisconsin community as being too liberal and permissive. As some progressive parents rushed in to defend it, they discovered that it was in fact a fairly conservative curriculum. Bonnie Trudell and I evaluated both *Values and Choices* and the favored curriculum of the New Right, *Sex Respect* (Mast, 1986), in terms of sex equity issues (Trudell and Whatley, in press). Even though these two are frequently set up in opposition to each other and are characterized as having huge differences, they actually share many messages and themes. The broad message in both is that abstinence, especially for young women, is the only choice, and this message is delivered by emphasizing the negative consequences for teenagers of having intercourse. The attacks on *Values and Choices* have been largely precipitated by the inclusion of a small amount of contraceptive information and an optional video sequence on homosexuality.[30]

Marianne Whatley asked what I think is the correct question when she titled her article "Whose Sexuality Is It, Anyway?" The primary goal of sex education should be providing the student with the tools and skills—cognitive and emotional, communicative and meditative, technical and moral—to construct a responsible, satisfying sexual life for her/himself both in the present and into the future.

Students need much more information than they are provided in usual sex education curriculums. But they not only need technical information about the development of sexuality in childhood and adolescence; they also need adults who will share with them experiences of value and meaning in sexuality. This is what children want from their parents in sex education: parents who are comfortable in talking to their children explicitly about sexuality in terms of their own lives. My own experience is that my children have always understood that a major aspect of their own security is the warmth and openness of the sexual relationship between my husband and myself. One constant complaint of college students in the classroom is of parents who never speak of sexuality and never give any indications to their children that they have a sexual relationship. Older students sometimes tell of parents who waited until the child is engaged or married before acknowledging the sexual component in the parental relationship. Children, even relatively adult children, need more than information about sex. They need to know about value in sex. How closely is sex—or gender—tied to identity? What is the role of pleasure? How are love and sexual pleasure related? How is reproduction connected to a sexual love relationship? How do children affect a couple's love?

Parental answers are not enough, of course; children and adolescents need to hear a variety of persons answer these kinds of questions before they are forced to choose between the answers. But they need parents—and teachers, and grandparents, and aunts and uncles, brothers and sisters, and friends—who can speak of such things. And few can. Few parents have the vocabulary for speaking to children of sex and love. Few have adequate correct information. And virtually none are comfortable with sexual discourse.

If as Christians we believe that we are all called to love our neighbors, then we should care that when we form couples around the intense love involved in sexual partnerships we are able to love each other well. A major purpose of sex education should be to make us better able to be good lovers of our partners. Another important purpose of sex education should be to prepare us to be good sex educators of our children. Both of these are seriously impeded by an emphasis on encouraging abstinence by focusing on the negative consequences of sex. Sex is not divine, it is not the most important aspect in human life, and it certainly does not solve all our problems. But until we construct sex education programs in which we acknowledge to our children that sex is pleasurable, that the pleasure in sex can be a powerful positive force by supporting love and relationship and community, they will continue to disregard sex education programs. As James Sears quotes James Whitson: "At the micro level, this results in 'reinforcing the notion popular among so many students that they cannot expect to learn anything real in school, since what they are presented in the classroom has no relationship to life in the real world'; at the macro level these school-based 'desexualized notions of human understanding and existence' contribute to an impotent body politic."[31]

The third problematic aspect in contemporary sex education programs is the assumption that sexuality is private. There is no real basis for such an understanding. Sexuality is clearly socially constructed. If it were not socially constructed it would not vary so tremendously from society to society, or from subgroup to subgroup. "Sexuality, then, is more a construct of ideology and culture than it is a collection of information about biology and the body; power and control are central to our modern understanding of sexuality and ourselves as sexual beings," writes Sears. When we ignore the social construction of sexuality and insist that sexuality refers to the private bodies of individual persons, we close off critical attention to existing sexual power structures and relationships. Gender roles, for instance, are not considered an appropriate topic for sex education courses. Klein writes:

> There is substantial evidence that sex equity and sex education experts have gone their separate ways and generally either ignored or distanced themselves from each other. Most sex educators in the U.S. have not explicitly taught sex-equitable sexual attitudes, knowledge, and behavior. Thus, they often reinforced the "double standard" or inaccurate stereotypes about males and females.[32]

But the failure to deal with issues of power and ideology concern not just gender equity, but also a host of other very real and important issues. Sexual violence, for instance, should be an important focus of sex education. Domestic battery, rape, child sexual abuse, and sexual harassment are both extremely common and terribly destructive activities in our society.

Homophobia is implicitly taught in our society when sex education programs fail to deal with sexual orientation and the little we know of its formation. Our society is heterosexist, and supports that bias by refusing to give young homosexual persons any information about themselves or others like them. It therefore reinforces for them their "abnormality."

Finally, another consequence of the failure to teach sexuality as socially constructed is that both men and women come to understand women as naturally victims. In her essay "Sexuality, Schooling, and Adolescent Females: The Missing Discourse of Desire," Michelle Fine writes of sex education programs:

> To avoid being victimized, females learn to defend themselves against disease, pregnancy, and "being used." The discourse of victimization supports sex education, including AIDS education, with parental consent. Suggested classroom activities emphasize "saying NO," practicing abstinence, enumerating the social and emotional risks of sexual intimacy, and listing the possible diseases associated with sexual intimacy. The language, as well as the questions asked and not asked, represents females as the actual and potential victims of male desire. . . .The naming of desire, pleasure, or sexual entitlement, particularly for females, barely exists in the formal agenda of public schooling on sexuality. When spoken, it is tagged with reminders of "consequences"—emotional, physical, moral, reproductive, and/or financial.[33]

The understanding of women as "naturally" victims not only has negative effects on women's later sexual enjoyment, but it necessarily affects women's ability to trust men, as well as encouraging men to see the use and abuse of women as "natural."

In this arena, sex education should aim at exposing victimization as abuse and sketching therapeutic measures for those who have been abused.

In conclusion, it is necessary to revamp virtually all the sexuality education programs in our society in order that they focus on providing to students in a holistic manner the skills and information necessary for them to be able to responsibly pursue sexual satisfaction as both adolescents and adults.

6. *Getting Clear About Bodyself and Bodyright*

Many writers in the Western world over the last quarter-century have emphasized the need to end body/mind dualism. But most of us still have difficulty understanding that the body *is* the self, that the mind is a part of that body, and that emotions, too, emerge from the bodyself. We resist adopting views of ourselves which incorporate the historically demonized body and its sexuality. Over 20 years ago, Harvey Cox characterized sex in *The Secular City* in terms that are still well recognized today:

> No aspect of human life seethes with so many unexorcised demons as does sex. No human activity is so hexed by superstition, so haunted by residual tribal lore, and so harassed by socially induced fear. Nowhere are the mythical denizens more obvious and nowhere the humanization of life more frustrated.[1]

For many U.S. women, the first, and for some the only, influence in their lives which has encouraged them to understand their bodies as themselves was the Boston Women's Health Book Collective's *Our Bodies, Ourselves*.[2] Its clear, informative, easy-to-read format and lists of resources helped women understand their female bodies and regain control of their bodies from both their sexual partners and the medical profession. For women and men interested in religion, Jim Nelson's books—beginning with *Embodiment: An Approach to Sexuality and Christian Theology* and including *Between Two Gardens: Reflections on Sexuality and Religious Experience; The Intimate Connection: Male Sexuality, Masculine Spirituality;* and *Body Theology*[3]—have all woven increasingly tight connections between body, emotion, relationship, and religious experience. The work of Beverly Wildung Harrison (*Making the Connections,* as well as dozens of other seminal articles and speeches) has insisted both on treating family, sexuality, and relationship within specific sociohistorical contexts and on the need to analyze the specific forms of these relationships with regard for justice.[4] Carter Heyward (*Touching Our Strength: The Erotic as Power and the Love of God*)[5] has further connected body, pleasure, and relationship with both justice and religious experience.

Other writers outside religious ethics, such as Linda Gordon and Betsy Hartman, have connected embodiment to moral responsibility. They describe the sociopolitical limitations on women's sexual and reproductive rights as not only restricting, endangering, and often damaging the concrete welfare of women, but also as seriously and illegitimately restricting the scope of their moral agency.[6]

This chapter will examine research findings on physical violence in sexual contexts and the process of recovering from it, and the role of Christian teaching in recovery from such violence. The thesis of the chapter is that social recognition of bodyright is a prerequisite for full personhood and moral agency in humans. Human persons have a moral right to control their own bodies because the inability to exercise that control, as demonstrated in victims of violence, especially sexual violence, seriously hampers their ability to become responsible moral agents.

Social Recognition of Bodyright

In some ways, the notion that all persons have a right to control their own bodies is taken for granted in our society. Modern philosophers such as Immanuel Kant and John Stuart Mill, working from very different understandings of the human person, society, and moral life, agreed on the centrality of personal autonomy.[7] There is no question that some version of autonomy remains important in many practical areas of contemporary ethics, though much of contemporary theology and philosophy begins with a critique of autonomy as having been overstressed in the modern period to the point that human sociality has been ignored and neglected. Torture is understood as criminal as well as immoral, regardless of the purpose of the torture or the identity of the torturer. Health care professionals are regularly required to obtain permission from patients before treating or experimenting on those patients' bodies or even on parts of those bodies after their removal.[8] Deliberate and unauthorized touching of the bodies of others constitutes a legal injury, whether that touch is the sexual touch of a boss on a secretary's rear end,[9] the assault of a mugger, or physical restraint of bystanders by protestors.

Not only does the law in our society protect citizens from other individuals who claim or seize control of our bodies, but the courts have recognized that society should not force us to use or care for our bodies in ways that either risk *or* save our lives or health.[10] For example, law cannot compel citizens to go into burning buildings to rescue persons trapped there, or to join rescue teams in mountain storms, or to donate blood, bone marrow, or organs. To do any of these things is virtuous, but supererogatory—they are goods that cannot be commanded. Even prisoners convicted of serious crimes cannot be involuntarily enrolled in medical experimentation on their bodies aimed at benefiting the common good.[11] In the same way, adults cannot be compelled to accept medical treatment, even when its refusal will cause their death. Some religious groups regularly refuse blood transfusions and surgery at the risk of death; the courts have generally allowed their refusals to stand, intervening only in the case of minor or incompetent patients.[12]

Regardless of these examples, I would argue that one of the most serious negative consequences of the heritage of mind/body dualism in the Christian West is the failure to recognize bodyright. The absence of bodyright in our culture is directly attributable to patriarchy. The absence of bodyright is clearest and most acute in the cases of children, of women, and of men who are in the military, especially when these are also racial/ethnic groups from lower economic classes. This fact supports the understanding of patriarchy as responsible for the absence of bodyright, for in full-blown patriarchies, the lives of women, children, slaves/servants, and warriors are owned by the patriarchs, whose interests they serve.

Even today persons in the military do not enjoy all of the rights guaranteed to citizens, beginning with the basic right of controlling their bodies. Military drafts periodically force an embodied person upon pain of incarceration or death to leave his ordinary life for the military, often to risk bodily injury or even life itself. The military does not legally require permission from soldiers in order to medically immunize, test, or treat their bodies. Soldiers can be ordered from one location to another, or reassigned from one job to another, some of them dangerous, without their consent. There is no recourse against such commands, and soldiers are punished for attempting to leave military service without authorization from military superiors. Within war, there are always situations where groups of soldiers are ordered to undertake action in which it is known from the beginning that their lives will be sacrificed, in order to allow others to succeed.[13] All aspects of one's body life are regulated in the military, from the clothing one is obliged to wear, to the salutes and responses one is obliged to make to superior officers, all upon threat of dire physical coercion. Bodyright is one of the many rights that are forfeited upon entry into the military.

In the lives of women in our society, there remains a great deal of patriarchal appropriation of women's bodyright. This has been especially true in terms of marriage, sexuality, reproduction, and medicine. Within marriage, Western Christian culture has understood women as called to submission to their husbands. St. Paul in I Cor. 7:3 – 4 wrote:

> The husband should give to his wife her conjugal rights, and likewise the wife to her husband. For the wife does not rule over her own body, but the husband does; likewise the husband does not rule over his own body, but the wife does.

Yet equal sexual rights over the spouse's bodyself were never effectively enforced. In practice, only husbands had ownership of wives' bodyselves because the context of the spousal relationship was general acceptance of the Roman household code so frequently but inconsistently quoted in the New Testament:

> Wives, be submissive to your husbands as to the Lord. For the husband is the head of the wife as Christ is the head of the church, his body, and is himself its Savior. As the church is subject to Christ, so let wives also be subject in everything to their husbands. Husbands, love your wives as Christ loved the church and gave himself up for her, that he might sanctify her, having cleansed her by the washing of water with the word, that he might present the church to himself in splendor, without spot or wrinkle or any such thing, that she might be holy and without blemish. Even so husbands should love their wives as their own bodies. He who loves his wife loves himself. (Eph 5:21 – 28)

This equation of loving of self with loving of one's wife seems scant protection for wives when we remember that loving oneself within the framework of body/soul dualism was understood as compatible with mutilation of one's body:

> And if your hand or your foot causes you to sin, cut it off and throw it away; it is better for you to enter life maimed than with two hands or two feet to be thrown into the eternal fire. And if your eye causes you to sin, pluck it out and throw it away; it is better for you to enter life with one eye than with two eyes to be cast into the hell of fire. (Mt. 18:8 – 9)

This particular understanding of self-love informed much of the tradition, from the practices of the early ascetics, through the procedures of the Inquisition and the conquest of the Americas. Love was not understood to forbid one from inflicting pain and suffering on the love object, but, in fact, love, whether of self or other, frequently *demanded* inflicting pain in order to produce virtue in the other. Inflicting body pain was legitimated because the body was *not* the self, but only the dangerous shell that the real self, the spiritual soul, inhabited.

Within the household code's understanding of the spousal relationship men were to use their headship to make women "holy and without blemish," which usually meant to make them better able to serve their masters as the Lord, as Ephesians 5:22

demanded. Appropriate subjection on the part of wives was *not* compatible with the exercise of the wife's conjugal rights referred to in I Cor. 7. But male headship over wives *was* compatible with the exercise of *husbands'* conjugal rights. In fact, male responsibility for overseeing proper submission in wives was understood to require punishing lack of meekness in wives. To this end, from the ancient world up to the present time, virtually all Western cultures have approved some physical chastisement of wives by husbands, with restriction limited only to the severity of the chastisement. For example, husbands were seldom allowed to kill their wives with chastisement,[14] and sometimes, as in much of the U.S. in colonial times through at least the late nineteenth century, husbands were restricted by law from beating their wives with a rod thicker than a man's thumb.

It is this heritage which so undermines the enforcement of legal statutes against conjugal battery today. Much of our population is still influenced, at least to some extent, by the understanding that it is the responsibility of men to discipline wives, that such discipline sometimes takes physical forms, that such discipline demonstrates a husband's ongoing care for his spouse, and that such discipline is private, within the sphere in which the husband is head. This attitude is basic for understanding why so many neighbors, relatives, friends, and police hesitate to intervene in family violence, citing "A man's home is his castle," in spite of concerns for the welfare of wives (and of children, too, who have been subject, like wives, to this same justification of battering as loving discipline).

Within patriarchies, women were/are given or sold between fathers and husbands. The purpose of women in patriarchies is both sexual and reproductive—as sexual object for the male, and as reproductive source of his heirs. To this end, women have not historically been allowed to control completely either their sexual or their reproductive functions. In our society until very recently, there was no legal recognition of marital rape, since sexual consent was permanently conferred with a woman's consent to marriage. The legalization of contraception and abortion in the twentieth century in our society conferred on women a degree of reproductive control over their bodies which until then husbands and the nation had held. Ongoing political attempts to prohibit legal abortions in the U.S. reflect this instrumental view of women paired with a sentimental absolutization of fetal life. In effect, women's reproductive bodyright is not only shared with social institutions which by law limit the exercise of that right, but that limited, legally recognized degree of bodyright is not secure.

The 1991 *Rust v. Sullivan* decision by the Supreme Court was perhaps the most egregious example of this instrumental view of women. That decision upheld a regulation forbidding institutions receiving federal funding from mentioning abortion to clients, thus eliminating the ability of medical personnel in those institutions to meet their professional obligation to treat women patients only after providing to them the full information upon which informed consent to treatment depends. Governmental restrictions on women's access to abortion in the U.S. since the 1973 *Roe v. Wade* decision steadily increased up to 1993. Existing restrictions at the time of the January 1993 Clinton inaugural included: 1) exclusion of abortion from the list of medical reproductive services paid for by the government for government employees, the military, and those on public assistance,[15] 2) allowing private insurers to exclude abortion from the list of medical reproductive procedures covered by group and private policies, 3) claiming that governmental interest in fetal life in the third trimester normally overrides the woman's right to abortion, 4) failing to ensure that all regions of the country provide abortion services as a part of the medical services provided to the population, 5) prohibiting federally funded clinics from discussing abortion with patients,[16] and 6) requiring waiting periods, parental notification, mandatory information programs, or other restrictions.[17]

The government limits women's right to contraception through the Federal Drug Administration's processes for controlling the sale of new drugs or health technologies. For example, the Reagan and Bush administrations prevented the FDA from considering the French drug RU-486, which acts as a contraceptive/abortifacient by preventing/terminating the implantation of the fertilized ovum. The government also limits women's access to contraception by maintaining a public climate of sexual ignorance. The failure to provide comprehensive sexual education in all schools of the nation, and the continued timidity of states and the federal government in the face of agitation by the religious right's opposition to sex education, together create a climate ripe for a variety of reproductive abuses by the medical profession.

The medical profession limits women's reproductive bodyright in a number of ways. The abuse of coercive sterilization of minority populations in this nation is well documented. Over a third of the Native American women of reproductive age who live on reservations have been sterilized, many of them without informed consent, some of them without their knowledge.[18] Public hospitals in urban centers have long practiced semi-routine sterilizations on African American, Chicana, and Puerto Rican welfare patients after delivery. Sometimes hysterectomies are used as sterilization procedures on poor minority women for purposes of providing surgical practice to interns and residents, even though the risk of death from hysterectomy is 10 – 100 times higher than from tubal ligation, the normal sterilization procedure in females.[19] Though there have been federal guidelines since 1979 designed to end such sterilization abuse, the guidelines are frequently ignored because there is no process for routine monitoring or enforcement. "Mississippi Appendectomies," in which the fallopian tubes are tied or the uterus removed without the patient's knowledge, are still practiced, and not only in the South.[20]

But sterilization is not the only area of contraception in which there is medical abuse. There is a strong tendency in both the medical establishment and the organizations which monitor and maintain the state and federal welfare establishment to treat minority women as incompetents incapable of controlling their own reproduction. For this reason, there is strong preference for the use of relatively permanent methods of contraception which do not require user initiative.[21] At the present time the five-year Norplant patch seems to be the path of choice within the medical and welfare establishments. Not only is Norplant one of the chemical methods of contraception against which there is more criticism because they are less safe over the long term than barrier methods, but it is even newer and less tested than other chemical means of contraception. Yet in many areas it is not only the most common prescription for welfare patients during the last year, but is often doctors' choice for minority women who are private, not welfare, patients.

After reading of this phenomenon last year, I asked two sections of my class in sexual ethics at a private religious university in the Midwest to respond to a confidential survey about contraceptive use. Of the 43 women in the two sections of the class, 28 reported that they had used some form of contraceptive at least once in the previous year. Of those 28, six women had had Norplant prescribed and implanted. All six of those women were African American; they constituted over two-thirds of the eight African Americans. Three of the six on Norplant were married with one or two children; one of the three single African American women on Norplant had never been sexually active, was not on welfare, and had seen her (white) doctor only for help in regulating heavy and irregular menstrual bleeding. A five-year dose of Norplant to regulate the menses in a 20-year-old? Few of the white women had ever heard of Norplant; among the white women using contraceptives, the majority used the pill, with a few using either condoms, condoms and sponge, or a diaphragm. The failure to educate the general population about sexuality, conception, and contraception allows such racist manipulation to continue unchecked in the medical/public assistance establishments.

But medical practitioners seem to understand minority women as only exaggerated versions of normally incompetent women. That is, they urge most women seeking birth control in this country to go on the pill, despite its known risks. Yet research shows that the majority of medical practitioners choose barrier methods for themselves and their spouses.[22]

The medical profession is guilty of more than ignoring bodyright in women in reproductive areas of care. The way contemporary private medical care is organized, medical education of the population is left to busy doctors contending with one to three patients every 15 minutes. Education loses out to treatment, and the patient is more or less dismissed with a probable cure, but with little personal understanding of his/her health problem or of the therapeutic process prescribed, and is sometimes sent off without warnings about possible physical reactions to the treatment itself.

While inadequate care is the rule for the entire patient population, it is even more true of *women* as patients. Women see doctors more frequently, and are consequently diagnosed with serious diseases and conditions at much earlier stages than are comparable male populations. Yet Robert J. McMurray's 1990 Report to the AMA, which reviewed studies on gender disparities in clinical decision-making,[23] reported that while women undergo more medical procedures than men for the same symptoms and conditions, they have less access to some of the major diagnostic and therapeutic interventions considered medically appropriate for their conditions. Compared to men with similar diagnoses, women were 30% less likely than men to receive kidney transplants, 50% as likely to be referred for diagnostic testing for lung cancer, and 10% as likely to receive cardiac catheterization. Also, the survey showed medical research to have largely ignored the study of diseases and medicines in women.[24]

Childhood is another area of human life in which bodyright is often slighted. It is clear that very young children cannot exercise the same degree of bodyright as adults. Children cannot be left to decide what they will eat and wear, where they will go, and what they will do from the moment of birth, for they are not capable of either making these decisions or of carrying them out by themselves. But one must ask what rights children are understood to have over their own bodies in our society. It is difficult to name them. Neither churches nor governments who present themselves as advocates for children take up bodyright beyond demanding basic food, shelter, education, and medical care.[25] Children are not understood to have any legitimate voice in the form that the food, shelter, education, or medical care take. Though most Americans are of the opinion that the "best interests of the child" govern decisions in court cases regarding child custody, the recent case of Jessica DeBoers forcibly pointed public

attention to the many cases in which the property rights of biological parents are decisive. There could be little other explanation for removing a two-and-a-half-year-old child from the adop-
tive parents who have cared for her since birth. No child welfare
sources, psychologists, or social workers would argue that this
move is in Jessica's best interests. Furthermore, it is difficult to
make a case for justice as requiring her return to biological parents when the biological mother had surrendered her own rights,
failed to inform the child's father of the pregnancy, and named as
father an unrelated man who also signed surrender papers.[26]

Children in general are understood to be controlled by parents in all aspects of bodily life. Parents can be and are defended
as acting appropriately in regulating what, when, and how children eat and dress, who they touch and don't touch, how children touch themselves, where they go to school, who they play
with, what city and neighborhood they are moved to, and what
activities they should be employed in at all times. In addition,
parents are given the right to physically chastise children so long
as that chastisement does not risk serious injury. Our society generally grants to children only the right not to be abused, but does
not allow the child a voice in deciding what constitutes abuse.

In Defense of Bodyright

It is ironic that Western societies have for centuries developed understandings of political and economic rights which both
found and limit modern social institutions, and yet the most foundational human right of all, that to bodyright, remains a relatively
late one to be developed, at least for the majority of the population. There are a variety of ways to ground arguments for
bodyright. Here, I will principally look to research on sexual victimization and particularly to the process of recovery from sexual
victimization.

Much of the theological/ethical advice that has been traditional for victims of sexual violence has revolved around forgiveness, reconciliation, and trust. For the most part, pastoral counsel-

ors, mostly clerical, encouraged women, children, and male victims to heal through an act of will. That is, the pastoral advice was to forgive and be reconciled with the perpetrator, and, through reconciliation, the victim would regain trust both in the specific perpetrator and in all the other possible perpetrators whom the victim fears. This has especially been the case when sexual violence has occurred within a family. Battered wives and children sexually or physically abused by parents have been urged to love, and to forgive their grievance against, the family member who abused them, especially when the alternative was to risk breaking up the family, as in jailing the abusive parent/spouse, or putting the victimized child in foster care. Battered wives are sometimes still encouraged, "Wives, be submissive to your husbands as to the Lord,"[27] and abused children still hear pastoral advice to "honor thy father and mother."[28]

Increasingly a consensus has formed among psychologists, social workers, counselors, and concerned pastoral workers who deal with victims of sexual violence. They have come to recognize that sexual violence is not only an assault against an individual's pride and a source of fear for one's future safety. Sexual violence can also seriously alter both an individual's sense of the surrounding world and its degree of safety or danger and can even more deeply damage its victims by seriously altering the victim's understanding of who she[29] is, of what her purpose and goals are, and of what she and others can expect of her. This should not be surprising if all instances of sexual violence have at their core a violation of bodyright.

Acts of sexual violence, whether we speak of a casual pat on the fanny from a boss to a secretary or a brutal rape, make a clear statement to the victim that "You are not in control of your body; I am." The more times the act is repeated, the more this claim is reinforced. The more the victim's resistance is overcome, either by physical coercion or threat, the more likely the victim is to accept the claim. Women who have been in situations of conjugal battery for decades learn not to contest their spouses' claim to own and control their bodyselves, and even come to accept their spouses' wishes and preferences because to do otherwise is to invite violence against themselves and sometimes against their children as well. Not only have such women been denied bodyright, but in that denial they have also been deprived of their right to the pleasures, aspirations, and preferences that make their lives their own. Women and children who suffer long-term violence are deprived of control of their bodies and lives and of the pleasure to be derived from securing one's wants and needs. They frequently come to lose any awareness of what their own needs and wants are. Their very feelings and emotions have been stolen from them by their abuser, who has forced them to respond to his wants and needs in place of their own. Over time they lose touch with their own emotions, with the very core of themselves. For this reason, many victims of physical/sexual abuse, upon being finally released from the situation of abuse, are unable to respond appropriately. Often feelings of relief that they can safely shed the false self the abuser forced them to adopt are tempered by feelings of emptiness and loss rooted in their inability to reclaim an authentic self.

Children who are sexually abused have the already restrictive social limits on children's bodyright even more strongly reinforced by their abuse. Abuse seems to rob children, and even the adults they become, of significant capacity for responsible moral agency if that abuse continues over long periods of time, or if the abuser was in a relationship of great intimacy and trust with the victim, or if the abuse involved clear coercion such as physical force or threats.[30] Sheila A. Redmond writes:

> Even if there appears to be little immediate negative impact, depression often results. Child sexual abuse is now being discovered as one of the initial traumatic causes behind such illnesses as multiple personality disorder and eating disorders such as bulimia and anorexia. It is included in the history of prostitutes and of the abusers themselves. These problems can surface immediately or, if the act is blocked from memory, the impact of the abuse may not be recognizable until the teen years or even later. Victims of child sexual abuse often show the same lack of self-esteem and inability to be involved in trusting relationships as do the children of alcoholics and children from backgrounds of physical violence. [31]

Psychologists Ronnie Janoff-Bulman and Irene Frieze state that sexual victimization in general exacts a severe psychological toll on victims by shattering common, basic assumptions about self and world, including: 1) the belief in personal invulnerability, 2) the perception of the world as meaningful and comprehensible, and 3) the view of self in a positive light.[32] This loss allows victims to easily foresee themselves as victims in the future, creating an anxiety which can be paralyzing. Janoff-Bulman and Frieze argue further that because victims learn to see themselves as "weak, helpless, needy, frightened, and out-of-control,"[33] their vulnerability is intensified.

Finkelhor and Browne studied one form of sexual victimization, child sexual abuse, and arrived at similar findings. They analyzed child sexual abuse in terms of four trauma-causing factors: traumatic sexualization, betrayal, powerlessness, and stigmatization.[34] They suggest that these "alter children's cognitive and emotional orientation to the world and create trauma by distorting children's self-concept, world view, and affective capabilities." Traumatic sexualization can produce compulsive sex play, frequent masturbation, sexual knowledge and interest inappropriate to age, promiscuity, inclination to prostitution, understanding of sex as a commodity, or sexual aversion. Betrayal often produces inability to evaluate the trustworthiness of others, and results from sexual abuse by intimates (the more intimate, the greater the betrayal)[35] *or* from the refusal of intimates to believe or act on, and sometimes from their punitive responses to, the child's report of abuse.

Feelings of general powerlessness result from the repeated invasion of a child's body space against the child's will. When familial or official disbelief allows the abuse to continue, the child's powerlessness is further demonstrated. Powerlessness from repeated victimization can cause children to expect abuse. Running away from home is a common response to repeated sexual abuse; tragically it, too, renders girls and some boys vulnerable to repeated sexual victimization.

Feelings of stigmatization in the victim may begin with the abuser's blaming the victim for the abuse, either by referring to the abuse as punishment for previous bad behavior or by accusing her of inviting sexual abuse by sluttish, seductive, evil behavior. Feelings of stigmatization may also result from the victim's awareness of public attitudes toward sexual abuse, or from the victim's experience of public stigmatization and avoidance after her abuse became known. However, Finkelhor and Browne suggest that nondisclosure does not necessarily lessen stigmatization, since the secrecy can itself heighten the victim's sense of being different and set apart. This sense of being different and shamed sometimes encourages victims to later seek out stigmatized levels of society, such as drug or alcohol abusers, criminal activity, or prostitution.[36]

Diana E. H. Russell suggests that the types of trauma reported in studies such as her own or those of Finkelhor/Browne and Janoff-Bulman/Frieze explain why it is that victims of child sexual abuse, and especially of child incest, are (re)victimized later in life at much higher rates than those who were not child sexual victims. She suggests that child victims learn to see the world as a place in which victimization is common, and to see themselves as likely victims of inevitable and unpreventable abuse. Feeling this way, child victims do not learn or use ordinary methods of self-protection, and even become unable to evaluate different degrees of danger in persons and situations.[37]

Russell further suggests that research on offenders and potential offenders adds another dimension to understanding the revictimization of child sexual victims. She notes that not all adults sexually involved with children are pedophiles in the strict sense, and quotes from K. Howells on research findings that "normal males show sufficient penile response to children to allow that children might become 'surrogate' partners when an adult partner is not available."[38] Some adults are titillated and even sexually aroused by knowing of a child's sexual victimization. Such adult sexual interest in child victims may be further increased by those victims who react to abuse by adopting sexually precocious behavior, which then further undermines adult internal inhibitions against acting out desires. Some adults who may not know of a person's previous victimization may still choose to prey on previous victims because they are attracted by the behavior cues of vulnerability in victims, cues such as low self-image or strong but unsatisfied need for affection, approval, and attention. Victims of child sexual abuse often display social vulnerability as well as emotional vulnerability (few friends and lack of closeness to family), which make them attractive prey to would-be offenders. Incest victims appear to be particularly at risk of being revictimized by male therapists and psychiatrists, according to Russell.[39]

Research on battered women and children has indicated similar patterns of revictimization. The U.S. Bureau of Justice conducted a National Crime Survey from 1978 to 1982. The study initially located and then tracked 2.1 million women who had been victimized by husband or partner violence at least once. During the first six-month period of the study, 32% of those women were attacked *again* by that same husband or sexual partner. Fifty-seven percent of the original assaults followed in the study were themselves repeat incidents.[40]

Research has indicated that there is a cycle to domestic violence, whether that violence takes the form of verbal assault, physical attack, or both.[41] The cycle of violence has three phases, all of which emanate from the offender: 1) the tension-building phase, 2) the assault, and 3) the contrition phase.[42] As the cycle continues, the offender's contrition phase shortens, and his apologies and pleas for forgiveness become rarer.[43] As the cycle repeats, it often becomes more intense, with verbal or psychological violence escalating into physical violence, and physical violence escalating sometimes to the point of homicide.

The cycle of violence continues because it satisfies the desires of the offender who wants to feel in control of his spouse and/or children. When he doesn't feel in control of the spouse or children he "loses control" of himself, and uses violence to regain control. Having regained control of the spouse and/or children through violence, he attempts to regain her/their good will through his contrition. Even during the contrition phase, however, the offender almost always blames his loss of control, his violence, on the spouse or children. In order to avoid any behavior that might trigger such violence, wives and children typically accede to even the most restrictive wishes of the batterer, which leaves the victims feeling alone and under siege. Children who remain in such patterns do so most often from a lack of alternatives. Women who stay in such cycles of violence sometimes truly lack alternatives, but often remain because the offender's periods of contrition bind them to the relationship. They learn to look forward to this stage of contrition when they feel loved, when "he is nice."[44]

It is well known that women who are murdered by their sexual partners had often been battered for years before the final homicide. A woman is beaten in her home every 15 seconds in the U.S. Violence in the home is the single largest cause of injury to women in the U.S.;[45] it is also the single largest cause of injury to pregnant women. A major portion of the medical difficulties of newborns are suspected to result from domestic violence against pregnant women. Breasts and pregnant bellies are a favorite target of wife/partner beaters.[46] Arias and Beach report that some degree of physical abuse of a spouse occurs in one marriage out of three, and at a similar rate in nonmarital sexual relationships.[47] Nor is domestic violence exclusively the province of the lower economic classes. At least one in ten professional men beat their wives.[48]

Women who are beaten by their husbands or lovers are also at risk to be murdered by them. The FBI estimates that one-third of all women homicide victims between 1976 and 1987 were murdered by husbands or ex-husbands.[49] The National Woman Abuse Prevention Project Report on Understanding Domestic Violence (1990) claims that 52% of all women murdered are killed by husbands, ex-husbands, or lovers. Local counts differ greatly from place to place. A Norfolk, Virginia, women's shelter counted 69 dead battered-women clients within the first nine months of 1987.[50] During the first two months of 1987, seven women were murdered by abusive spouses in the metropolitan Denver area. By the end of the year, the number was 19.[51] American homicide statistics compiled by the Centers for Disease Control in Atlanta were analyzed by psychologist Angela Browne and sociologist Kirk Williams. They found an increase during the 1980s in the number of women being killed by abusive partners in 35 states; in 25 states, most of the murdered women were killed after they separated from or divorced their male partners.[52] Because the general purpose of domestic violence is male control of women, the most severe violence—homicide—seems to be prompted by occasions or situations in which women reject and begin to distance themselves from control by their partners, such as separation and divorce.

Healing from Bodyright Violations

Violence against women and children has many effects, and numerous examples have been mentioned in the above descriptions of this abuse, its incidence, and effects. There is a separate literature on the process of treating, and on the healing process in, victims of sexual violence. The process of healing in victims of sexual violence varies according to a number of factors. The starting point of the healing process, and the type of initial intervention recommended, will depend upon whether the rape, battery, harassment, or child sexual abuse was very recent, and whether there was an isolated incident or a long-term pattern of sexual victimization. Since the majority of sexual abuse is not reported, and occurs within existing relationships—families, sexual relationships, work relationships, or more general social relationships such as neighbors—a great deal of victimization is not interrupted by outside intervention, and continues over time. Such extended forms of sexual abuse as are found with marital rape, conjugal battery, child incest, and sexual harassment are often brought to an end by historical factors which may be independent of the victimization, such as family breakup, a move, work transfers, firings, layoffs, or resignations, or by various changes in the situation introduced by the increased age of a child victim. It is not surprising, then, that a great deal of the literature concerning healing from sexual violence focuses on adults whose sexual victimization occurred years ago, often when they were children or young adults.[53]

The earliest form of sexual violence to receive contemporary attention was rape. Descriptions of rape trauma syndrome and its healing process now have an extensive literature. Much of the early literature focused on stranger rape, largely because the most identifiable population of research subjects were victims who had reported rapes to the police and offenders who had been convicted of rapes. Because of that focus it was not originally clear that the vast majority of rapists are not the stranger rapists who are most likely to be reported, tried, and convicted. Nor was it clear that the pseudosexual motivation of stranger rapists may not hold nearly so true for date or marital rape, and that silent rape syndrome is a more common response to rape than reporting rape.

More recently a great deal of attention has been paid to both marital rape and date/acquaintance rape and to the ways in which both the motivation of offenders and the effect on victims can differ from those in stranger rape, and may require modifications in therapy. Also recently, a large literature about healing adult victims of child sexual abuse, especially incest, has arisen, with an ensuing controversy over the claimed incidence of, methods of detecting, and professional expertise in child sexual abuse. Nevertheless, there are some agreed-upon commonalities in the healing process in all these types of sexual violence.

Counselors, pastors, and therapists who deal with victims in the immediate aftermath of sexual violence are counseled that they are dealing with persons who either may be feeling great pain and anxiety, or may be numb and disoriented. Whether they have just survived a beating, a rape, child sexual abuse/incest, or sexual harassment, the first thing survivors require is safety. Fear, especially of losing one's life, is the most widely reported feeling following rape, and fear of being still at risk lingers in other forms of sexual assault as well.[54] Only from a position of safety can victims feel free to tell their story and receive the support that they require.

Victims must not only be safe—they must be made to *feel* safe. Their perceptions of safety should be supported, even if those perceptions require arrangements which may not seem necessary and may even seem irrational to others. For example, some victims feel unsafe in the presence of any male after a violent attack by either a strange male or a date or male relative. Victims attacked in their homes may not feel safe in their homes, even in the presence of police or friends and relatives, both immediately after the attack and later. The first step in recovery is to make the victim feel safe. That may mean removing the victim to another location temporarily, or even in assisting her to move to another home or work location if serious fear persists. It is not helpful to tell victims that such fears are irrational and should be overcome when those fears are limited and more or less easily avoided by activity such as moving. The energy required to overcome such fears may be better expended on other things. Of course, if the victim's fears—of men, of being alone, of being in public—persist, and interfere in her relationships with husband, sons, father, co-workers, or neighbors, then she will need to work on overcoming those fears after the immediate crisis has passed. Within this process, her feelings should be respected, and she, not some outside "rational" judge, should set the pace.

While it is obvious that a victim who has been physically damaged should receive timely medical attention, it is also sometimes the case that a victim of sexual violence needs to be reassured by medical personnel concerning her survival and condition. To this end, it is important in cases of rape or child sexual abuse that information or preventative treatment for sexually transmitted diseases (STDs) or pregnancy be given in such a way as to reassure the victim, and not raise fears of new, previously unenvisioned dangers. Sometimes medical examination can also have the effect, and sometimes for the victim the intention as well, of pointing out that the attack was truly violent and did leave bruises, lacerations, or other evidence of violence. In a society which tends to distrust or dismiss the word of women about violence aimed against them, many women need to be able to point to corroborating evidence of the violence visited on them.

Once the victim has been made to feel safe, the next step should be dictated by the victim. Some victims have a need to tell their story immediately; for others, shock may persist and interfere with their ability or desire to communicate clearly. If a criminal investigation of the incident(s) is occurring, the police will insist on an account and, in the case of rape and sometimes in child sexual abuse, on an immediate physical exam.

Police officials, counselors, victim advocates, and pastors of victims are trained to keep in mind at all times that the victim has sustained a major injury, and that healing entails restoring to the victim her sense of being in control of the activities and treatment of her bodyself. If it is necessary to subject a disoriented victim to interrogation and medical exam, those processes should be conducted with the utmost care in order to return to the victim control of her bodyself and her life. She should be given as much choice as possible in the ordering of these activities. Ideally, she should be given choices as to who should do the interrogation (male or female), who should be present (one or many, including a friend or advocate), and where it should be done. In cases of domestic violence against women, effective police policy dictates that police, having interrupted an attack, not attempt to interrogate the victim and batterer together.[55] The victim needs not only to feel safe from the batterer, which is difficult in his presence, but she needs to be reassured that the batterer is the offender and she the victim. When police understand their role in domestic violence scenes as mediators of the couple's "spat" or as judges whose role is apportioning blame between the husband and wife, the wife is often not protected enough to fully tell her story, partly because she must anticipate what will occur when the police leave, but also partly because the police, by their initial impartiality, have supported the batterer's claim that the wife shares part or all of the blame for the beating.[56]

Similarly, victims of sexual violence should not be forced to undergo medical exam by someone to whom they object (a male, for example), or without a friend or relative present. Victims should be informed as to each step in the procedure and the purpose of each step, and whenever possible should be invited to take part in the procedure, should they so desire. Many victims report terrible alienation after experiences of having a strange doctor, usually male, give them a physical exam, including a pelvic exam, after a sexual assault. Some doctors act as if the patient were not present, as if it were not her ravaged body being explored for damage, but only a thing. It has become a truism for many victims that such examinations feel like a repeat of the original violence.

Whether the victim is a young child or an elderly woman, the physician should introduce herself/himself, explain the purpose and procedure for the exam, give the victim all the personnel options possible, and obtain her consent to procedure and personnel before she is asked to undress. Male physicians, of course, should have female medical personnel present with the victim at all times. During the exam itself, the examining physician should speak to the victim, both describing to her what the exam is disclosing about the condition of her body and asking her cooperation whenever possible. For example, appropriate questions during the exam might include: "I know this is a terrible thing to put you through right now, Sally (to a child), so I'll be as quick and as gentle as possible. You need to tell me if anything hurts or makes you feel uncomfortable, OK? Would you like someone to hold your hand while we do this? Can you feel any pain anywhere on your body now? Where were you most aware of pain during the attack?" Or, "You have a large purple bruise on your right hip, Mrs. _____. It looks recent. Do you know how you got that bruise? There is a little dried blood in the folds of the labia, but I don't see any external cuts. When was your last menstrual period? Two weeks ago? Were you aware of any bleeding anywhere on your body during or after the attack? I'm going to have to insert this instrument into your vagina (or anus) to check for bleeding or tears in the tissue. It's a little cold. Can you hold very still for just a minute? Do you want to wait a few minutes before we do this? We could take the blood specimen first, if you prefer. How about a cup of coffee? Would you like your sister to come in now?"

While the most important need is to demonstrate that control of the exam is at least shared with the victim, and that the victim's bodyself is respected, some victims will benefit from conversation that distracts them from feelings of powerlessness and anxiety, while others may find such conversation demeaning, a denial of the seriousness of the attack. The individual victim's responses are the best clues for anticipating her needs.

The response of many medical personnel to requests for more enlightened treatment of victims of violence is that they do not have the time to do this kind of "hand-holding" and have not been trained to do it, either. But though victims of sexual violence can be additionally traumatized by the absence of such care, the absence of such care in the lives of ordinary patients who have never been sexually victimized also has the cumulative effect of undermining bodyright. All persons, not just victims of sexual violence, need hospitals, doctors, and nurses to acknowledge that our bodies are us, that we are in charge of the care of our bodies, that we are entitled to all information about our bodies, and that their role is to care for the welfare of the patient's embodied self—not for some (body)machine that is merely owned and possessed by the patient. It should not be a matter of rearranging medical care to spare the tender feelings of victims of sexual violence, but of rearranging medical care in general to respect the bodyselves and bodyright of patients.

If the medical establishment in this nation really respected bodyright, then it *would* train doctors both in humane interpersonal response to various kinds of suffering, and to be better medical educators of their patients; it would *not* schedule two or three patients every 15 minutes, hospital emergency rooms *would* be better staffed, and hospital nurses who are increasingly occupied with paperwork, not personal care, *would* have assistants trained to do more than deliver trays and change beds.

Men as Victims of Sexual Violence

Men are sometimes the victims of sexual violence by other men, especially in situations such as prisons, where male access to women is restricted. Men are also sometimes the victims of sexual violence by female partners, most often in domestic battery. There are no conclusive statistics on male battery by women. Since the violence of one partner frequently begets violence in the other, research frequently fails to disclose original or principal batterers. Present research suggests that 10 – 11% of family violence is female on male,[57] though all research makes clear that male violence against females is much more likely to cause serious injury.[58] Women's violence against men is not only less likely to inflict serious injury or death, but is also less likely to be reported. Because men are socialized to be in control, they are often too embarrassed to report violence against them by women, lest it give the impression that they require protection against a woman. In cases of male-male rape, men are even less likely to report than are women because they feel tainted by the stigma attached to homosexuality, despite the fact of their coercion. There is less research on the recovery process for male victims of sexual violence. Both male rape and female battery of males tend to produce crises around masculinity. Some male rape victims fear that their rapist was responding to unconscious homosexual "signals" from them; others fear that having been degraded and "feminized" will have made them into homosexuals despite their wishes. These fears are not rational, and do not necessarily disappear with more accurate explanations of gender identity and sexual orientation. Male victims of female battery sometimes feel a similar emasculation, especially if their battery included a serious injury that became public. For some men, masculinity is so closely tied to mastery over women that full recovery from sexual victimization entails extensive reconstruction of sexual identity. Male victims of rape, whether by males or females, especially those who experience erection or ejaculation, share the impaired sexual functioning, confusion, self-disgust, and emotional distress of women suffering from rape trauma syndrome.[59]

For these reasons, when sexual violence occurs against men, it can be just as devastating as sexual violence against women and children. Because Western society encourages men to exercise greater control over their bodies, and especially their sexual selves, than women, forcible loss of that bodily control more easily undermines a man's sense of masculinity and agency. While therapy for male victims must also revolve around restoring to men a sense of being in control of their bodies, that restoration is often different than for women, since many men—especially white middle-class men in this society—have been socially conditioned to expect levels of control, especially sexual control, that few women can envision. While sexual assault of a woman is often perceived as the final blow in a long series which undermined her sense of autonomy and agency, sexual assault of a man is more likely to be experienced as a solitary and unforeseen knockout punch which obliterates his sense of bodyself and publicly denies his bodyright.

There is a growing body of evidence demonstrating that when physical violence is divided into categories of more and less severe, women may match men in the demonstration of less severe violence, especially in throwing or breaking objects.[60] Psychologists interpret violence by women as due to many of the same causes as male violence, such as lack of communication skills, possessiveness, the absence of stress-relief, and social permission. The difference between male and female social permission is that, while men have historically had permission to "discipline" women and to lose their tempers, women have been taught to see themselves as weak and ineffective, incapable of hurting men. This feeling of powerlessness is a source of great frustration to some women. Paradoxically, because the social definition of women as powerless nullified the need to train women to use physical power responsibly, some women feel free to express their anger and frustration in violence which they do not believe can cause serious harm.[61]

Victims' Innocence and Rage

Alongside the immediate need to begin restoring to victims of sexual violence control over their bodies, there is a need to support feelings of rage and convictions of innocence in victims. Whether the abuse has been repeated or not, whether the abuser has blamed them for the abuse or not, victims of sexual violence live in a society in which they are regularly blamed for their own abuse. Victims of conjugal battery are blamed for provoking the husband's anger, victims of rape are blamed for provoking a man's sexual desire, victims of sexual harassment are accused of overreacting to attention meant to be complimentary, and sexually abused children are even accused of seducing their offenders. The fact that sexual violence is seldom, if ever, addressed by churches conveys the idea that sexual violence does not happen to good church members. The silence of churches regarding both the sinfulness and the pervasiveness of sexual violence in our society confirms feelings of shame, alienation, and guilt in the victims of sexual violence. Those who deal with victims throughout the healing process need to constantly be on guard not to reinforce these feelings in any way. Questions such as "What were you wearing when he attacked you?" "Why *hadn't* you made his dinner?" "Why *didn't* you leave him?" or "Why *didn't* you tell your mother?" all serve to imply that the victim was in some way responsible for her own abuse.

Victims of sexual violence need to be reassured of their own innocence. They need to hear that nothing that they said or did, short of violence, could have legitimated the violence against them, and that even their own use of violence would only have justified a proportional, defensive violence. Victims need to be treated as victims, as persons unjustly treated. The essence of the injustice perpetrated on them is the violation of their bodyright.

Therapeutic interaction with victims of sexual violence will inevitably involve the victim's attempt to make sense of the abuse by asking why it happened and what she could have done to avoid it. It is important to distinguish four different messages that the victim needs to hear, and not to conflate them. Those four messages are:

1) The victim is not responsible for the rape/beating/sexual molestation/sexual harassment. Unless she first attacked the bodyright of the perpetrator, she did not invite or deserve any violence. Walking home from the gym alone at night, or believing a parent's threat to kill you if you tell, might not be wise, but they are neither crimes nor sins.

2) The sexual violence visited on victims is socially supported. Victims need to understand the complicity of our society in

sexual violence if they are to move beyond victimization and heal from their injuries. That healing will require rejecting major aspects of the sexual socialization process in our society. This is true for children as well as for adults. Child victims must be told that social complicity takes forms such as blindness to child sexual abuse and to the signals put out by victims, as well as failure to teach children to recognize and report sexual abuse.

3) Victims need not be powerless and easily violated in the future.[62] There are many things that an individual can do to protect herself, and many ways that society can be pushed to better protect victims by altering socialization processes. However, victims have no obligation to restrict their life and activities in significant ways in order to protect themselves from future abuse. Not every potential safeguard is worth its cost to one's quality of life; insist that the burden of assuring individual safety be understood as a social, not merely an individual task.

4) Though victims need not be powerless, no one can be invincible. There is no absolute protection against sexual violence or any other kind of evil. The more communal our protection, the stronger it will be, but in the end, our very humanity makes us vulnerable to suffering and injustice. There is a certain degree of randomness in evil which, like rain, falls on the innocent and the guilty.

Frequently victims will walk through their abuse time and time again, attempting to discover what they could have done to avoid the violence. It is important for them to realize that though there are things they could have done to lessen the risk of their victimization, not having taken those precautions does not make them responsible for their victimization. A nurse who accepted a transfer onto the night shift rather than lose the job she needed to support her children is not therefore responsible for being raped at gunpoint in the hospital parking lot after her shift ended. We are not always free to make the choices we think are the safest. Also, since the majority of sexual violence takes place in the home or at the hands of family members, the very existence of a "safe" place from sexual violence is in doubt.

For many victims, reflection on what they could have done to avoid the sexual violence reveals that precautions would not have *prevented* the sexual violence but only changed the identity of the victim, reminding us again of the randomness of sexual violence. While this is clear for cases of stranger rape and stranger child abuse, it is often more difficult for other sexual victims to see. But research often shows that a battering spouse battered previous spouses and lovers, and will batter future spouses; when circumstances snatch one child from the clutches of a perpetrator of child incest, frequently another sibling or cousin is substituted; when one sexually harassed secretary is fired, quits, or transfers, the harasser will usually harass another.[63] While perpetrators of sexual violence are frequently without criminal records, and may not be known for violence in any non-sexual contexts,[64] they are, much more often than not, *habitual* perpetrators of sexual violence.

Victims' Rage

Rage is another reaction common in victims. There has been a great deal written over the past few years about the positive nature of anger and rage. Perhaps best known is Beverly Wildung Harrison's essay "The Power of Anger in the Work of Love: An Ethic for Women and Other Strangers,"[65] which makes the point that anger arises as a response to injustice, injustice perpetrated against the self or someone or something dear to the self, and functions as a source of energy for redressing the injustice.

It is this understanding of righteous anger that many therapists refer to when they insist that victims be encouraged to express anger. The understanding is that anger which is not expressed will eventually be turned toward the self. The self will accept the blame for the victimization, which will be interpreted as appropriate treatment. This self-blaming saps the energy of the self, and is frequently expressed as depression.

It is clear that victims need to be encouraged to express anger, but especially in the early stages of recovery anger must be carefully and explicitly directed toward the victimizer. The expression of anger in itself is often, but not necessarily, therapeutic. Withholding anger and blame at serious injury can over time lead to self-blame and the creation of deep depression; expression of anger can prevent such depression. But some expressions of anger can be used to maintain a situation of injustice by allowing victims to periodically blow off some steam in ways that serve neither to call the offender to account nor to restore the bodyright of the victim. Sometimes the expression of rage only heightens rage by rehearsing initial but mistaken interpretations of the victimization, which then become unchangeable.[66]

The expression of rage is healthy when it is appropriately directed at the perpetrator of the injustice, so that the victim is absolved and the perpetrator publicly accused of responsibility for the abuse. This should be a first step in redressing the injustice of sexual violence. *Within a therapeutic process*, expressions of anger, even frequent venting of anger in very visceral ways (punching a bag, primal screams, etc.), even when not aimed specifically at the perpetrator, can serve a very useful purpose in combatting depression. But this expression of anger is only useful when the injustice is already being addressed, when the perpetrator has already been named and accused, so that the source of the anger is clear and accepted.

Sometimes victims may express what seems like anger toward the person who hears their account of the violation, whether that is a family member, a friend, a therapist, or a therapy group. Many times that anger—or its equally likely flip side, withdrawal—is really a reaction to fear that those who hear the story of their abuse may dislike, be repulsed by, or fail to believe them after hearing their story. Some victims, especially child victims of incest, *expect* to be disbelieved or even punished for telling their stories; their expression of anger at the hearers of their story masks their hurt and pain and their need to be believed and supported.

This response of anger toward those who hear the story of abuse is also common among victims of sexual harassment. Victims who acquiesced to demands for sexual favors in order to save their jobs, or grades, often project onto others not only rage which should properly be aimed at the harasser, but also rage stemming from feelings of guilt for having capitulated to the demands of the harasser. Such rage is not therapeutic; it is not the first step in the healing process described by Harrison or Fortune.[67] Progress through the healing process requires that victims honestly face their feelings of guilt, come to see that the offender—not the victim—is the guilty party, and gradually come to learn and trust that others will place blame appropriately. Of course, in many situations, the victim's fear that others will blame her are, unfortunately, very realistic. In such cases, hearers may have to struggle to convince the victim that they believe and support her, and that there are many other people who will listen, believe, sympathize, and not condemn.

When the perpetrator of the violence was someone in an intimate relation with the victim, the feelings of the victim are likely to be very ambivalent. It is important that both positive and negative feelings be supported. That is, an adolescent girl sexually abused by an uncle may have years of happy memories of her special interaction with this uncle before the abuse began. Those memories should be acknowledged and not denied, though they do not mitigate the later abuse by the uncle. To repress real and positive memories of abusers is to radically oversimplify for the victim the reality of abuse and evil. Dealing with this level of emotional complexity may be difficult for very young children, whose conceptual framework may not be large enough to understand that they are at risk from "good people" as well as "bad people." Even for many adult victims, reaching an accurate understanding of their relationship with an intimate abuser may take some rather sophisticated analysis, because hindsight often suggests that some positive memories of the perpetrator may have been deliberately designed by the perpetrator to create trust and confidence in the victim, which the perpetrator could call on to aid in the continuation of the abuse and the maintenance of secrecy concerning the abuse.

Selfhood and Recovery from Sexual Violence

All the above treatments of victimization and recovery from sexual violence make clear that sexual violence transforms the victims' relationship to others, world, self, and often God, but that the principal injury is to victims' self-concept. The victim feels stripped of self-esteem, dignity, strength, the love and respect of others, the ability to trust others, the ability to feel secure, and even the ability to trust herself and her own judgment. For many victims, the inability to trust themselves and their own judgment reflects self-blame. They remind themselves that they *did* decide to marry this man who beat and/or raped them, to trust this parent or relative who abused them, to leave open the door through which the rapist entered. Many of them feel additional guilt because they experienced involuntary sexual response to the abuse, which makes them feel complicit in their abuse.[68]

Victimism

All these aspects of human personhood which have been stripped from the victim must be restored to her. This restoration requires certain kinds of treatment from the persons around them during the healing process. One of the great dangers of both the initial crisis period and the long-term recovery process after sexual violence is that the friends and family of the victim, as well as the victim herself, succumb to "victimism." While it needs to be made clear to victims that they *are* victims of sexual violence—they are innocent, and the perpetrator is guilty—it is a mistake to understand victimhood as a permanent part of their identity. Their victimization was a historical event, like a car accident, or the death of a friend, or the end of a relationship. It was tragic, it caused great damage and suffering, but it can and should be left behind. It can be overcome. It will probably never be forgotten, but it need not remain a source of trauma.

When friends and family insist on treating victims of sexual violence as fragile dependents in need of protection, on tip-toeing around them and taking on victims' routine decision-making out of a perception of victims as necessarily preoccupied with their victimization, friends and family do those victims no favors, but rather help perpetuate their injuries.

Just as all initial interaction with victims of sexual violence, even in the crisis phase, needs to focus on providing simple short-term options to the victim so that she can begin to reexert control over her body and her life, so the long-term recovery process must structure a process within which the victim, a piece at a time, conquers her fears, regains a sense of being strong, in control, worthwhile, and capable of wise judgment and deep trust in others.

Real support from family and friends will *not* take the shape of deciding for the victim that "It has been three months now, Mary, don't you think you should be recovered enough to be able to ride in an elevator with a strange man?" Rather, real support will take the form of helping the victim clarify for herself the shape of the healing process going on within her, and what should be its next step: "Jane, you expected to have a lot of fear about returning to school and facing your friends, but you say the teachers and kids made you feel welcome and special. Do you think there is anything else you may be dreading that might turn out to be not so hard? What do you think might be your next step in getting your life back to normal? No, you don't need to see your father (uncle, grandfather) if you don't want to. What do you want to do? Are you thinking about him? What are you feeling about him? Is there anything you want to do with those feelings, or is there something else you want to talk about or do first?"

Nor should the primary focus in recovery be on getting back to one's normal routine. All too often we reassure ourselves that things are fine when victims have gone back to work or school, when housewives take up their housework again, when the time schedules of our daily routines are reestablished. Routines in themselves are not sufficient to heal victims, and may not allow the time and energy that must go into healing. On the other hand, many recovering victims of sexual violence find that when all the areas of damage and pain have been probed and understood, and when a series of steps toward healing have already been made, resuming partial or even full routines (returning to school or work, to responsibilities as principal caretaker of children, etc.), can be helpful to, and not a flight from or obstacle to, the final stage of healing.

The *immediate* resumption of these routines not only may hide great traumas that may become disruptive and destructive of victims' lives in the future, but simply may not be possible. Sometimes the only way to truly heal from the trauma of sexual violence is to resist the adoption of former routines, because those routines include some of the structural aspects of the abusive relation. For example, a friend of mine had adopted a three-year-old, Elizabeth, who she discovered almost immediately had been repeatedly sexually abused by an adult male friend of her neglectful parents. Elizabeth began seeing a child therapist, both with and without her new mother, and heard in many different ways that she was good, that the adult had done wrong, that he had no right to touch her at all, much less to hurt her and threaten her. Six months later, having heard my friend despair of Elizabeth ever losing the belligerence and contrariness which seemed the result of the abuse, I visited them. Immediately after I arrived my friend instructed Elizabeth, who knew me but not well, to greet me with a hug and kiss. Elizabeth refused rather defiantly—and continued to refuse. After five minutes of vain coaxing, her mother finally sent her to her room until she would change her mind.

I tried to explain to my friend that her message to Elizabeth in this incident was that Elizabeth did not have the right to say who she kissed and touched, or who kissed and touched her, and that this undermined the message she had been given about her abuse. But my friend's perspective was that she was only insisting that Elizabeth respect her elders and be appropriately affectionate. It was, she argued, "good for her, since too much of her experience of touch was painful and sexual." My friend was focusing on abuse as bad because it inflicted pain, suffering, and physical damage, or violated sexual taboos, instead of abuse as the theft of a person's right to control her own body, her own self. The problem is that our society does not recognize a child's bodyright—and that failure not only sets children up for child sexual abuse, but also makes children's recovery from child sexual abuse virtually impossible.

What Elizabeth needed to hear was adult permission and even encouragement for her to set the limits concerning access to her own bodyself. And she needed adults to respect those limits. Ideally, Elizabeth's permission should be necessary for anyone to touch her bodyself, whether the proposed touch is a matter of grooming, affection, medical or dental care, or instruction in motor skill development. Sometimes with children we must violate their wishes for their own good—to inoculate them, to give emergency medical treatment, to prevent them from running into the street after a ball, for example. But violations should be infrequent, very brief, in the clear and immediate interest of the child, and in some way necessary, as well as always explained to the child.

Children and Bodyright

A great deal of the adult coercion of children occurs because adults do not understand children as sufficiently important to warrant the adult spending time to explain why the child should agree to and cooperate with some proposed activity. It is simply easier to restrain children when they refuse the shot from the nurse, or to dress them in the outfit the adult thinks is more appropriate, or to threaten them with punishment if they refuse Aunt Bessie's kisses and cheek-pinching. But when adults act in this way, they send the message that bodyright is not respected, that only physical power has rights—and that children, too, can exert power over the bodies of others when they get bigger and more powerful.

According to Alice Miller, a Swiss psychotherapist, the more punitive and violent the parenting, the greater the tendency for children to distance themselves from their real pain, projecting it onto others by punishing their own children or other more vulnerable persons, and to be unable to empathize or identify with victims of oppression.[69] But in some ways, she says, the parent who treats the child with both abuse and affection creates even more destructive responses in the child, for such children cannot separate love and abuse, and will give others, including their own children, a fusion of love and abuse because they have no capacity for love that is nondestructive. The emotional intensity constructed by this fusion of love and abuse is so strong that treatment is difficult; the fusion of love and abuse for many is more compelling and attractive than even supportive, nonabusive love and intimacy.

It is important to recognize that while Miller describes abusive patterns of child-rearing, she sees them reflected to a lesser degree in normal child-rearing practices. A severe critic of child-rearing, Miller describes parenting in Western culture as control-oriented. Parents shape the child into a being who reflects the parents' needs or wishes by forcing the child, whether through reinforcement or physical coercion, to minister to the needs of the parent.[70] For example, for some years I forced my children to dress for church in ways that met my image of how the church community should see my family. In so doing, I refused to allow my children to present to the community the self they felt they were or wanted to be. When parents control large parts of children's lives over long periods of time, children learn to bury their own feelings and needs, and to rely on the false selves that mirror their parents' needs and wishes. Just as my friend declared that the problem with Elizabeth was Elizabeth's refusal to be polite, parents often feed their own interpretations back to the child. Eventually, after many such incidents, a child comes to accept that the issue at stake is one of courtesy and respect for elders, and not one of body control: whose body is it, and who should control it? The child is increasingly distanced from her own feelings, her own perspective, and substitutes over time the feelings and perspectives of the parent. The primary cost to the child and to the adult the child will become is capacity for intimacy.

This lack of capacity for intimacy is crippling. It can take the form of disliking and avoiding genital sex, which in itself can cause a great deal of suffering for persons in sexual relationships, since sexual activity can both express and sustain, and also feed and multiply, love between persons. But lack of capacity for intimacy also takes nonsexual forms. Lack of capacity for intimacy has negative effects on the ability to become intimate with God, as well as on ability to create and sustain close friendships. Personal lack of capacity for intimacy allows individuals no escape from loneliness and solitude. Among Christians, called by Jesus' two great commandments to love God and neighbor, lack of or diminished capacity for intimacy can prevent true Christian discipleship. Without the capacity for intimate love, it is difficult to develop the interest in and empathy for others which call us to work for justice. Diminished capacity for love and justice certainly undermine any potential for moral agency.

Denial of Bodyright in Work

The repression of bodyself and the denial of bodyright are not only disturbingly present in child-rearing practices, but are also present in many other aspects of our culture, including that part of our lives which occupies our largest block of time, work. Repression in work has many sources. While the denial of bodyself and bodyright is clearest in the structure of work in the working class, other forms of repression are present even in some of the best-paid, most respected forms of work.

Bodyright is denied to much of the working class in much the same way that it is denied to children. Industrial workers are controlled in terms of when they come to and leave work, a control that is exacerbated by many companies' insistence on mandatory overtime; what they wear on the job; when they may use the bathroom; what tasks they perform, the speed at which they perform the tasks, and the order in which they do them. Some companies restrict workers' ability to talk with other workers; others require exposure to toxic materials without informing workers of the risk to their health, their reproductive capacity, or the health of their offspring. Our capitalist society tends to interpret hourly work in terms of employer's temporary ownership of the bodyself of a worker as if it were a machine or a tool. Salaried employees retain more control of their bodyselves, surrendering to employers only the production of those bodyselves. However, salaried workers whose work is intellectually creative are often shackled by contract clauses which assign all ideas of the employee to the employer as "intellectual property." Restrictions on hourly workers are usually more numerous and petty. Many clerks, typists, and telephone personnel are frequently subject to dress codes and directives about haircuts and facial hair, even individual orders to wear make-up, usually in the name of corporate image or morale. This kind of appropriation of bodyright by those holding authority in the workplace sets the ground for sexual harassment in the workplace as well, both by causing workers to be unsure of the location of the line between legitimate and illegitimate prerogatives of superiors over the bodyselves of workers, and by encouraging workplace authorities to take for granted their control of employee bodyselves.

Christian Theology: Support for Abuse, Obstacle to Healing?

Sheila A. Redmond suggests that Christianity has taught five beliefs which both encourage child sexual abuse and inhibit healing from it or from other forms of sexual violence. Those five are: 1) the value of suffering, 2) the virtue of forgiveness, 3) the necessity—especially for females—of remaining sexually pure, 4) individual need for redemption, and 5) the virtue of obedience to authority. Because Christian children accept these values and beliefs, Redmond asserts, their process of recovering from sexual violence is obstructed. Redmond writes of the Christian value of suffering as understood by child victims:

> Victims of sexual assault suffer from self-destruction of the ego. One suffers because one has done something bad and is being punished. If one becomes truly repentant and humble, gives over one's soul to the control of the deity, then every-

thing will be all right. Implicitly, the assault is destroying the integrity of the self. What better way to empty the soul and become humble than by being sexually assaulted as a child? This attitude toward suffering can then be used as a reason for not admitting the damage caused by the molestation. One can be blessed by stoically accepting this kind of assault.[71]

According to Redmond, the problem with emphasizing forgiveness to child victims of sexual abuse is that

> a necessary component of resolving the trauma of the assault is articulation of rage, anger, and hatred at being used, at the powerlessness of their positions as children. This militates against any demand for too early an emphasis on forgiveness and understanding the perpetrator and his crime as anything but unjustified and unforgivable.[72]

Premature demands that the victim forgive the perpetrator are often the rule in cases of family violence, including cases of incest, marital rape, and conjugal battery. There are a variety of reasons. One is concern for the stability of the family. Often there is pressure both from inside and outside the family for the victim to forgive as a way of minimizing, resolving, and disposing of the abuse in ways that preclude criminal prosecution or other intervention of the law. It is frequently argued that the family will not be helped by having the father sent to prison, or having the child removed to a foster home, or having the marriage break up and the husband receive a police record. Premature forgiveness by victims is often demanded by both family members and friends who do not want to have to take sides between the accused and the accuser and by other relatives who not only do not want to take sides but who also do not relish the notoriety by association that can accompany more official and/or therapeutic approaches to sexual victimization. Sometimes family members even argue that early forgiveness is the best solution for the victim herself, in that she is spared the trauma and embarrassment of having her "shame" become known and her virtue and reputation impugned.

The third Christian teaching attacked by Redmond, sexual purity, is one particularly aimed at women. Women have historically been understood in Christianity as having a carnal, specifically reproductive purpose which not only makes them more vulnerable to sins of the flesh, especially sexual sins, but makes those sins of the flesh more horrendous, since they impinge upon her God-given purpose. The emphasis on virginity, especially in Roman Catholicism, and on chastity in Christianity in general, is of special relevance to women. For much of the tradition, a woman who had lost her virginity had lost her virtue, which was of much more importance than her life. As late as the 1950s Maria Goretti was canonized a saint in the Catholic church because in 1902 she had chosen to forfeit her life rather than her virginity.[73] For a girl child, exposure to such teaching ensured that experience of child sexual abuse or rape would carry implications of permanent uncleanness and evil for the victim.

Redmond's fourth Christian teaching charged with obstructing healing from child sexual abuse is the universal human need for redemption. The understanding that each of us is born with sin and needs to be justified can easily produce feelings of guilt and unworthiness in individuals. When feelings of guilt and unworthiness are understood as normal, and as confirming Christian doctrine, it becomes difficult to understand the guilt and feelings of unworthiness stemming from sexual violence as negative and in need of resolution.

Lastly, Redmond represents Christianity, especially the biblical tradition of Christianity, as both encouraging obedience to authority figures, and presenting patriarchal models of authority. Christianity has taught children to "honor thy father and thy mother," wives to "be submissive to their husbands as to the Lord," Jesus as the meek child of God who accepts an order to die on the cross, and persons with power as representing God's own position of power vis-à-vis the individual human. Within this framework, resistance to sexual violence against an authority figure—a parent, a husband, a priest or minister, a boss, a teacher— becomes rebellion against God.

Rita Nakashima Brock focuses on christological aspects of Christian support for abuse.[74] This christological focus of Brock's is closely related to Redmond's critique of Christian teaching on the value of suffering, since the passion and death of Jesus Christ has been paradigmatic for Christian understanding of suffering. Of Redmond's five problematic Christian teachings, the goodness of suffering *does* seem to demand the closest attention. There is at least some basis in traditional Christian revelation for resisting premature forgiveness and making forgiveness dependent upon contrition and reparation, and for differentiating forgiveness and reconciliation. In the same way, it is possible to use liberatory aspects of the Christian tradition to partially offset both the sexist cult of purity for women and the tradition's support for authoritarianism. Contemporary treatment of original sin as sin of the world, or social sin, rather than as a major moral flaw in the individual (a nurture rather than nature approach to original sin) similarly avoids much of the problem Redmond describes as resulting from the need for redemption.

But there is no way to avoid the centrality of the Christian belief that Jesus Christ suffered and died before resurrecting, and that he is the incarnated Word, the exemplar for Christians. If his suffering itself were not good in itself, Christians still must affirm the virtue of his willingness to risk suffering and death by continuing his liberating activity on behalf of the reign of God, despite opposition from all organized parts of his society.[75] We can make distinctions between voluntary and involuntary suffering, between suffering as an end and suffering as a means, but these only mitigate and do not remove the problem, and are distinctions not easy to convey to a laity untrained in theology.

Brock suggests that Christians shift their focus from trinitarian doctrines and doctrines of atonement to focus on the child as the primary image of divinity. But she does not explain what to do with scripture and tradition regarding the crucifixion, death, and resurrection of Jesus Christ. I agree with Brock that understanding the presence of God in the ministry of Jesus demands a focus on the effect of Jesus' interaction with those he healed, exorcised, fed, and otherwise aided, rather than on the person of Jesus himself. But I suspect that, while much of our world, especially white, middle-class America, may be in drastic need of an emphasis on divine vulnerability, the image of the vulnerable child is not sufficient to support the needs and hopes of suffering humanity. As James Cone often points out in contemporary theological debate, the religious needs and faith of the wounded and oppressed peoples of the world are not filled by a God who is dead, or by a God who is powerless and cries at their suffering. These wounded and oppressed need and want a God who not only cries with them, but is powerful enough to save them when they cannot save themselves by themselves.[76] Cone does not defend all depictions of God's uses of power within Christian tradition; he is sensitive to the complexity of Jesus' rejection of dominion as a model for the exercise of power. But he insists that Jesus' rejection of dominion was supported by a ministry of empowerment, of enabling, which finds its locus in a God of power, even if that divine power is not the power to intervene in human history independent of historical human persons.

At the level of individual spirituality, I suspect that human experience of divinity includes as much of the God of power as it does the vulnerable child. How many persons and groups plagued by crushing poverty, cruel oppression, addictions, or despairing depression have been enabled to continue the struggle against sin and evil by reminding themselves that the power to resist is "not I, but God in me"?

On the other hand, many who have worked in spiritual direction with victims of sexual violence have discovered that the God of Christianity is permanently tainted for these victims by the images of divine domination in the tradition. Many victims of father-daughter incest can never respond positively to God as father. For many other victims of sexual violence, the images of divine power (king, lord, master, judge) are offensive and the notion of God is itself negative because they represent power over human persons. While this is understandable, it is not inevitable or necessary. Christians need to purge the tradition of images of God as dominion, as autonomous power over others. We have alternative visions in the tradition: God, the loving parent, who created our bodyselves and calls them into full adulthood as co-creators of the universe, and Jesus the Christ who suffered the violation of his bodyself out of commitment to dignity, justice, and love for other bodyselves. If the image of God were so purged, then God as parent could be a resource for victims of their parents, rather than a support for the abuse and an obstacle to healing. A purged image of God could assure the child victim that her/his parent is not acting in accordance with God's model of a good parent, and is offending against both God and the child. The present ambiguity in the image of the divine, and the consequent support for abuse, does not require our choosing between a powerless and a powerful God, but rather our choosing between a God who both knows vulnerability and shares power, directing it toward justice and healing, and a God who jealously hoards power, using it for purposes of exercising dominion over and exploiting others.

Conclusion

The phenomenon of sexual violence and recovery from its victimization point to two areas of necessary change in Western Christian culture: 1) recognition and respect for bodyright, and 2) insistence that the image of God includes only creative, collaborative, enabling, and therapeutic power oriented to life and its fullness. These are not minor changes in our religious tradition or our secular culture. Purging the image of God will be a long, gradual affair of sifting through scripture and the theological tradition piece by piece and self-consciously rejecting divine images of domination for use in prayer, song, or liturgy, while making a point at all levels of Christian education to indicate the inadequacies of divine images of domination, and how they entered the tradition without serious critique because they were tied to prevailing social structures and institutions.

Moving our culture toward more complete respect for bodyright will require even more massive changes. A starting point would be for ordinarily competent individuals to be understood to have complete control over their own bodies, and for such individuals to understand themselves as part of an integral human community and a common biosphere. Individual decisions regarding personal bodyselves could be overruled by properly authorized persons, after consultation with the individual, only:

1) when it did the individual no harm, 2) when it benefited the common good, and 3) for very temporary periods.

Such a reform would require a thorough reform of military life to restore to members of the armed services their basic civil rights regarding the body. If members of the military were accorded the same rights as civilians over their bodies, then, for example, soldiers irreversibly injured by being required to handle hazardous materials such as Agent Orange would be entitled to the same legal and medical recourse as civilians injured on the job; they would also have the same right to know in advance the dangers of handling those materials, as right-to-know laws are increasingly guaranteeing to civilians in cities and states across the nation.

In such a reform, a military draft would be impossible, dangerous military actions would require volunteers, and the peacetime military would no longer unilaterally control the health, dress, relationships, job details, or location of members of the armed services. It would be no more serious an offense for an enlisted person to strike an officer than for an officer to strike an enlisted person. Members of the armed services would need to give permission, after informed consent, for experiments or tests to be done on their bodies or body products, just as civilians must. In the temporary emergency of war, bodyright would need to be abridged, but abridgment would be limited as situationally necessary and bodyright not abolished altogether.

If bodyright were respected, sexual relationships, including marriage, would also change. There would be no more owning of the other's body, no more understanding sex in terms of the marital debt, no more acceptance of domestic battery as fulfilling an obligation to discipline wives or children. Sex would occur when mutually desired by both partners. All decisions and methods of decision-making would be negotiated by the partners. Traditional sex roles would be without authority; roles would be mutually agreed upon by the partners. All sexual unions, including marriage, would be based in mutuality.

Work would also be structured differently, so that workers exercised a great deal more responsibility over their bodies and body activity. Petty types of control over the bodies of workers which are not necessary to the work would be eliminated. In many types of work, policies would be negotiated with workers. Mandatory overtime in which the employee has no scheduling authority would be a thing of the past. On the other hand, there might very well be mandatory drug and alcohol testing in forms of work in which users endangered the lives of others and/or themselves, so long as just provisions were made for promulgation of policy dealing with false positives and mistaken reporting.

But the greatest challenges in such a reform would occur in child-rearing practices. The emphasis in child-rearing would radically shift from the present focus on achieving socially desirable behavior in one's children to successfully transferring power and responsibility to one's children. For most parents today, the process of parenting is understood as one in which the parent makes the decisions—what the child should eat, learn, wear, say, desire to be—for the duration of the child's minority, in the hopes that during these years the child will accept piece by piece the values, style, skills, and aspirations which have been inculcated. Somewhere between the ages of 18 and 25, most children become independent of the parent's power. In the dorms of college campuses all over the nation, this sudden coming into power over one's bodyself and life has been for decades celebrated with months/years of drunkenness and experimental sex—though drunkenness and experimental sex are certainly not limited to college students. For most young people there has been no gradual preparation for responsibility for their bodyselves.

Recognition of bodyright would dictate that beginning with the very first years of a child's life a child's wishes should be solicited, heard, and considered in any decision about the child's bodyself. Children should always have explained to them what is occurring to their bodyselves and why. They should not be made to eat when they are not hungry, but neither should they be allowed to consistently substitute nonnutritious snacks for meals. Children should not be made to adopt a parent's dress choices, but neither should they be allowed to wear shorts in the snow. Young children need to be given a range of options they can comprehend in as many areas of their lives as possible, and their choices in these areas should be respected. They may not have the right to decide not to go to Grandma's at Easter, but they do have the right to say no if Grandma wants to hold them on her lap all afternoon. As children get older, they should have more choices in more areas of their life. When children cannot be allowed to decide an issue involving bodyright, such as whether or not blood should be drawn for testing, adults should take care to explain why it is necessary to overrule them, and offer them as many choices as possible regarding the blood test. There is no question that granting children bodyright will complicate parenting. But if children are to develop moral self-esteem, personal and social responsibility, and the ability to engage in self-giving, intimate relationships with others, they need to have their bodyright widely respected. If adults treat the bodyself of the child as a thing, and not a person, adults teach the child to see herself as a thing, and to see other persons as things, and to imagine that God, too, sees her and other persons as things to be manipulated.

7. *Regrounding Spirituality in Embodiment*

A spirituality is a specific way of living in relation to ultimate value. Early Christians understood "The Way," meaning the path of following Jesus Christ, as their distinctive spirituality. Though Jesus Christ remains the preeminent model for Christian spirituality, contemporary recognition of the dual need to glean as much of Jesus' deeds and teachings as possible from the incomplete, sometimes unclear, and occasionally contradictory accounts passed to us, and to discern into what contemporary options those deeds and teachings translate today, make following that model complicated. The relative paucity of scriptural references to sexuality by or about Jesus has unfortunately eased the way for dualistic segregation of spirituality and sexuality in the tradition.

But sexuality is intimately connected with many aspects of ultimate human concern, including both life and death, and love and intimacy.

Preceding chapters dealing with embodiment, emotional and relational development, healing, inclusiveness, intimacy, and human dignity have hinted at some parameters for a spirituality. In these last pages, I will add some final remarks about these themes and their implications for traditional Christian spirituality.

Perhaps the first thing to be observed is that the dominant cultural narrative in our post-modern society—the narrative of therapeutic well-being—is, in many ways, an inadequate reaction to many of the more repressive, neurotic, and masochistic (and of course, then, sometimes sadistic) inclinations in traditional Christian spirituality. I can remember my physician father being called during the 1960s to the local motherhouse of Catholic nuns to stitch up lacerations inflicted on their own backs by some of the more zealous sisters during Lent. At the time, these sisters and persons like them were admired by many fellow Catholics, both within the convent and outside it, for their willingness to share the pain of Jesus. My father himself, being a physician, felt some ambivalence about such activities, but stopped short of condemning the practice. In the same way among some contemporary Latin American/Filipino populations, the processions on Good Friday occasionally include devotees who have had themselves physically nailed to a cross in order to share the sufferings of Jesus. Nor is veneration of bodily suffering exclusively Catholic. Innumerable Protestants, many of them clergy, have confided to me that they concede to Catholics a corner on what they call "spirituality" and "moral rigor." This is undoubtedly one factor in the ongoing slippage in membership among liberal Protestant denominations; evangelical, fundamentalist, and Catholic churches are gaining new members (though Catholic churches, too, have lost members, especially among college-educated young since the 1960s[1]). The churches that are gaining are perceived—even by many who do not agree with them on specific teachings on sexuality and sex education, sex roles, biblical interpretation, or doctrine—as retaining a rigorous spirituality. The churches which are losing members are perceived as having abandoned traditional spirituality along with traditional moral and theological teaching, and as having no real replacement for either. These "liberal" churches are understood as "permissive," wishy-washy, and even morally opportunistic.

The understanding of Christian spirituality as embracing body pain developed in early Christianity from a complex set of influences, in addition to the passion and crucifixion of Jesus Christ. The persecution of early Christians by the synagogues and then by the Roman Empire led Christians to respect and admire the faith and courage of the martyrs and their willingness to embrace suffering and death. Veneration of the martyrs for the salvation they earned through their suffering and death over time too often turned into the veneration of suffering and death as desirable ends in themselves. This confusion contributed to a tendency to interpret the divinity and virtue of Jesus Christ in terms of his accepting, and even often seeking, pain and death, some results of which we examined in the previous chapter.

By the time the risk of persecution for professing Christian faith was removed following the establishment of Christianity as the religion of the Empire, an ascetic monastic movement had emerged as the path for those Christians who desired a more challenging Christian spirituality.[2] This monastic movement understood itself as the path for the few, for the truly zealous, for those wanting to follow more completely the difficult Way of the Jesus whose path led through the cross. The monastic spirituality forged over the centuries came to be understood not merely as the higher spiritual path, but in many ways as the only truly spiritual path. For while it was recognized that following the celibate religious or clerical lifestyle was not necessary in order to be saved, it soon became taken for granted that access to salvation lay in approximating as closely as possible monastic practices and lifestyle, regardless of one's formal state in life.[3]

Monastic spirituality therefore structured the basic model of Christian spirituality. It is ironic that this is what many Protestants, even theologically trained clergy, are unconsciously recognizing when they confide that they envy Catholics their great spiritual tradition, and regret that Protestant churches have never really developed spirituality as a theological or practical field. Such statements are not, of course, completely true. It would be ridiculous to say that neither Luther nor Calvin taught a spirituality, or that the theological successors of the reformers never addressed spirituality. But the spirituality of the reformers was only marginally different from the previous Catholic tradition. This should not be surprising, in that the reformers did not see themselves as beginning new churches so much as purifying the existing church of the rampant corruption which had arisen. That corruption seemed impossible to overcome within the existing structures of pre-Reformation Catholicism, due in large part to the self-interest of the hierarchy, especially the papacy, in continuing many of the most blatant corruptions. The dominant position among the reformers toward spirituality was to reground Christian spirituality in the traditions which had existed before the onset of corruption. Thus Protestant spirituality came to be grounded in scripture, especially the New Testament, and in early theologians, such as the Fathers of the Church, who had reflected on those scriptures.

When the Fathers seemed to diverge from scripture, commitment to *sola scriptura* was usually decisive. The reformers' most significant departure from the perspective of the Fathers concerned ascetic practices around sexuality, especially celibacy. For a number of reasons, including both widespread corruption around the practice of celibacy and the initial emergence of more companionate marriage patterns among the urban commercial class, which was the most fervently supportive of reform, the reformers, beginning with Luther, insisted on marriage as the usual state of life even for ministers and celibacy as an exception limited to the very few specifically gifted with that charism.

But this defense of marriage and rejection of celibacy only modified traditional Christian spirituality; it did not challenge the basically ascetic cast of traditional spirituality. While sexuality had been largely demonic in pre-Reformation Christianity, the Reformation, at least in its dominant forms, domesticated marital sexuality. While the reformers agreed with the Roman Catholics that the primary end of sex was reproduction,[4] the Calvinist tradition brought to New England by the Puritans additionally understood sex as an important manner of cherishing and loving the spouse. What this meant for ordinary Christian spirituality in American Protestantism was that marital sex was not understood as a barrier to worship, prayer, or reception of baptism or Holy Communion. Few married couples were warned away from sex, or interrogated about it by clergy, as continued to occur among Catholics.[5] On the other hand, neither did sexuality become for any of the Protestant churches a significant avenue for either experiencing or expressing the truths of revelation. The general model of Christian spirituality in Protestantism reflected the past monastic tradition in its emphasis on solitary prayer, sacrificial suffering as the path to salvation, personal access to revelation, the divine presence, and divine grace, and the inferiority of the material to the spiritual and of the human body to the human mind/soul. Nonmarital sexuality still carried with it the scent of brimstone. The practical goodness of marital sexuality was more or less limited to its ability to prevent serious sexual sin; preachers' references tended to quote Paul on it being better to marry than to burn.[6]

Protestant modifications to previous Christian spirituality focused on the elevation of marriage as a vocation (despite, ironically, its demotion from sacramental status), the rejection of clerical celibacy, and an intensification of individualism in the search for salvation flowing from attempts to undo papal/institutional control over salvation through control of seven sacraments. There was no reexamination of either sexuality or body pleasure and their meaning in Christian life. New images of domesticated marital sex as good,[7] and marriage as companionate union of (unequal) co-workers, were added to the pool of traditional images of sex and marriage, but few if any of the inherited ascetic images and attitudes were purged from that pool.

What this has tended to produce in late twentieth-century North America is rationalist discontent with "superstitious" (Catholic) fears of the body and sex, as well as a parallel discontent with the lack of coherence in (Protestant) Christian teachings and attitudes toward sexuality. Both these dissatisfactions are understandable. But a return to past consistent and rigorous dualist approaches to sex and morality is no longer truly possible. Many people rally around those who suggest such a return in the face of contemporary North American religious pursuit of therapeutic well-being.[8] Even many unsophisticated Christians without much theological training are rightly suspicious of the well-publicized, commercially supported message that the gospel offers us peace and comfort, that faith is the path to satisfying individual desires. The Way that led the early Christians to suffering and death seems hardly synonymous with personal well-being, peace, and comfort.

There is a place for peace and comfort in our lives. We need to be replenished periodically. We need to be supported in difficult times. We need to be reminded of the unconditional love of God for us. But these needs must be kept in tension with the call to love our neighbor, especially the preferential option for loving the needy neighbor. Our peace, comfort, and contentment should be sought within the common good, not at the cost of either causing or tolerating injustice to others. In terms of our sexuality, too, we need sources of support and sources of challenge. We know that intimate relationships play a major role in the process of self-creation and perfection, beginning from our earliest human interactions as infants and continuing throughout our adult lives.

The task of forging a Christian spirituality which can both do justice to the Incarnation and draw on human sexuality for the energy and vision to create and support just and loving communities remains equally challenging for Protestants and Catholics. After many centuries, it still remains tragically ironic that a religion which holds as its central belief that divinity became fully and humanly embodied and then endured bodily suffering even unto death in order to redeem all embodied human persons is, among world religions, perhaps the most ambivalent about the goodness of the human body, its development, its activities, and its appetites.

One important aspect of the Christian spiritual tradition which was negatively impacted by the ascetic dualism which prized the mind/soul and disdained the human body was the relationship of God and humanity. Instead of understanding Jesus Christ as the bridge connecting God and humanity, the dominant strains of Christian spirituality, influenced by dualism, adopted a docetic christology which has served to widen the gulf between Creator and created. A Jesus Christ understood as divine, as having human appearance but not substance, is compatible with the biblical depiction of the intimacy between Jesus and the Father. But the starting point of the Gospel writers and of the communities from which the Gospels emerged—that Jesus of Nazareth was, like them, fully human—is lost, and with it, the ability of Jesus' relation with God to serve as a model for other humans. The certainty of St. Paul that Jesus was the first to be resurrected, but not the last or only,[9] echoed in early creeds, has been lost.

The sexuality of humans has come to be understood as evidence of the inferior physicality—materiality—of humans compared to the spiritual being of God.[10] The materiality of humanity, which involves both temporality and mutability, has been crucial to the great power void understood to lie between the Creator and the created.[11] In the face of human powerlessness and ultimate lack of control over our very selves, humility in the face of the divine has been deemed appropriate. Humans are to be humble because we are less than both God and the angels, and some groups of humans—for example, women, children, and for much of the tradition, slaves—are to be especially humble because they are even less than other humans.

Much of our liturgical stress has focused on achieving proper human humility. It is not for nothing that we are reminded at funerals that "You are dust and unto dust you will return." Similarly, innumerable churchmen and theologians have taught us to pray in ways that insist on our utter worthlessness in the face of God's greatness. Some of the most popular hymns in Christian history magnify the greatness of God as one who exhausts goodness while imaging humanity as totally corrupt, powerless, and dependent. Many such liturgical manifestations of Christian spirituality are entirely appropriate. We humans *are* liable to sin, and we *do* experience graced moments of revelation in which we clearly recognize both the seriousness of the evil we knowingly choose and our own fallibility in recognizing good. In such moments, it is appropriate to be overwhelmed by the goodness and power of God which serve as resources for our own efforts at conversion. But two common aspects of the traditional treatment of humility are not appropriate: 1) rejecting or ignoring human dignity, and 2) condemning or discouraging human initiative.

Valerie Saiving (Goldstein)'s classic feminist essay "The Human Situation: A Feminine View," published in the *Journal of Religion* in 1960,[12] pointed out that Christian depictions of sin in terms of pride and ambition serve a useful moral purpose for males, whose gender socialization in the West predisposes them toward reaching out, doing, achieving, possessing, making their mark on the world. Religious warnings against pride and reminders of the social limits to ambition serve, in tension with gender socialization, to delineate the parameters of acceptable behavior, ruling out both irresponsible, dependent passivity and unbridled individual ambition at the expense of others. But the same Christian definition of sin only reinforces the messages of gender socialization for women. For women there is no creative tension between dependent and independent, between controlling others and abdicating responsibility for one's own life. Christian definitions of sin reinforce female socialization in pressing women toward irresponsible passivity and dependence.

Christian tradition within existing patriarchy has understood the God/human relationship in oppositional terms. If God is good and perfect, then humans are sinful; if God is all-powerful, humans are impotent; if God is creator, the most humans can legitimately hope to be is stewards. We have also been taught that God *polices* this unequal relationship.

When our tradition has referred to our God as a jealous God, it has not always referred to human temptations to worship other gods. Sometimes the reference has been to human aspirations to be like God. The tower of Babel (Babylon) story in Genesis 11:1 – 9 seems to parallel the message in the story of the Fall in Genesis 3: God is jealous of human attempts to "make a name for themselves"[13] or live forever[14]—attempts to be like God. Too much of our prayer over the centuries has been designed to appease an insecure, jealous God who resists sharing creativity and responsibility with humans, and desires instead confessions of worthlessness, professions of praise, sacrificial offerings, and abject obedience. It is this understanding of God as requiring a huge gulf between God and humans that has underlain myriad arguments against scientific exploration, intervention, and technology. For centuries we have heard not only atheists and agnostics engage in paeans to human science and technology as replacing the unlimited power and creativity of God, but, from far too many representatives of religion, also arguments that: "If God had wanted the races to mix, He wouldn't have separated them with oceans, mountains, and deserts," "If God had wanted humans to fly, He would have given them wings," "God made smallpox (or cholera or bubonic plague or AIDS) with a purpose; we should not attempt to interfere with immunizations or cures," or "Who do these scientists think they are, interfering in the way God distributed DNA to 'improve' the Creator's work?"

But our tradition also contains more positive descriptions of the divine will or relationship with humans. The God of the Israelites and of Jesus professes to be uninterested in sacrifice and praise from humans; God demands human faithfulness that takes the form of active justice, of caring for the weak and oppressed:

> I hate, I despise your festivals; I take no delight in your solemn assemblies. Even though you offer me your burnt offerings and grain offerings, I will not accept them; and the offerings of well-being of your fatted animals I will not look upon. Take away from me the noise of your songs, I will not listen to the melody of your harps. But let justice roll down like the waters, and righteousness like an overflowing stream. (Amos 5:21 – 24)

The God who deigns to wrestle with Jacob (Genesis 32: 22 – 31), to pass between the rocks so that Moses can view God safely (Exodus 33:12 – 23), and to debate with the stricken Job (Job 38:1ff) is not jealous of human creative power and responsibility, but rather is supportive of honest human attempts to understand and cooperate with God, to learn the limits and responsibility of humanity. It is into this latter strain that the Gospels fall, for the Good News of Jesus Christ was not a call to passively await God's action in history, but rather a call to accept responsibility for preparing self and world to cooperate with God's saving action in history. To be creative is not to coopt God's creativity; to make responsible decisions is not to reject the Creator's power and authority. Augustine is right that "our hearts are restless till they rest in thee, O Lord." But growing *toward* God inevitably entails also growing more *like* God. This is not a moral problem, but an experience of gift.

When the Yahwist creation story insists that humans were made in the image and likeness of God, it calls us to act in a divine manner: justly, lovingly, responsibly. Insistence that only God has dignity and worth raises obstacles to our own self-love, undermines our ability to believe in God's love for us as individuals, and accustoms us to view victimization of ourselves and others with callousness. The U.S. army officer who observed in Vietnam that "we had to destroy the village in order to save it" has been all too frequently paralleled in the churches by pastors and theologians who have counted as nothing massive human suffering inflicted in the name of God, in order to "save" the very persons injured. The many different liberation theologies from around the world which have begun to give voices to groups which have been theologically mute throughout most of history are making ever clearer that examples of spiritual riches which the tradition touts as achieved through acute suffering are unrepresentative and misleading.[15] The sufferings endured under poverty, enslavement, and subordination serve at least as often to create despair, cruelty, and death as they do to produce faith, courage, and love.

As North American Christians learn from the poor and victimized around the world and in our midst, we become more and more aware of the essential integrity of body experience and spirituality. As this awareness grows, we must become more critical of the insensitivity of our inherited tradition to the integrity of body experience and spirituality. Many elements of classical Christian spirituality are tainted by ascetic distortions of the God/human relationship which entered the tradition linked to valuable spiritual insights. For example, *The Confessions of St. Augustine* is perhaps the classic Christian conversion story. And yet in reading Augustine's account in the *Confessions* of the life and virtue of his mother, St. Monica, with whom he credits his own conversion, modern Christians feel something amiss:

> [W]hen she arrived at a marriageable age, she was given to a husband and served "him as her lord." (Eph. 5:21) She strove to win him to you, speaking to him about you through her conduct, by which you made her beautiful, an object of reverent love, and a source of admiration to her husband. She endured offenses against her marriage bed in such wise that she

never had a quarrel with her husband over this matter. She looked forward to seeing your mercy upon him, so that he would believe in you and be made chaste. But in addition to this, just as he was remarkable for his kindness, so was he given to violent anger. However, she had learned to avoid resisting her husband when he was angry, not only by deeds but even by words. When she saw that he had curbed his anger and become calm and that the time was opportune, then she explained what she had done, if he happened to be inadvertantly disturbed.

In fine, when many wives, who had better-tempered husbands but yet bore upon their faces signs of disgraceful beatings, in the course of friendly conversation criticized their husbands' conduct, she would blame it all on their tongues. Thus she would give them serious advice in the guise of a joke. From the time, she said, they heard what are termed marriage contracts read to them, they should regard those documents as legal documents making them slaves. Hence, being mindful of their condition, they should not rise up in pride against their lords. Women who knew what a sharp-tempered husband she had to put up with marveled that it was never reported or revealed by any sign that Patricius had beaten his wife or that they had differed with one another in a family quarrel, even for a single day. When they asked her confidentially why this was so, she told them of her policy, which I have described above. Those who acted upon it, found it to be good advice and were thankful for it; those who did not act upon it, were kept down and abused.[16]

In this account, Monica's virtue and wisdom are manifest in her voluntary acceptance of the status of slave, and they are not negated by her blaming victims of violence for their own victimization. How can this be reconciled with human dignity, with the fact that humans were made in the image and likeness of God's own self, or with the gospel of Jesus Christ? While no one should be blamed for acquiescing to violence against them, whether in order to avoid pain, injury, or death or to comply with belief in nonresistance to evil, neither should they be blamed for *naming* violent abuse as wrong.

Too often within our tradition we have interpreted Jesus of Nazareth as accepting with embodiedness the status of slave in order to save the human race.[17] This sacrifice on his part has then been interpreted to require that humans imitate that slave status,[18] as if that were the appropriate status of humans before the Lord. This has frequently been what we have meant by humility. But the life of Jesus is not the life of a slave. It was, in fact, his claiming of power and authority which served to antagonize the organized groups in his society to kill him. Jesus gathered around himself a group of followers who were phenomenally successful in spreading his gospel precisely because he mediated to them so well the presence of the Divine One whom they all sought. While attempts to replace that Divine One with alternatives of our own conjuring is rightly condemned, we should attempt to become holy, as God in heaven is holy. Paul was right to teach: "Be imitators of God, as beloved children." True Christian humility is not abasing ourselves in denying our own dignity, but learning to live with accurate recognition of our true achievements and faults—that is, in learning to share God's view of us. Paul wrote:

> For if those who are nothing think they are something, they deceive themselves. All must test their own work, then that work, rather than their neighbor's work, will become a cause for pride. (Gal. 6:3 – 4)

It would be wrong to interpret Paul to mean that all persons are as nothing. Paul himself spends a great deal of time and effort in the Epistles wrestling with temptations both to claim no achievements for himself, and to claim full responsibility for the successes in which he has had a role. He struggles to understand how he can be both dependent upon God's grace in all, and yet responsible for his own actions.[19] Similarly, in comparison to the other apostles, Paul wants to both acknowledge that they are all co-workers in the same historical project, and defend himself against slights by citing his own efforts and sufferings. This struggle in Paul is paradigmatic. We are all called to true humility: an accurate understanding of our relationship to God and others. We are called to recognize the many ways that each of us is both inseparable from God and others and dependent upon them for that which we lack. At the same time, we are called to recognize the talents entrusted to us, and develop and use them so that we become cocreators with God, sustaining and expanding God's providence for others. False humility, grounded in negative assessments of human embodiment, serves as an excuse for sloth and irresponsibility. We are the children of God, just as we are the children of our parents. Being children of God does not mandate our remaining minors. That God our divine parent does not grow old and therefore more dependent, like human parents, is no excuse for us to remain permanent children.

We are not faced with a choice of becoming adults and putting God aside, or remaining minors forever. It is possible to be an adult and still be faithful to a parent, still offer the respect and honor due a good parent, and still carry forward joint projects with that parent. In fact, with God, as with our human parents, we often discover that disowning them is more easily said than done, for God and human parents live within our very selves because we take on the traits of those we have loved.

Contemporary Christians are creating new forms of spirituality based in reflection on embodied human experience. Forms of spirituality always reflect the particular historical situation in which they arise. For example, it is not suprising that, in the aftermath of the massive social, political, economic, and technological changes which came together in the 1960s and 1970s, spiritual attention turned to individual needs for peace, comfort, and personal security as realized in the search for therapeutic well-being. At the same time, there are much larger, longer-lived trends in spirituality, as in history in general. Until the twentieth century, Christianity and much of the Western world in general have demonstrated for nearly 2,000 years an otherworldly, ascetic spirituality in which materiality, and especially sexuality, were suspicious, if not actually sinful. Present inroads on that tradition insist that: 1) bodily experience can reveal the divine, 2) affectivity is as essential as rationality to true Christian love, 3) Christian love exists not to bind autonomous selves, but as the proper form

n between beings who become human persons in
4) the experience of body pleasure is important in
ability to trust and love others, including God. But it
clear whether our own age will turn out to be the
pivo... nt at which Christian spirituality transforms itself by
wholeheartedly embracing the body and materiality, or whether
our age is more of a historical blip, such as the Renaissance, in
which antimaterialist asceticism is briefly arrested.

Endnotes

Chapter 1

1. In the present, see John Paul II, general audience of October 8, 1980; for earlier historical examples, see Uta Ranke-Heinemann, *Eunuchs for the Kingdom of Heaven: Women, Sexuality, and the Roman Catholic Church* (1988 German edition, tr. Peter Heinegg; New York: Doubleday, 1990), Chapter 10.

2. Augustine, *De Trinitate*, 7:7, 10; Rosemary R. Ruether, "Virginal Feminism in the Fathers of the Church," in *Religion and Sexism*, ed. Rosemary R. Ruether (New York: Simon and Schuster, 1984).

3. See, for example, Lev. 19:20-22, Lev. 21:10-21, Deut. 22:28-29, Ex. 21:4-11, Ex. 4:22.

4. Luther, *Lectures on Genesis*: Gen. 3:16, *Luther's Works*, vol. I, ed. J. Pelikan (St. Louis: Concordia, 1958), 202.

5. Thomas Aquinas, *Summa Theologiae* 1:92:1 ad 1 (New York: McGraw-Hill, 1964), vol. 13, 35-39.

6. William Masters and Virginia Johnson, *Human Sexual Response* (Boston: Little, Brown, 1966) and *Human Sexual Inadequacy* (Boston: Little, Brown, 1970); Alan Bell and Martin Weinberg, *Homosexualities: A Study of Diversity Among Men and Women* (New York: Simon and Schuster, 1978); Alan Bell, Martin Weinberg, and S. Hammersmith, *Sexual Preference: Its Development in Men and Women* (Bloomington, IN: Indiana University Press, 1981).

7. J. Kestenberg, "Orgasm in Prepubertal Children," *Medical Aspects of Human Sexuality* 13, no. 7 (1979): 92-93.

8. M. Levitan and A. Montagu, *A Textbook of Human Genetics*, 2d ed. (New York: Oxford, 1977).

9. For example, see Margaret Mead, *Sex and Temperament in Three Primitive Societies* (New York: Morrow, 1963).

10. Lisa Sowle Cahill, *Between the Sexes: Foundations for a Christian Ethics of Sexuality* (Philadelphia: Fortress and Paulist, 1985), 5.

11. Elisabeth Schüssler Fiorenza, *In Memory of Her: A Feminist Theological Reconstruction of Christian Origins* (New York: Crossroad, 1983), xviii-xix.

12. Elisabeth Schüssler Fiorenza, "Contemporay Biblical Scholarship: Its Roots, Present Understandings, and Future Directions," in Francis A. Eigo, O.S.A., ed., *Modern Biblical Scholarship: Its Impact on Theology and Proclamation* (Villanova, PA: Villanova Press, 1984), 21-22.

13. Marie Fortune, *Sexual Violence: The Unmentionable Sin* (New York: Pilgrim, 1983), 48-53.

14. Ibid., 54-55.

15. Ibid., 54-56; Florence Rush, *The Best Kept Secret* (Englewood Cliffs, NJ: Prentice-Hall, 1980), 17.

16. Judges 11:30-40.

17. Schüssler-Fiorenza, *In Memory of Her*, 29-30.

18. James Nelson, *Between Two Gardens: Reflections on Sexuality and Religious Experience* (New York: Pilgrim, 1985), 18-20.

19. Hugo Echegaray, *The Practice of Jesus* (Maryknoll, NY: Orbis, 1984), 29-30, 81-82, 84-85, 94-95.

20. Acts of the Apostles 11:1-18.

21. John XXIII, "*Notre joie est grande*," October 20, 1960, *Actae Apostolicae Sedis* 52 (1960): 897.

22. Mt. 11:18-19; Mk. 2:18-22.

23. Vincent Genovesi, S.J., *In Pursuit of Love: Catholic Morality and Human Sexuality* (Wilmington, DE: Michael Glazier, 1987), 154-155; Philip Keane, S.S., *Sexual Morality: A Catholic View* (New York: Paulist, 1977), 98; John Shelby Spong, *Living in Sin? A Bishop Rethinks Human Sexuality* (San Francisco: Harper and Row, 1988), 45-46.

24. Those few include James Nelson's *Embodiment: An Approach to Sexuality and Christian Theology* (Minneapolis: Augsburg, 1978) and his *The Intimate Connection: Male Sexuality, Masculine Spirituality* (Philadelphia: Westminster, 1988) and Andre Guindon, *The Sexual Creators: An Ethical Proposal for Concerned Christians* (Lanham, MD: University Press of America, 1986).

25. See, for example, Spong, Keane, and Genovesi, above, as well as Andre Guindon's *The Sexual Language: An Essay in Moral Theology* (Ottawa: University of Ottawa Press, 1977).

26. For example, Vincent Genovesi's *In Pursuit of Love: Catholic Morality and Human Sexuality* divides into two halves. The first half consists of chapters on Christian living, conscience and the magis-

terium, theology of sin, and human sexuality. The organization of the second half is traditional, and revolves around the traditional sins: premarital sexuality, contraception, homosexuality, masturbation, and abortion. The first quarter of Phillip Keane's *Sexual Morality: A Catholic Morality* is devoted to theological anthropology, the changing role of women, and an· overview of relevant traditional moral themes; the rest of the book is organized into chapters around masturbation, homosexuality, the limitation of sex to marriage and the limitations on sex within marriage, celibacy, the 1975 Vatican document on sexual ethics, and a chapter on "other sexual issues" which includes critical treatment of traditional moral maxims, new sexual technology, and sexual offenses (abuse). Gennaro Avvento's *Sexuality: A Christian View* (Mystic, CT: Twenty-Third Publications, 1982) spends four chapters on developing secular and Christian views of sexuality, the development of conscience, and "The Emerging Woman" before devoting the remaining 12 chapters to contraception (4 chapters), sterilization, masturbation, artificial insemination, sex for singles, extramarital sex, homosexuality, and abortion. Helmut Thielicke's *The Ethics of Sex* (Grand Rapids: Baker, 1964), though older than any of the above and thus unable to draw on the extensive secular literature on sexuality since 1964, is nevertheless less organized around traditional Christian sexual sins than any of the above. It does, however, draw the most rigid distinctions between men and women. Thielicke devotes only one-third to treatment of birth control, abortion, homosexuality, and artificial insemination, and two-thirds to biblical anthropology, eros and agape, the plasticity of human sexual behavior, a historical survey of Christian treatments of marriage, and the contemporary shift toward equality of the sexes. Is this the result of differences in Catholic and Protestant treatment of sexuality? Perhaps. The Anthony Kosnick, et al., *Human Sexuality: New Directions in American Catholic Thought* (New York: Paulist, 1977), which was commissioned by the Catholic Theological Society of America, follows Thielicke in outline—it is not until the fifth and final chapter that the book takes up the traditional sexual sins. But that final chapter begins on page 99 and ends on page 239! The point here is that it is very difficult to break the historical conditioning that makes us organize our thinking about sexual ethics around traditional sexual sins, even when we no longer understand some of them as serious or perhaps even sinful.

27. T. Langfeldt, "Childhood Masturbation: Individual and Social Organization," in L. L. Constantine and F. M. Martinson, eds., *Children and Sex* (Boston: Little, Brown, 1981).

28. R. A. Spitz, *Autoeroticism: Some Empirical Findings and Hypotheses (on three of its manifestations in the first year of life)*, vol. 3/4, *The Psychoanalytic Life of the Child* (New York: International Universities Press, 1949). Still the authoritative work.

29. Shere Hite, *The Hite Report* (New York: Dell, 1977), 73-78; John Money and C. Bohmer, "Prison Sexology: Two Personal Accounts of Masturbation, *Journal of Sex Research* 16 (1980): 258-266. In addition, masturbation is a central feature of most sex therapy programs, e.g., Helen S. Kaplan, *The New Sex Therapy* (New York: Bruner-Mazell, 1974) and *How to Overcome Premature Ejaculation* (New York: Bruner-Mazell, 1989); and J. R. Heiman and J. Lo Piccolo, *Becoming Orgasmic: A Sexual and Personal Growth Program for Women,* rev. ed. (Englewood Cliffs, NJ: Prentice-Hall, 1988).

30. F. L. Whitam, "The Homosexual Role: A Reconsideration," *Journal of Sexual Research* 13 (1977): 1-11; C. Silverstein, *Man to Man: Gay Couples in America* (New York: William Morrow, 1981), 102-103; and A. Bell, M. Weinberg, and S. Hammersmith, *Sexual Preference: Its Development in Men and Women* (Bloomington, IN: Indiana University Press, 1981), 186-190.

31. See, for example, the Medellin document on peace (by Gustavo Gutierrez) in *Renewing the Earth: Catholic Documents of Peace, Justice, and Liberation,* eds., David J. O'Brien and Thomas A. Shannon (New York: Doubleday, 1977).

32. One of the earliest and best-developed explanations was that of Piet Schoonenberg, S.J., *Man* (sic) *and Sin,* trans. J. Donceel (Notre Dame, IN: University of Notre Dame Press, 1965), 4-5.

33. Heterosexism is a characteristic of Western societies, in which law and public policy assume that all persons are naturally heterosexual, and are oriented to marriage and children. These assumptions are reflected in laws and policy about what persons are considered to be the "natural" guardians of the incompetent sick, who has visiting rights in institutions, who are considered heirs for the intestate, who can file joint income taxes, who can be claimed as dependents, etc. Homophobia, while closely related, is usually understood as fear and hatred of gays and lesbians by individuals and groups of individuals.

34. Diana Russell, *Rape in Marriage* (Riverside, NJ: Doubleday, 1982).

35. C. Safran, "What Men Do to Women on the Job: A Shocking Look at Sexual Harassment," *Redbook* (November 1976): 148ff (88% victimization rate); L. Ploy and L. Stewart, "The Extent and Effects of the Sexual Harassment of Working Women," *Sociological Focus* 17 (1984): 31-43 (50% victimization rate); A. Grieco, "The Scope and Nature of Sexual Harassment in Nursing," *Journal of Sex Research* 23 (1987): 261-266 (82% victimization rate).

36. Diana E. H. Russell, *The Secret Trauma: Incest in the Lives of Girls and Women* (New York: Basic Books, 1986), 216.

37. Russell, *Secret Trauma* (38% of the women who had not been victims of child incest had suffered rape or attempted rape as adults, compared to 68% of those who had been victims of child incest); F. Mims and A. Chang, "Unwanted Sexual Experiences of Young Women," *Psychosocial Nursing* 22 (1984): 7-14 (50% were victims of rape or attempted rape); P. DeVast et al., "The Presence of Sexually Stressful Events Among Females in the General Population," *Archives of Sexual Behavior* 13 (1984): 59-67 (24% victims of rape or attempted rape); L. Koss et al., "The Scope of Rape: Incidence and Prevalence of Sexual Aggression and Victimization in a National Sample of Higher Education Students," *Journal of Consulting and Clinical Psychology* 55 (1987): 162-170 (15% raped, 25% more victims of unwanted sexual intercourse); S. Feldman-Summer and G. Norris, "Differences Between Rape Victims Who Report and Those Who Do Not Report to a Public Agency," *Journal of Applied Psychology* 14 (1984): 562-573 (50% victims of rape or attempted rape).

38. Margaret Heckler, U.S. Secretary of Health and Human Services, Spring 1985 *Report on Child Sexual Abuse* (1 in 4 girls, 1 in 9 boys sexually abused); Russell, *Secret Trauma* (28% of girls under 14 sexually abused); Gail Wyatt, "The Sexual Abuse of Afro-American and White Women in Childhood," *Child Abuse and Neglect: The International Journal* 9 (1985): 507-519 (36% of girls under 14 sexually abused).

39. October 1989 survey reported September 6, 1990, *Cincinnati Enquirer,* A6, "Misconceptions About Sex Abound, Survey Shows."

40. Krista Ramsey, "Ohio Lacks Required Sex Curricula," *Cincinnati Enquirer,* Sunday, January 19, 1992, A1. In this investigative story, Douglas Kirby, director of research for California-based Educational Training and Research Inc., describes the typical U.S. sex education program as an "organ recital" method. In junior high there are several days spent on learning the names and functions of various

biological parts, a few classes on body changes at puberty, and brief discussions on STDs and contraception. In most districts, high school sex education consists of a half-year health course in which only 12 – 18 hours (two to three weeks) are related to sexuality, and those deal with reproduction only. Most states have no state law requiring sex education. Kentucky in 1990 *repealed* its law requiring all districts to teach some sex education.

41. P. S. Reichelt, "Public Policy and Public Opinion Toward Sex Education and Birth Control for Teenagers," *Journal of Applied Social Psychology* 16 (1986): 95-106; E. R. Mahoney, "Sex Education in the Public Schools: A Discriminant Analysis of Characteristics of Pro- and Anti-Individuals," *Journal of Sex Research* 15 (1979): 264-275.

42. P. Scales and D. Kirby, "Perceived Barriers to Sex Education: A Survey of Professionals," *Journal of Sex Research* 19 (1983): 309-326.

43. Ibid.

44. F. Sonenstein and K. Pittman, "The Availability of Sex Education in Large City School Districts," *Family Planning Perspectives* 16 (1984): 1, 19-25.

45. S. Spencer and A. Zeiss, in "Sex Roles and Sexual Dysfunctions in College Students" (*Journal of Sex Research* 23 (1987): 338-347), showed only 13% of university students report sexual dysfunctions. But other statistics indicate the problem is greater: C. A. Darling and J. K. Davidson in "Enhancing Relationships: Understanding the Feminine Mystique of Pretending Orgasm" (*Journal of Sex and Marital Therapy* 12 (1986): 182-196), report that 66% of women and 33% of men report faking orgasm; Crooks and Baur report premature ejaculation rates among university students at 50% occasionally, and another 25% regularly (*Our Sexuality*, 159); the table of J. Ende et al. (1984) in Crooks and Baur, *Our Sexuality*, 553, shows 25% of women report anorgasmia during routine sexual histories by physicians.

46. J. Ende et al., 1984, table in Crooks and Baur, *Our Sexuality*, 553.

47. J. Annon, *The Behavioral Treatment of Sexual Problems,* vol. 1 (Honolulu: Enabling Systems, 1974).

48. Kaplan, *The New Sex Therapy*, 289; Masters and Johnson, *Human Sexual Inadequacy,* 95-96.

49. Crooks and Baur, *Our Sexuality,* 556.

50. Ibid.

51. Charles Gallagher et al., *Embodied in Love: Sacramental Spirituality and Sexual Intimacy* (New York: Crossroad, 1986), 32-35.

52. G. Fox, "The Family's Role in Adolescent Sexual Behavior," in T. Ooms, ed., *Teenage Pregnancy in a Family Context* (Philadelphia: Temple University Press, 1981); G. Sanders and R. Mullis, "Family Influences on Sexual Attitudes and Knowledge as Reported by College Students," *Adolescence* 23 (1988), 837-846.

53. James T. Sears, "Dilemmas and Possibilities of Sexuality Education: Reproducing the Body Politic," in *Sexuality and the Curriculum: The Politics and Practices of Sexuality Education*, James T. Sears, ed. (New York: Columbia Teachers College Press, 1992), 10; A. Kenney, S. Guardado, and L. Brown, "Sex Education in the Schools: What States and Large School Districts Are Doing," *Family Planning Perspectives* 21 (1989): 2:59.

54. D. Haffner, *Sex Education 2000: A Call to Action* (New York: SIECUS, 1990).

55. See Kenney et al., "Sex Education and AIDS Education," *Family Planning Perspectives* 21 (1989): 2:61.

56. Ibid.

57. See the Quebec Conference of Bishops, Social Affairs Committee, "Heritage of Violence: A Pastoral Reflection on Conjugal Violence," translated by Antoinette Kinlough (Montreal: L'Assemblée des les Éveques du Quebec, 1989), sections 3.1.2, 3.4.3, and 3.4.5, which incorporates a critique of the understanding of women as made for motherhood, and therefore as objects to be used, of less worth and dignity than men.

58. Norman Pittenger, *Making Sexuality Human* (Philadelphia: Pilgrim Press, 1970), 9.

59. Albert Jonsen and Stephen Toulmin, *The Abuse of Casuistry* (Berkeley: University of California Press, 1988), Chapter 16ff.

60. Nelson, *Intimate Connection*, Chapter Four and 105-111; Nelson, *Between Two Gardens*, Chapters Two and Twelve.

61. Gallagher et al., *Embodied in Love*, Chapter One (and throughout).

Chapter 2

1. Alan Bell and Martin Weinberg, *Homosexualities: A Study of Diversity Among Men and Women* (New York: Simon and Schuster, 1978), 328-330. Since the impact of AIDS, anal intercourse is even less common.

2. In Hunt's 1974 survey, only 2% of lesbians had ever used a dildo. Morton Hunt, *Sexual Behavior in the 1970s* (Chicago: Playboy Press, 1974), 318-319.

3. S. Daniels, "Critical Issues in Sexuality and Disability," in D. Bullard and S. Knight, eds., *Sexuality and Physical Disability: Personal Perspectives* (St. Louis, MO: Mosby, 1981).

4. S. Lieblum and R. T. Seagraves, "Sex Therapy with Aging Adults," in S. Lieblum and R. Rosen, eds., *Principles and Practice of Sex Therapy* (New York: Guilford, 1989).

5. E. Jones, J. Forrest, N. Goldman, S. Henshaw, R. Lincoln, J. Rosoff, C. Westoff, and D. Wulf, "Teenage Pregnancy in Developed Countries: Determinants and Policy Implications," *Family Planning Perspectives* 17 (1985): 53-63.

6. William Masters and Virginia Johnson, *Human Sexual Response* (Boston: Little, Brown, 1966), 66; Shere Hite, *The Hite Report: A Nationwide Study of Female Sexuality* (New York: Dell, 1976), 190.

7. A. Kinsey, W. Pomeroy, C. Martin, and P. Gebhard, *Sexual Behavior in the Human Female* (Philadelphia: Saunders, 1953), 163-164, 391.

8. Helen Singer Kaplan, *The New Sex Therapy: Active Treatment of Sexual Dysfunction* (New York: Brunner/Mazel, 1974), 397; Carol Tavris and Susan Sadd, *The Redbook Report on Female Sexuality* (New York: Delacorte Press, 1975), 74-80; C. Ellison, "A Critique of the Clitoral Model of Female Sexuality," paper presented to the American Psychological Association, Montreal, September 4, 1980.

9. For example, in an interview of David Wells, major Canadian pornography publisher, in the documentary "Not a Love Story," Wells presents as well-known market research the conclusion that "what all men want most—the greatest male turn-on—is to have a naked woman kneeling at his feet, performing fellatio." While the universalism of this statement is certainly suspicious, to the extent that a great deal of erotic fantasy seems rooted in adolescent desires, it is probably true that many men never completely outgrow adolescent forms of sexual desires.

10. David Sue, "Erotic Fantasies of College Students During Coitus," *Journal of Sex Research* 15 (1974): 299-305.

11. C. D. Bryant and C. E. Palmer, "Massage Parlors and 'Hand Whores': Some Sociological Observations," *Journal of Sex Research* 11 (1975): 227-241; E. G. Armstrong, "Massage Parlors and Their Customers," *Archives of Sexual Behavior* 7 (1978): 117-125.

12. The official Roman Catholic position is that the physically unitive aspect and the reproductive aspect of sexual activity cannot be intentionally separated—which rules out both artificial contracep-

tion and in vitro fertilization (Paul VI, *Humanae Vitae*, #12, *Actae Apostolicae Sedis* 60 (1968): 488-489).

13. I heard Frances Kissling, director of Catholics for a Free Choice, present this three-stage schema at the "North/South Dialogue: Reflections on Religion, Ethics, and ·Reproduction" in Mexico City, December 1992.

14. For a review of the critique of developmentalism, see Ronald H. Chilcote, "A Critical Synthesis of the Dependency Literature," *Latin American Perspectives* 1 (1974): 4-29.

15. The bulk of Betsy Hartman's *Reproductive Rights and Wrongs: The Global Politics of Population Control and Reproductive Choice* (New York: Harper and Row, 1987) is devoted to detailing these abuses. In Indonesia, for example, Hartman describes how the local level of male hierarchy (village headmen) is utilized by government officials to pressure villagers into compliance with population control programs. In return the headmen are rewarded with personal honors and gifts, as well as with rewards for the village, such as access to agricultural credit (pp. 74-83).

16. Susan Power Bratton, *Six Billion and More: Human Population Regulation and Christian Ethics* (Louisville, KY: Westminster, 1992), 25, 182; also see Hartman's treatment of the use of the military to force sterilizations in Bangladesh in 1983, and of the sterilization requirement for receiving emergency food after the 1984 floods in the same country (Hartman, *Reproductive Rights and Wrongs*, 214-217).

17. For example, Phillip Berryman quotes two regional groups of Brazilian Catholic bishops which issued statements in May 1973 using government statistics to point out the redistribution of wealth upward in Brazil over the preceding years of developmentalism. Phillip Berryman, *Liberation Theology* (New York: Pantheon, 1987), 123.

18. For example, Mexico was a leading example of developmentalism at work for well over a decade, with annual growth rates of GNP of 7 – 10%. Yet in August 1982, Mexico was the first of the developing nations to declare its inability to make debt payments. Brazil, which led the world in GNP growth for over a decade, suspended payment of its debt in January 1983. This was only the beginning of the debt explosion—for the suspension of interest payments led to the rapid rise in the amount of principal due, as overdue interest was added to principal. Penny Lernoux, *In Banks We Trust* (New York: Doubleday, 1984): 226-227.

19. Lernoux, *In Banks We Trust,* 229.
20. After more than a decade of recognition that the debt burdens of many poor nations were impossible to pay off, even if the mass of the population were plunged into the most abject poverty possible for decades into the future, First World nations began during the early 1990s a nation-by-nation process of debt renegotiation. Options exercised by the lender nations included a combination of debt forgiveness, swap for debt, and more lenient scheduling of debt repayment designed to free up governments of developing countries. The Craxi proposal, named for Benito Craxi, whom U.N. Secretary Peres de Cuellar had appointed in December 1989 his personal debt representative, presented the U.N. General Assembly with a strengthened and updated version of the U.S. Brady Initiative. That Brady Initiative had already reduced the commercial debt of some severely indebted middle-income countries by 1991, according to the World Bank's report on debt, *World Debt Tables: 1990-1991,* released in February 1991. The nation-by-nation process of renegotiating (forgiving/swapping/extending terms on) external public debt under this Craxi/Brady plan began in 1991, but the results are as yet unclear. "Future of the Global Economy: Challenges of the 90's" and "Debt: An Issue of Responsibility," in *U.N. Chronicle* (September 1990): 41-46, 53; "Development Strategy for the 1990's Aims to Reverse Economic and Social Decline," *U.N. Chronicle* (March 1991): 85-86.
21. Alexandra Toufexis, "Too Many Mouths: The Problem—Swarms of People Are Running Out of Food, Space," *Time* (January 7, 1989): 48-50.
22. M. Potts, "The Challenge of the 1990's," *IPPF Medical Bulletin* 25 (1991): 1-4.
23. E. Diczfalusy, "Contraceptive Prevalence, Reproductive Health, and International Morality," *American Journal of Obstetrics and Gynecology* 166 (1992): 1037-1043.
24. See, for example, Dom Moraes' *A Matter of People* (New York: Praeger, 1974), which surveys a number of individuals of various professions in the developing nations regarding population control programs funded by developed nations.
25. Ten percent of all plant species are found in the Amazon. Half the 4.5 million plant and animal species on the earth occur only in rain forests of which the Amazon is the largest. James Lockman, "Reflections on the Exploitation of the Amazon," in Carol S. Robb

and Carl J. Casebolt, eds., *Covenant for a New Creation: Ethics, Religion, and Public Policy* (Maryknoll, NY: Orbis, 1991): 167-169.

26. Bratton, *Six Billion and More*, 21.

27. See Hartman, *Population Rights and Wrongs*, in note 15.

28. At the 1974 United Nations-sponsored International Conference on Population in Bucharest, the United States' anti-natalist position was strongly attacked by representatives of many poor nations on the grounds that economic development would bring about fertility decline by itself. They insisted that, instead of urging population control measures, the U.S. should be pursuing capital and technology transfers to the poor nations (Jane Menken, ed., *World Population and U.S. Policy: The Choices Ahead* [New York: W. W. Norton and Co., 1986], 8). The Reagan administration, in its opposition to abortion, came to restrict the distribution of any U.S. funds to any organization or institution which provided, recommended, or offered information about abortion. This restriction, continued by the Bush administration, crippled many population control programs in developing nations, far beyond the reach of abortion provision, in that it refused funding to any agency or program that provided, advised, or educated about abortion directly or indirectly. With the 1993 end of that restriction by the Clinton administration, it will now be necessary to monitor population programs for such abuses much more strictly.

29. Bratton, *Six Billion and More*, 176-181.

30. Beginning with ecologist Paul Ehrlich's *The Population Bomb* (New York: Ballantine, 1968).

31. John B. Cobb and Herman E. Daly, *For the Common Good: Redirecting the Economy Toward Community, the Environment, and a Sustainable Future* (New York: Simon and Schuster, 1987), 252-256.

32. Cobb and Daly, *For the Common Good*, 1-2.

33. Christoph E. Buechtemann and Juergen Schupp, "Repercussions of Reunification: Patterns and Trends in the Socio-economic Transformation of East Germany," *Industrial Relations Journal* 73 (Summer 1992): 7, 90ff; Alistair Horne, "No Three Cheers," *National Review* 44 (February 17, 1992): 3, 76-77, Peter Lee, "The Dream Becomes a Nightmare," *Euromoney* (February 1992): 44-48; William S. Ellis, Gerd Ludwig, and Steve McCurry, "The Morning After: Germany Reunited, *National Geographic* 180 (September 1991): 3, 2ff.

34. Andrea Cezeaux, "East Meets West to Look for Toxic Waste Sites," *Science* 251, no. 4994 (February 8, 1991): 67-73; "East Germany

Closes Toxic Waste Dumps," *European Chemical News* 54, no. 1408 (February 5, 1990): 28.

35. On poor nations as dumping grounds: Joel Millman, "Exporting Hazardous Waste," *Technology Review* 92 (April 1989): 3, 6ff; Debora McKenzie and Roger Milne, "If You Can't Treat It, Ship It," *New Scientist* 122, no. 1658 (April 1, 1989): 24-25; "Angola: An Offer Luanda Just Can't Refuse?" *Africa Report* 34 (March-April 1989): 2, 5. On poor neighborhoods as dumping grounds: Gary Boulard, "Combatting Environmental Racism," *The Christian Science Monitor,* March 17, 1993, p. 8, col. 7; Eugene I. Meyer, "Environmental Racism: Why Is It Always Dumped in Our Backyard?" *Audubon* 94 (January-February 1992): 1, 30-32.

36. As of this writing the latest major incident is the May 29, 1993, deaths of 5 Turkish children and the injury to three other members of the same family in a racially motivated attempt to burn them out of their home in Solingen, Germany (in western, not eastern Germany).

37. See Daniel Callahan, *Setting Limits: Medical Goals in An Aging Society* (New York: Simon and Schuster, 1987), who argues this, but goes on to demand that the aged, as both a powerful political bloc and the most privileged recipients of health care, must be persuaded to accept limitations on their access to health care in order to control costs and spread the benefits more equitably. Callahan sees this as a difficult task, and his book is the first step in beginning the social dialogue required in order to reach any sort of consensus.

38. This was for many years the defense used by the Catholic church to demographic criticisms of church opposition to artificial birth control. See John XXIII, *Mater et Magistra,* #193 and 198-199, and Paul VI, *Humanae Vitae,* #23, in Joseph Gremillion, ed., *The Gospel of Peace and Justice: Catholic Social Teaching Since Pope John* (Maryknoll, NY: Orbis, 1976).

39. Julian Simon, *The Ultimate Resource* (Princeton, NJ: Princeton University Press, 1981), 221-22.

40. Jerrie DeHoogh et al., "Food for a Growing World Population," *Technological Forecasting and Social Change* 10 (1977): 1, 31.

41. Cobb and Daly, *For the Common Good,* 2.

42. Werner Fornos, *Gaining People, Losing Ground* (Washington, DC: Population Institute, 1987).

43. There are a number of sources documenting these groups' lack of interest in promoting alternative energy sources, as well as a simi-

lar lack of interest from groups in the nuclear energy field. Among them: John M. Blair, *The Control of Oil* (New York: Pantheon, 1976); John Gever, Robert Kaufmann, David Skole, and Charles Vorosmarty, *Beyond Oil* (Cambridge, MA: Ballinger, 1987); Richard Munson, *The Energy Switch: Alternatives to Nuclear Power* (Cambridge: Union of Concerned Scientists, 1987).

44. In my local *Cincinnati Enquirer* over the last two weeks, there has been a steady stream of articles about the reservations in first the House and then the Senate regarding the budget bill in general, and most specifically about the energy tax: "House vote a vote of confidence: Reluctant Democrats expected to come through on energy tax," *Cincinnati Enquirer,* May 23, 1993, p. A1; "Arms Twist, tempers boil over the tax bill," *Cincinnati Enquirer,* May 27, 1993, p. A1; "Clinton's budget squeaks through," *Cincinnati Enquirer,* May 28, 1993, p. A1; Carl M. Cannon and Karen Hosler, "Hinting at Compromise: Clinton may give a bit on energy tax," *Cincinnati Enquirer,* May 29, 1993, p. A1; Steven Greenhouse, "Industries May Avoid BTU taxes," *Cincinnati Enquirer,* May 30, 1993, A1.

45. Bratton, *Six Billion and More,* 74.

46. Bratton both recounts incidence of late marriage in earlier epochs and gives the modern example of Sri Lanka. In that nation development efforts have created a situation in which the average age of female marriage is 25, infant mortality is severely decreased, literacy greatly increased, and almost as many girls as boys are educated—all relatively rare in poor nations. Bratton, *Six Billion and More,* 35.

47. Jill Armstrong and Eduard Bos, "The Demographic, Economic, and Social Impact of AIDS," in Jonathon Mann et al., eds., *AIDS in the World: A Global Report* (Cambridge, MA: Harvard University Press, 1992), 202-204.

48. Ethiopian social planner Maaza Bekele asserts that "It . . . seems unrealistic to expect that poverty-stricken, hard-working African mothers—many close to death before the age of 35—can be expected to limit the number of their children when only one out of three or four survive. . . . [These women] cannot run the risk that their major creative contribution to humanity (given that the rest of their life is pure drudgery) will be denied them. In each woman is the grain of hope that life for her offspring will be better than hers." The Hunger Project, *Ending Hunger: An Idea Whose Time Has Come* (New York: Praeger, 1985), 86.

49. In China, for instance, the recent opening to adoption of Chinese infants by Westerners has demonstrated how the one-child policy combined with the social preference for sons over daughters has produced hundreds of thousands of abandoned girl babies, and stories of rural infanticide. Some have suggested that the fact that all the abandoned adoptable children are girls may account for the new willingness of the Chinese government to allow non-Chinese to adopt Chinese babies. It is not known to what extent this willingness of Chinese couples to abandon girls in attempts to try again for a son will affect the balance of the sexes in China, and census figures on sex ratios since 1990 are not available. However, in India, where a similar preference for sons over daughters is implemented apart from official population control policy under the impetus of poverty and the availability of sonagrams and selective abortion, the 1991 census revealed a shortage of over 22 million girls over the expected number, and a sex ratio of only 929 women for every 1000 men. (William Stief, "India's Endangered Women," *The Progressive*, 56:8 (August 1992): 43; Rhona Mahoney, "On the Trail of the World's 'Missing Women,'" *Ms.*, 2:5 (March-April 1992): 12; Bhupesh Mangla, "India: Missing Women," *The Lancet*, 131:1780 (September 14, 1991): 10; Bruce Porter, "China's Market in Orphan Girls," *The New York Times Magazine*, April 11, 1993.) 1984 floods in the same country. (Hartman, *Reproductive Rights and Wrongs*, 214-217.)

Chapter 3

1. N. MacLufsky and F. Naftolin, "Sexual Differentiation of the Central Nervous System," *Science*, 211 (1981): 1294-1303.
2. For example, E. Macoby and C. Jacklin's study of research on sex differentiation, *The Psychology of Sex Differences* (Stanford, CA: Stanford University Press, 1974), noted that females tend to associate in smaller groups than males and to have much less clear and rigid dominance hierarchies than males (Chapter 6, especially pp. 225-226).
3. Laurie Arliss, *Gender Communication* (Englewood Cliffs, NJ: Prentice-Hall, 1991), Chapter 12, "Women at Work," especially p. 171; Rita Mae Kelly, *The Gendered Economy: Work, Careers, and Success* (Newberry Park, CA: Sage, 1991), Chapter Three, "Women, the Economy, and Careers."
4. Kelly, *The Gendered Economy*, 83; Kinsey and subsequent researchers, for example, found significant differences in rates of

male and female masturbation: for boys 21% of 12-year-olds, and 82% of 15-year-olds; for girls 12% at 12 years, and 20% at 15 years old. Alfred Kinsey et al., *Sexual Behavior in the Human Male* (Philadelphia: Saunders, 1948); and *Sexual Behavior in the Human Female* (Philadelphia: Saunders, 1953).

5. Arliss, *Gender Communication*, 103; Mácoby and Jacklin, *The Psychology of Sex Differences*, 274.

6. Kelly, *The Gendered Economy*, 86-92, 188-192; Arliss, *Gender Communication*, 208-209.

7. See the Introduction and Chapter One of Elisabeth Schüssler Fiorenza, *In Memory of Her: A Feminist Theological Reconstruction of Christian Origins* (New York: Crossroad, 1983).

8. John Shelby Spong, *Living In Sin? A Bishop Rethinks Human Sexuality* (San Francisco: Harper and Row, 1988), Chapter 7. See also Chapter 6, "The Case Against Authority."

9. Mt. 19:9 and Lk. 16:18.

10. Jn. 8:1-11.

11. Lk. 10:38-41, Jn. 11, 12:1-3.

12. Lk. 8:2-3.

13. See Chapter 5 in Schüssler Fiorenza's *In Memory of Her*, "The Early Christian Missionary Movement."

14. Rom. 16:7.

15. Beginning, Schüssler Fiorenza suggests, with the controversy in the early church of Jerusalem described by Luke in Acts 6 (*In Memory of Her*, 165-166).

16. I Cor. 7.

17. Acts 15:20.

18. Elaine Pagels, *The Gnostic Gospels* (New York: Random House, 1979), argues that an important criterion used in excluding prospective documents from the canon was treatment of women's leadership.

19. See James Hitchcock, "Two Roads to Secularization," and Carl F. H. Henry, "Dismantling a Noble Heritage," in William Bentley Ball, ed., *In Search of a National Morality: A Manifesto for Evangelicals and Catholics* (Grand Rapids, MI: Baker, 1992), 17-40.

20. Kathryn Tanner's *The Politics of God: Christian Theologies and Social Justice* (Minneapolis, MN: Fortress, 1992), 127-32, explains how Christian theologies of the transcendence of a just and loving God rule out clear-cut hierarchies and other forms of domination.

21. Marie M. Fortune, *Sexual Violence: The Unmentionable Sin* (New York: Pilgrim, 1983).

22. I Tim. 2:15.
23. The priestly version in Gen. 1:1-2:3.
24. The Yahwist version of Gen. 2:4-2:24 ff. See Phyllis Bird, "Images of Women in the Old Testament," in Rosemary R. Ruether, ed., *Religion and Sexism* (New York: Simon and Schuster, 1984), 73.
25. Gen. 22.
26. Judges 11.
27. Schüssler Fiorenza, *In Memory of Her*, 30-32.
28. For a discussion of this centralization process, see my "Renewal or Repatriarchialization? Responses of the Roman Catholic Church to the Feminization of Religion," *Horizons: The Journal of the College Theology Society*, 10/2 (1983): 231-251.
29. See Chapter 2, note 8, for sources.
30. For a discussion of this critique of physicalism, see Anthony Kosnick et al., *Human Sexuality: New Directions in American Catholic Thought* (New York: Paulist, 1977), 114-122. This text was commissioned by the Catholic Theological Society of America, and was later criticized by the Vatican.
31. Here I have slightly anticipated Chapters 4 and 5, which deal with the role of sexual pleasure and its relation to grace.
32. See, for example, Thomas Aquinas, *Summa Theologiae,* ed. and trans. Blackfriar Dominicans, 60 vols. (New York: McGraw-Hill Book Co., 1964), 2a2ae 26, 9-12, who argued that the proper objects of love are both those having a more excellent good, and those to whom we are more closely united. Aquinas followed Aristotle, who understood both love and friendship in terms of mutuality (*Niomachean Ethics*, Bk. VIII, 1157b).
33. See Anders Nygren's treatment of Luther on self-love as vicious, in *Agape and Eros*, trans. Philip Watson (New York: Harper and Row, 1969), 712-713, and also Sören Kierkegaard, *Works of Love*, trans. Howard and Edna Hong (New York: Harper and Row, 1964), 133-134. The Christian tradition before Luther did not exclude the self from consideration in love so rigorously.
34. See David Barash, *The Whisperings Within: Evolution and the Origin of Human Nature* (New York: Penguin, 1979), 102-104, who credits Sarah Hrdy with the original research. Barash's book makes some of the more modest sociobiological claims for biological influence on human behavior.
35. Barash, *The Whisperings Within*, 104.
36. Barash, *The Whisperings Within*, 104-105.

37. See, for example, Robert L. Trivers, "Parental Investment and Sexual Selection," in D. Campbell, ed., *Sexual Selection and the Descent of Man* (Chicago: Aldine, 1972), and Barash, *The Whisperings Within*, 46-88, 108-109.

38. This was certainly clear in Pius IX's *Syllabus of Errors*. But even in the 20th century Pope Pius XI and Pope Pius XII took very negative positions regarding change. Christine E. Gudorf, *Catholic Social Teaching on Liberation Themes* (Washington, DC: University Press of America, 1980), 6-16.

39. Gudorf, *Catholic Social Teaching*, 16-17.

40. Paul VI's *Populorum progressio* and *Evangelii nuntiandi*, and John Paul II's *Sollicitude rei socialis* and *Centesimus anno* are the definitive examples of this more critical attitude. English editions of all four are found in Thomas Shannon and David O'Brien, eds., *Catholic Social Thought* (Maryknoll, NY: Orbis, 1991).

41. Thus Pius XII in his August 1950 encyclical *Humani generis* accepted the theory of evolution for Catholics provided that it was understood as embracing monogenism and not polygenism (evolution producing one set of human parents, and not many simultaneous ones). *Acta Apostolicae Sedis* 42 (1950): 562-563; trans. A. C. Cotter, *The Encyclical 'Humani generis'* (Weston, MA: Weston College Press, 1952), #5-7.

42. Bernard Lonergan, "Theology in Its New Context," in William F. J. Ryan and Bernard J. Tyrell, eds., *A Second Collection* (Philadelphia: Westminster Press, 1974), 60f.

43. For a discussion of this point in Catholic thought with reference to Lonergan, see Michael J. Himes, "The Human Person in Contemporary Theology: From Human Nature to Authentic Subjectivity," in Ronald P. Hamel and Kenneth R. Himes, OFM, eds., *Introduction to Christian Ethics: A Reader* (New York: Paulist, 1989), 54-56.

44. This is a point made by sociobiologist E. O. Wilson, "Ethics and Sociobiology," in Jonathon Harrison, ed., *Challenges to Morality* (New York: Macmillan, 1993), 221. But the impossibility of a uniform code of ethics should not be interpreted as resulting in a weaker, less rigorous, or less meaningful ethics. Changeability in itself is not negative, either in the character of God or the character of creation, so long as there is some continuity and consistency within the change. Growth, dynamism, and development can all be understood as enhancing being.

45. Thomas Aquinas, *Summa Theologiae*, 2a2ae, 66:2; 1a2ae 94:6; 1a, 98:1.

46. Jessie Bernard, "The Paradox of the Happy Marriage," in Vivian Gornick and Barbara K. Moran, eds., *Woman in Sexist Society: Studies in Power and Powerlessness* (New York: New American Library, 1971), 145-162.

47. Mary Hobgood, "Marriage, Market Values, and Social Justice: Toward an Examination of Compulsory Monogamy," in Susan E. Davies and Eleanor H. Haney, eds., *Redefining Sexual Ethics* (Cleveland: Pilgrim, 1991), 115-126.

48. S. Ryan Johansson, "The Moral Imperatives of Christian Marriage: Their Biological, Economic, and Demographic Implications in Changing Historical Contexts," in John Coleman, S.J., ed., *One Hundred Years of Catholic Social Thought: Celebration and Challenge* (Maryknoll, NY: Orbis, 1991), 135-154.

49. Poorer nutrition was the basic reason for comparatively lesser health, and it was responsible for later maturation, smaller stature, longer (infertile) recovery periods between pregnancies, higher miscarriage and maternal mortality rates, and smaller babies with higher infant mortality. (S. Ryan Johansson, "The Moral Imperatives," in *One Hundred Years,* 138-140.)

50. Beverly W. Harrison, "The Effect of Industrialization on the Role of Women," in Beverly W. Harrison, *Making the Connections: Essays in Feminist Social Ethics* (Boston: Beacon, 1985), 42-53.

51. Philippe Aries, *Centuries of Childhood* (New York: Vintage, 1960).

52. For a complete survey of papal teaching on the role of women, see my *Catholic Social Teaching on Liberation Themes* (Washington, DC: University Press of America, 1980), Chapter Five.

53. For an overview, see Randall J. Hekman, "The Attack on the Family: A Response," in Wm. Bentley Ball, ed., *In Search of a National Morality: A Manifesto for Evangelicals and Catholics* (Grand Rapids, MI: Baker, 1992).

54. Karl Marx, *Capital,* vol I (New York: Modern Library, 1936), 536, and Marx and Frederick Engels, *The Communist Manifesto,* in *A Handbook of Marxism* (New York: International Publishers, 1935), 42.

55. See Hilda Scott, *Does Socialism Liberate Women?* (Boston: Beacon Press, 1979), especially Chapters Eight and Nine.

56. See Sheila Rowbotham's discussion of marxist socialism on the family and sexuality in Chapter 13 of *Hidden from History: Rediscovering Women in History from the 17th Century to the Present* (New York: Vintage, 1974), especially 67-68.

57. Ibid., Chapter Nine.

58. See in particular the discussion around Daniel Moynihan's "The Negro Family" and the more recent examples of the same phenomena in Margaret Cerullo and Marla Erlien, "Beyond the 'Normal' Family: A Cultural Critique of Women's Poverty," in Rochelle Lefkowitz and Ann Withorn, eds., *For Crying Out Loud: Women and Poverty in the U.S.* (New York: The Pilgrim Press, 1986), 248-261.

Chapter 4

1. Augustine, *The City of God,* Ch. 14, in *The Fathers of the Church,* vol. 14, trans. G. Walsh and G. Monahan (New York: Fathers of the Church, Inc., 1952), 395-404; Thomas Aquinas, *Summa Theologiae* I 98, 1,2.

2. Augustine, *On Marriage and Concupiscence,* in Philip Schaff, ed., *The Nicene and Post-Nicene Fathers* I: 17 (Grand Rapids, MI: Wm. B. Eerdmans, 1971), 270-271.

3. J. Ende et al., "The Sexual History in General Medical Practice," *Archives of Internal Medicine* 144 (1984): 3, 558-561. 1984; C. Ellison, "A Critique of the Clitoral Model of Female Sexuality," delivered to the American Psychological Association, 4 Sept. 1980, Montreal.

4. Thomas Aquinas, *Summa Theologiae* Iau IIae 34, vol. 20, Blackfriars ed. (New York: McGraw-Hill, 1975), 65-77.

5. Since 1990 in Poland the power of the Catholic church within the Solidarity government has seen sex education abolished in the public schools on just these grounds. In addition, there is some degree of censorship being exercised within publishing, even academic publishing, which prevents dissemination of, and hinders the gathering of, information about such topics as incest, domestic battery, and marital rape on the grounds that to acknowledge such activities is to encourage them. While in Poland delivering a series of lectures in Polish universities, sexology conferences, and the Polish Academy of Science in October 1992, I not only heard representatives of the bishops defend this agenda, but met many doctors and professors whose books had been taken out of print or refused for publication by the church-controlled Ministry of Education on the grounds that their sexual topics were "inappropriate."

6. *The World's Women: Trends and Statistics 1970-1990* (New York: United Nations, 1991), 16.

7. See James B. Nelson's excellent treatment of this and other aspects of male sexuality throughout his *The Intimate Connection: Male Sexuality, Masculine Spirituality* (Philadelphia: Westminster, 1988).

8. Nelson, *Intimate Connection*, 34-35.

9. The socialization of males to repress body feeling is generally agreed to be one major source of men's shorter lives. The failure of men to disclose is linked to higher stress and anxiety rates, which relate to some of the most common mortal diseases of adults. Men do not get medical help as often or as soon as women, and serious conditions tend to be diagnosed at much later stages, often too late. Sidney Jourard, "Some Lethal Aspects of the Male Role," in Joseph H. Pleck and Jack Sawyer, eds., *Men and Masculinity* (Englewood Cliffs, NJ: Prentice-Hall, 1974), 21-29.

10. Sheila A. Redmond, "Christian 'Virtues' and Recovery from Child Sexual Abuse," in J. C. Brown and C. R. Bohn, *Christianity, Patriarchy, and Abuse: A Feminist Critique* (New York: Pilgrim, 1989), 72.

11. Timothy O'Connell, *Principles for a Catholic Morality* (New York: Paulist, 1978), 155-157. Philip S. Keane in *Sexual Morality: A Catholic Perspective* defines premoral evil as the limitations that exist in all human action which must be taken into account when choosing between actions, and implicitly treats premoral goods as the corresponding goods that exist in all human actions. (*Sexual Morality: A Catholic Perspective* [New York: Paulist, 1977], 46-51.)

12. See the excellent survey of both moral theologians and psychologists on this issue in Vincent Genovesi, *In Pursuit of Love: Catholic Morality and Human Sexuality* (Wilmington, DE: Michael Glazier, 1987), 302-318.

13. William H. Masters, Virginia E. Johnson, and Robert C. Kolodny, *Human Sexuality,* 4th ed. (New York: HarperCollins, 1992), 339.

14. Masters, Johnson, and Kolodny, *Human Sexuality,* 562-563.

15. For one of the most competent treatments of this issue within the context of treatment for sexual dysfunction, see Robert Crooks and Karla Baur, *Our Sexuality,* 5th ed. (Indianapolis, IN: Benjamin Cummings, 1993), 252-254.

16. E. Kanin, "Date Rapists: Differential Sexual Socialization and Relative Deprivation," *Archives of Sexual Behavior* 14 (1985): 219-231.

17. This entire section is heavily dependent upon Ernest Wallwork, *Psychoanalysis and Ethics* (New Haven: Yale University Press, 1991), Chapter Six.

18. See O'Connell, *Principles for a Catholic Morality,* Chapter 8, "Conscience."

19. Wallwork, *Psychoanalysis and Ethics,* 184-190.

20. Mk. 10:29-31, 8:34-37.

21. J. J. C. Smart, "Extreme and Restricted Utilitarianism," in Thomas K. Hearn, Jr., ed., *Studies in Utilitarianism* (New York: Appleton-Century-Crofts, 1971), 251.

22. Ibid., 252-253.

23. Thomas Aquinas, *Summa Theologiae,* Ia IIae 34.

24. Thomas Aquinas, *Summa Theologiae* Ia IIae, 8:1, 5:1 and 2, 5:3, 5:4; Sigmund Freud, *A General Introduction to Psychoanalysis,* trans. J. Riviere (New York: Pocket, 1952), 365. For the most complete form of this argument, see Albert Ple, *Duty or Pleasure? A New Appraisal of Christian Ethics* (Paris: Les Éditions du Cerf, 1980; New York: Paragon, 1987), Ch. 7-8.

25. B. Myers, "Mother-Infant Bonding: Status of This Critical-Period Hypothesis," *Developmental Review* 4 (1984): 240-274; Robert Crooks and Karla Baur, *Our Sexuality,* 303; Jessie Potter, "The Touch Film."

26. S. Rice and J. Kelly, "Love and Intimacy Needs of the Elderly," *Journal of Social Work and Human Sexuality* 5 (1987): 89-96.

27. Aquinas, for example, followed Aristotle in believing that male semen contained whole and complete little men, who needed only nurture in the womb. These little men became defective—that is, female—under certain specific conditions, including the presence of southerly (moist) winds during pregnancy. (*Summa Theologiae* Ia, 92 a1, and *In II sent.* 20, 2,1; *De veritate* 5, 9, ad 9; also see Albert the Great, *De animalibus* 1, 250.)

28. Jeffrey S. Turner and Laura Robinson, *Contemporary Human Sexuality* (Englewood Cliffs, NJ: Prentice-Hall, 1993), 425-426, 429.

29. Crooks and Baur, *Our Sexuality,* 480.

30. Crooks and Baur, *Our Sexuality,* 510-511.

31. For purposes of analyzing the different pleasures involved in the sexual response cycle, I have combined the Masters and Johnson model with that of Helen Singer Kaplan, collapsing sexual desire, excitement, and plateau into a single stage of arousal, and retaining the resolution stage of Masters and Johnson for their stated reasons. This modification retains the emphasis of both Kaplan and Masters and Johnson on the biphasic nature of human sexual response. Helen Singer Kaplan, *The New Sex Therapy* (New York: Brunner-Mazel, 1974), Chapter One.

32. Charles A. Gallagher, George A. Maloney, Mary F. Rousseau, and Paul F. Wilczak, *Embodied in Love: Sacramental Spirituality and Sexual Intimacy* (New York: Crossroad, 1986), 12.

33. Nelson, *Intimate Connection,* 70.

34. Lack of orgasm may seriously slow down resolution. Without orgasm vasocongestion lingers, leaving heavy, swollen feelings in the genitals and pelvis which can be very uncomfortable. These effects may last longer than 30 minutes. Without the release of orgasm, the individual may feel emotionally cheated, resentful, or ashamed, as well as sexually dissatisfied.

35. Diana E. H. Russell, "The Incidence and Prevalence of Intrafamilial and Extrafamilial Sexual Abuse of Female Children," *Child Abuse and Neglect* 7 (1983): 133-146.

36. Diana Russell, *Rape in Marriage* (New York: Macmillan, 1983), 57, 64.

37. Ibid.

38. Del Martin, *Battered Wives* (San Francisco: Glide, 1976), 11.

39. Constance A. Bean, *Women Murdered by the Men They Love* (New York: Haworth, 1992), 141. Also see the Quebec Assembly of Bishops, Social Action Committee, "A Heritage of Violence: Pastoral Reflections on Conjugal Violence," Montreal, Quebec, 1989, 19, which states that pregnancy is often a trigger for violence in the home.

40. Ibid., 58-61.

41. I do not mean to suggest that lesbian sex is free of violent abuse. Women are abusers as well as victims. The Texas study of Shupe et al., for example, revealed that 10% of women initiate instances of domestic abuse. Anson Shupe, William A. Stacey, and Lonnie Hazelwood, *Violent Men, Violent Couples: The Dynamics of Domestic Violence* (Lexington, MA: Lexington Books, 1987), Chapter 3.

42. B. Leigh, "Reasons for Having or Avoiding Sex: Gender, Sexual Orientation, and Relationship to Sexual Disorder," *Journal of Sex Research* 26 (1989): 199-208.

43. S. Harter, P. Alexander, and R. Niemeyer, "Long-term Effects of Incestuous Child Abuse in College Women: Social Adjustment, Social Cognition, and Family Characteristics," *Journal of Consulting and Clinical Psychology* 56 (1988): 5-8; B. Gomez-Schwartz, J. Horowitz, and M. Sauzier, "Severity of Emotional Distress Among Sexually Abused Preschool, School-age, and Adolescent Children," *Hospital and Community Psychiatry* 36 (1985): 503-508.

44. J. Giles Milhaven, "Sleeping Like Spoons," *Commonweal* 116 (4/7/1989): 205-207.
45. Anders Nygren, *Agape and Eros*, trans. Phillip S. Watson (New York: Harper and Row, 1969), 712-14. See also Sören Kierkegaard, *Works of Love*, trans. Howard and Edna Hong (New York: Harper and Row, 1964), 68, 143-44.
46. See my "Sacrifice, Parenting, and Mutual Love," in B. Andolsen et al., *Women's Consciousness, Women's Conscience: A Reader in Feminist Ethics* (Minneapolis: Winston-Seabury, 1985), 175-191.
47. P. W. Blumstein and P. Schwartz, *American Couples* (New York: Morrow, 1983).
48. Hugo Echegaray, *The Practice of Jesus* (Maryknoll: Orbis, 1984), 52.
49. Echegaray, *Practice of Jesus*, 59-60.
50. Echegaray, *Practice of Jesus*, 43-46.
51. Echegaray, *Practice of Jesus*, 65-67.
52. Ex. Echegaray, *Practice of Jesus*, 84; the Gospel of Luke on women, especially Lk. 10:38-42.
53. Ex. Mt. 8:1-3, 14-15.
54. E.g., Lk. 19:1-9 (Zaccheus); Lk. 7:37-50; Mt. 9:10-13.
55. See Chapter One's discussion of the decision in Acts to admit Gentiles to the church.
56. Echegaray, *Practice of Jesus*, 82; but especially Elisabeth Schüssler Fiorenza, *In Memory of Her: A Feminist Theological Reconstruction of Christian Origins* (New York: Crossroad, 1983), 118-123ff.
57. Ex. Lk. 5:30-33.
58. According to Matthew, the 12 disciples attended with Jesus; Mark merely says "the Twelve." Luke describes the attendees generally as the apostles, and John even more generally as the disciples. Mt. 26:20; Mk. 14:17; Lk. 22:14; Jn. 13:5.
59. Schüssler Fiorenza, *In Memory of Her*, 147-151.
60. Mt. 13:44; Mt. 13:33; Mk. 4:30-32; Mk. 4:3-9.
61. Lk. 5:3-11; Jn. 2:1-10; Mk. 14:13-21; Mt. 22:1-10.
62. This is why learning that a partner has faked orgasm often arouses such anger and hurt.
63. Beverly W. Harrison and Carter Heyward, "Pain and Pleasure: Avoiding the Confusions of Christian Tradition in Feminist Theory," in Brown and Bohn, eds., *Christianity, Patriarchy, and Abuse*, 148-173.
64. David Sue, "Erotic Fantasies of College Students During Coitus," *Journal of Sex Research* 15 (1974): 299-305.

65. Thus many researchers divide rape into four categories: sexual gratification rapes, anger rapes, power rapes, and sadistic rapes. Crooks and Baur, *Our Sexuality,* 717-719.

66. A. N. Groth and B. Hobsen, "The Dynamics of Sexual Assault," in L. Schlesinger and E. Revitch, eds., *Sexual Dynamics of Anti-Social Behavior* (Springfield, IL: Thomas, 1983), 163, 165, 167-168. Date rape is a form of acquaintance rape also called sexual gratification rape.

67. L. L. Holmstrom and A. W. Burgess, "Sexual Behavior of Assailants During Reported Rapes," *Archives of Sexual Behavior* 9 (1980): 427-439.

68. A. N. Groth, A. W. Burgess, and L. L. Holmstrom, "Rape: Power, Anger and Sexuality," *American Journal of Psychiatry* 134 (1977): 1235-1243.

69. Marie M. Fortune, *Sexual Violence: The Unmentionable Sin* (New York: Pilgrim, 1983), 9; Film: "Rape: Face to Face."

70. Fortune, *Sexual Violence,* 9.

71. G. Fischer, "College Student Attitudes Toward Forcible Date Rape: Cognitive Predictors I," *Archives of Sexual Behavior* 15 (1986): 457-466.

72. A. Parrot, in a presentation at the meeting of the Society for the Scientific Study of Sex, San Diego, CA, Sept. 1985.

73. R. Giarrusso, "Adolescents' Cues and Signals: Sex and Assault," in P. Johnson, chair, *Acquaintance Rape and Adolescent Sexuality,* symposium papers published by the Western Psychological Association, San Diego, CA, 1979.

74. C. Muhlenhard and S. Andrews, "Open Communication About Sex: Will It Reduce Risk Factors Related to Rape?" paper presented at Association for Advancement of Behavior Therapy, Houston, 1985.

75. C. Muhlenhard and A. Felts, "An Analysis of Causal .Factors for Men's Attitudes About the Justifiability of Date Rape," unpublished research paper of 1987, reported in Nancy W. Denney and David Quadagno, *Human Sexuality,* 2d ed. (St. Louis: Mosby Year Book, 1992), 602.

76. For example, see the advice given in human sexuality texts which deal with rape prevention. Nancy W. Denney and David Quadagno in *Human Sexuality* write: "Men use a variety of strategies to obtain sex from unwilling women. Rapaport and Burkhart (1984) and Muhlenhard and Linton (1987) both found that the most common strategy was ignoring the woman's protests, rather than using violence. Unfortunately, a woman's verbal protests are usually not

enough to constitute a rape in the eyes of the law, particularly if the rapist is an acquaintance. The court requires that the woman use a reasonable amount of resistance (i.e., fighting back rather than crying and pleading)." (Denney and Quadagno, *Human Sexuality*, 603.)

77. Harrison and Heyward, "Pain and Pleasure," in Brown and Bohn, eds., *Christianity, Patriarchy,* 160-168.

78. E. Donnerstein and L. Berkowitz, "Victim Reactions in Aggressive Erotic Films as a Factor in Violence Against Women," *Journal of Personality and Social Psychology* 41 (1981): 710-724; E. Donnerstein and D. Linz, "Sexual Violence in the Media: A Warning," *Psychology Today* (January 1984): 14-15; E. Donnerstein, D. Linz, and S. Penrod, *The Question of Pornography* (New York: Free Press, 1987).

79. See the treatment of sexuality in James B. Nelson's *Embodiment: An Approach to Sexuality and Christian Theology* (Minneapolis: Augsburg, 1978) for an extended treatment of power in sex.

80. Lk. 9:46-48; Lk. 22:24-30.

81. As in Eden: Gen. 2:15-3:22, or at Babel: Gen. 11:1-9.

82. René Girard, *Violence and the Sacred,* trans. Patrick Gregory (Baltimore: Johns Hopkins Press, 1977), Ch. 1-2.

83. See my "Ending the Romanticization of Victims," in *Victimization: Examining Christian Complicity* (Philadelphia: Trinity Press International, 1992).

84. See my "The Power to Create: Sacraments and Men's Need to Birth," *Horizons* 14/2 (1987): 296-309. The seventh Catholic sacrament, Holy Orders, confers the authority to administer the other six.

85. Augustine, *On Marriage and Concupiscence* I:19 in *The Nicene and Post-Nicene Fathers,* vol. 5; *On the Good of Marriage,* Ch. 3 in *The Fathers of the Church,* vol. 17.

86. Rosemary R. Ruether, "Misogynism and Virginal Feminism in the Fathers of the Church," in Ruether, ed., *Religion and Sexism* (New York: Simon and Schuster, 1974), 161-166.

87. The following section is based on John Boswell's *Christianity, Social Tolerance, and Homosexuality* (Chicago: University of Chicago, 1980), Chapter 5.

88. Boswell, *Christianity,* 124.

89. Boswell, *Christianity,* 125, on Plutarch's *Moralia.*

90. Thomas Aquinas, *Summa Theologiae* I, 92 1.

91. Augustine, *De Gratia Christi et de Peccato Originalia* II, 40 in *Patres Ecclesiae*, vol. 34, *Sancti Augustini* (Paris: Paul Mellier, 1842), 181.
92. *The World's Women*, 67.
93. *The World's Women*, 68.
94. We do not have evidence of this trend in many parts of the world, because we do not have any statistical evidence on levels of sexual activity over time in these areas. But what evidence there is of trends supports an upward trend in level of sexual activity. Of course, not all of the increase in sexual activity is positive. For example, while some West African societies had traditional bans on marital intercourse between the last weeks of pregnancy and the time the child was weaned 2 to 3 years later, those bans have been eroded, especially for men. Today a combination of increased economic distress causing many women to become part-time or full-time commercial sex workers, and the exposure of many men to sexual customs and conventions, including periodic work-connected travel, from the industrialized world has produced a situation in which men observe the traditional bans with their wives but may increase the number of sex partners outside marriage. (I. O. Orubuloye, "Patterns of Sexual Behavior of High Risk Groups and Their Implications for STDs and HIV/AIDS Transmission in Nigeria," 20, delivered to the AIDS and Reproductive Health Network meeting in Rio de Janeiro, Brazil, April 22-25, 1993.)
95. Blumstein and Schwartz, *American Couples*, 195-196; R. Doddridge et al., "Factors Related to Decline in Preferred Frequency of Sexual Intercourse Among Young Couples," Psychological *Reports* 60 (1987): 391-395; Morton Hunt, *Sexual Behavior in the 1970's* (Chicago: Playboy Press, 1974), 186-206.
96. Janice Raymond, "Female Friendship and Feminist Ethics," *Women's Consciousness*, 167-168.

Chapter 5

1. William H. Masters, Virginia E. Johnson, and Robert C. Kolodny, *Human Sexuality*, 4th ed., (New York: HarperCollins, 1992), 46; also see Chapter 25.
2. See Beverly W. Harrison and Carter Heyward, "Pain and Pleasure: Avoiding the Confusions of Christian Tradition in Feminist Theory," in J. C. Brown and C. R. Bohn, eds., *Christianity, Patriarchy, and Abuse: A Feminist Critique* (New York: Pilgrim, 1989), 148-173.

3. According to the 1989 research of Charlotte Muhlenhard and Lisa Hollabaugh, 39.3% of 610 female undergraduates had engaged in token resistance at least once. "Do Women Sometimes Say No When They Mean Yes? The Prevalence and Correlates of Women's Token Resistance to Sex," *Journal· of Personality and Social Psychology,* 54 (1989): 872-879.

4. Robert Crooks and Karla Baur, *Our Sexuality,* 5th ed. (Indianapolis: Benjamin Cummings, 1993), 248-249.

5. Population Council Bulletin, 1993.

6. C. Brisset, "Female Mutilation: Cautious Forum on Damaging Practices," *The Guardian,* 18 Mar 1979, 12-15.

7. E. Warner and E. Strashin, "Benefits and Risks of Circumcision," *Canadian Medical Association Journal* 125 (1981): 967-976, 952.

8. Rita M. Gross, "Menstruation and Childbirth as Ritual and Religious Experience Among Native Australians," in Nancy Falk and Rita M. Gross, eds., *Unspoken Worlds: Women's Religious Lives in Non-Western Cultures* (San Francisco: Harper, 1980).

9. K. Rapaport and B. Burkhart, "Personality and Attitudinal Characteristics of Sexually Coercive College Males," *Journal of Abnormal Psychology* 93 (1984): 216-221; C. Muhlenhard and M. Linton, "Date Rape and Sexual Aggression in Dating Situations: Incidence and Risk Factors," *Journal of Counseling and Psychology* 34 (1987): 186-196.

10. Nancy W. Denney and David Quadagno, *Human Sexuality,* 2d ed. (St. Louis, Mosby Year Book, 1992), 601-606.

11. Marianna Valverde, *Sex, Power, and Pleasure* (Philadelphia: New Society, 1987), 36-37.

12. C. Darling and J. Davidson, "Enhancing Relationships: Understanding the Feminine Mystique of Pretending Orgasm," *Journal of Sex and Marital Therapy* 12 (1986): 182-196.

13. Blumstein and Schwartz, *American Couples,* 214-216; J. Loulan, *Lesbian Sex* (San Francisco: Spinsters Ink, 1984), 20.

14. Valverde, *Sex, Power, and Pleasure,* 90.

15. Blumstein and Schwartz, *American Couples,* 216.

16. Valverde, *Sex, Power, and Pleasure,* 86-89; C. Tripp, *The Homosexual Matrix,* 2d ed. (New York: McGraw-Hill, 1987), 152.

17. Crooks and Baur, *Our Sexuality,* 290; L. Peplau, "What Homosexuals Want in Relationships," *Psychology Today* (March 1981): 28-38; Tripp, *Homosexual Matrix,* 153. In terms of sexual activity, surveys of sex researchers have shown that lesbians and gay men utilize significantly more variety and inventiveness in sexual practices,

that they spend longer on foreplay, are less goal-oriented, are less sex-role limited, and spend more time in lovemaking than do heterosexual couples. (Masters, Johnson, and Kolodny, *Human Sexuality*, 396-398.)

18. Tripp, *Homosexual Matrix*, 153-154; Blumstein and Schwartz, *American Couples*, 214-217.

19. Masters, Johnson, and Kolodny, *Human Sexuality*, 398.

20. The clients at sado-masochist business establishments are disproportionately professional—the very class most affected by more egalitarian sexual practices. (Robert J. Stoller, *Pain and Pleasure: A Psychoanalyst Explores the World of S&M* [New York: Plenum Press, 1991], 114.) These clients are diverse in that some insist on same-sex partners, others on opposite-sex partners, and for others the sex of the partner is incidental to the S&M itself. (Stoller, *Pain and Pleasure*, 16.)

21. Helen Singer Kaplan, *The New Sex Therapy* (New York: Bruner and Mazell, 1974), 123.

22. Ibid., 132.

23. Ibid., 289.

24. Ibid., 292.

25. Ibid., 305.

26. The September Yankelovich study of women's attitudes towards abortion found that Catholic women in the U.S. were as likely as Protestant women to obtain abortions; over half of the Catholic women surveyed personally knew someone who had had an abortion; of those, two-thirds of the respondents said that obtaining the abortion was the right thing to do. At the same time, 65% of Catholic women, and 54% of Protestant women, thought that abortion was morally wrong in general. Yet when asked about specific situations, half of Catholic women felt that abortion was morally acceptable in the case of contraceptive failure, and more than half said abortion was morally acceptable for an unmarried teenager, a woman on welfare who can't work, or a married woman with a large family. More than three-fourths of all Catholic women thought that abortion was morally acceptable when a woman is raped, the victim of incest, carrying a fetus with a severe defect, or when the woman's health is threatened. Reported in *A Church Divided: Catholics' Attitudes About Family Planning, Abortion, and Teenage Pregnancy* [Washington, DC: Catholics for a Free Choice, 1986], 12. The lack of agreement among Catholic theologians is equally pronounced. See, for example, Patricia Beattie Jung and

Thomas A. Shannon, eds., *Abortion and Catholicism: The American Debate* (New York: Crossroad, 1988).

27. Information on sexually transmitted diseases is virtually always outdated before it is published. This information reflects Center of Disease Control information from 1992.

28. Thirty-one homosexual men who tested negative on the ELISA antibodies test were found to have the AIDS virus, and 27 of them continued to test negative on ELISA and the Western blot test for 7-36 months after the virus was isolated in them. David Imagawa et al., "Human Immunodeficiency Virus Type 1 Infection in Homosexual Men Who Remain Seronegative for Prolonged Periods," *New England Journal of Medicine* 320, no. 22 (June 1, 1989): 1458-1462.

29. James T. Sears, "Dilemmas and Possibilities of Sexuality Education: Reproducing the Body Politic," in James T. Sears, *Sexuality and the Curriculum: The Politics and Practices of Sexuality Education* (New York: Columbia Teacher's College Press, 1992), 12-17.

30. Marianne H. Whatley, "Whose Sexuality Is It, Anyway?" in Sears, *Sexuality and the Curriculum*, 79.

31. Sears, "Dilemmas and Possibilities," in *Sexuality and the Curriculum*, 19.

32. Susan Shurberg Klein, "The Issue: Sex Equity and Sexuality in Education," *Peabody Journal of Education* 64 (1987): 4, 1.

33. Michelle Fine, "Sexuality, Schooling and the Adolescent Female: The Missing Discourse of Desire," *Harvard Educational Review*, 58 (1988): 1, 32-33.

Chapter 6

1. Harvey G. Cox, *The Secular City: Secularization and Urbanization in Theological Perspective* (New York: Macmillan, 1966), 167.

2. Boston Women's Health Book Collective, *Our Bodies, Ourselves* (New York: Simon and Schuster, 1976).

3. James B. Nelson, *Embodiment: An Approach to Sexuality and Christian Theology* (Minneapolis: Augsburg, 1978); *Between Two Gardens: Reflections on Sexuality and Religious Experience* (New York: Pilgrim, 1984); *The Intimate Connection: Male Sexuality, Masculine Spirituality* (Philadelphia: Westminster, 1988); and *Body Theology* (Louisville: Westminster, 1992).

4. See specifically Beverly Harrison's presidential address, "The Dream of a Common Language: Towards a Normative Theory of Justice in Christian Ethics," in Larry Rasmussen, ed., *The Annual of the Society of Christian Ethics 1983*, as well as *Our Right to Choose:*

Toward a New Ethic of Abortion (Boston: Beacon, 1983) and *Making the Connections: Essays in Feminist Social Ethics* (Boston: Beacon, 1985).

5. Carter Heyward, *Touching Our Strength: The Erotic as Power and the Love of God* (San Francisco: HarperCollins, 1989).

6. For example, see Linda Gordon, *Women's Body, Women's Right: Birth Control in America*, rev. ed. 1990 (New York: Penguin, 1977), and Betsy Hartman, *Reproductive Rights and Wrongs: The Global Politics of Population Control and Reproductive Choice* (New York: Harper and Row, 1987).

7. As Beauchamp and Childress point out, Kant's view of autonomy was much more restricted than Mill's in that only reason was allowed to direct the autonomous will; desire or habit was regarded as direction from outside the personal will. (Tom L. Beauchamp and James F. Childress, *Principles of Biomedical Ethics* [New York: Oxford, 1979], 59). Kant and Mill, from their different approaches to modern thought, illustrate the centrality of the isolated, autonomous, unrelational human person in modernity. While post-modern thought has severely criticized and rejected the idea of human autonomy in favor of an understanding of human persons as inherently social and interdependent, the language available to discuss bodyright in the post-modern age has inevitably been infected with modern notions of autonomy. Here I have continued to speak of respect for individual "control" over one's body. No one is ever in total control of one's own body, since the body exists within a community, where its existence and activities affect the bodies and lives of, and are affected by those of, others. Beverly Harrison, in the Ethics Section of the November 1993 AAR meeting, suggested that "integrity" replace language of "control over one's body," which reflects notions of autonomy and domination. But I am not sure within this specific context that "integrity" conveys to contemporary audiences the primacy of *decision-making* regarding one's body and its activity that is implied in bodyright. Therefore, I have continued to use, despite its clear problems, control language.

8. See the discussion of autonomy and especially informed consent in Beauchamp and Childress, *Principles*, Chapter 3, especially the discussion of U.S. court cases and decisions (65ff).

9. Title VII of the 1964 Civil Rights Act, which prohibits discrimination in employment on the basis of sex, has also been interpreted by the courts as prohibiting unwelcome advances or requests for sexual favors. In 1980 the Equal Employment Opportunity Commis-

son, using the Civil Rights Act as a source, issued guidelines which impose punitive liabilities on companies and institutions for harassment by supervisors unless the companies/institutions have acted to prevent and punish such activity. Those guidelines were revised in 1986.

10. See the distinction between moral obligation and moral value in Hans Jonas, "Philosophical Reflections on Experimenting with Human Subjects," in Thomas Shannon, ed., *Bioethics*, 3d ed. (New York: Paulist, 1987), 264-266.

11. Karen Lebacqz and Robert Levine, "Respect for Persons and Informed Consent to Participate in Research," in *Bioethics*, 340-341.

12. See Beauchamp and Childress, *Principles*, 82-85.

13. Hans Jonas uses the example of conscripted soldiers in suggesting that there is always a kind of trade-off of individual lives for the many in any society, and that this fact should not be used to justify unjust exercises of power, but rather recognized as a limit on the achievement of any common good. Hans Jonas, "Reflections," *Bioethics*, 257-258.

14. Rosemary Radford Ruether, "The Western Religious Tradition and Violence Against Women in the Home," in Brown and Bohn, eds., *Christianity, Patriarchy*, 34-35; R. E. Dobash and R. Dobash, *Violence Against Wives: A Case Against the Patriarchy* (New York: Free Press, 1979), 137; Elizabeth Badinter, *L'un et L'autre, Des Relations Entre Des Hommes et Femmes* (Éditions Odile Jacob, 1986), 191-205.

15. In July 1977, passage of the Hyde Amendment stopped the use of Medicaid funds for abortions for women on public assistance, who had been the recipients of approximately one-third of abortions in the U.S. (Crooks and Baur, *Our Sexuality*, 367). The decision to exclude abortion from the medical care provided for military and other government employees was an executive decision under Presidents Reagan and Bush which is being reversed under President Clinton.

16. The 1991 *Rust v. Sullivan* decision by the Supreme Court upheld the legislation imposing a gag rule on all the 4000 clinics which received federal funding. The clientele of these clinics is largely low-income women. One of President Clinton's first actions as president was to order the lifting of the gag rule.

17. The Supreme Court decision in *Planned Parenthood v. Casey* in June 1992 allowed all these restrictions to stand, though it rejected the requirement of spousal consent.

18. Boston Women's Health Book Collective, *The New Our Bodies, Ourselves* (New York: Simon and Schuster, 1984), 256-257.

19. Ibid.

20. Ibid.

21. It is necessary to be very careful in making this criticism, for although the same charge can readily be made against contraceptive services made available to poor women in other nations by U.S.-funded programs, the situations are not necessarily the same. Medical providers tend to assume that women, and especially poor, nonwhite women, are not competent to oversee any contraceptive methods which require agency. In populations where women have possibilities for some degree of autonomous agency, such attitudes impede the exercise of responsibility by women, and undermine women's health. But in many areas of the world, health workers report that women who want contraception demand long-term, physician-controlled methods because they can obtain neither the spousal cooperation required for barrier methods nor spousal permission for shorter-term chemical means such as the pill. Both spousal violence against women and lack of legal and social recognition of women's bodyright underlie women's demands for methods such as Norplant. With a Norplant patch she will not have to worry about becoming pregnant for five years, and there are no pills, diaphragms, or condoms to be refused or destroyed by a spouse. Women's lack of sexual and reproductive autonomy is becoming much better understood through the social scientific research emerging from the attempt to track and contain the AIDS epidemic around the world. See, for example, Christopher J. Elias and Lori Heise, *The Development of Microbicides: A New Method of HIV Prevention for Women*, Working Paper No. 6 (New York: The Population Council, 1993), 22-33.

22. Alexandra Dundas Todd, *Intimate Adversaries: Cultural Conflict Between Doctors and Women Patients* (Philadelphia: University of Pennsylvania Press, 1989).

23. Robert J. McMurray, "Gender Disparities in Clinical Decision-making," Report to the American Medical Association Council on Ethical and Judicial Affairs, 1990, as reported in Susan Sherwin, *No Longer Patient: Feminist Ethics and Health Care* (Philadelphia: Temple University Press, 1989), 223-224.

24. Ibid.

25. For example, see Randall J. Hekman, "The Attack on the Family: A Response," in William B. Ball, ed., *The Search for a National Mo-*

rality (Grand Rapids: Baker/Ignatius, 1992), 131-143. Hekman argues an evangelical/Catholic case against divorce, working mothers, income taxes, gay rights, and the green movement on the basis of the interests of children, but he is not open to the idea of children's rights, and in fact opposes efforts to end corporal punishment, without making any attempt to delineate how legitimate and abusive corporal punishment should be separated.

26. "Who's Looking After the Interests of Children?: A Devastating Tug of War Highlights the Need for Child-Friendly Custody Laws," *Newsweek* (August 16, 1993): 54-55.

27. See "Letter from a Battered Wife" in Del Martin's *Battered Wives* (San Francisco: Glide, 1976), one of the earlier treatments of conjugal violence. But even recent church statements on conjugal violence, such as the the U.S. National Conference of Catholic Bishops' "When I Call for Help: Domestic Violence Against Women," October 1992, and the Social Affairs Committee of the Assembly of Quebec Bishops' "Heritage of Violence: A Pastoral Reflection on Conjugal Violence," Montreal 1989, acknowledge this inadequate pastoral response as still occurring.

28. See Marie Marshall Fortune's *Sexual Violence: The Unmentionable Sin* (New York: Pilgrim, 1983).

29. While it is certainly not the case that all victims of sexual violence are female, since the overwhelming majority are, I will refer to the victim as "she."

30. R. Krugman, J. Bays, D. Chadwick, C. Levitt, M. McHugh, and J. Whitworth, "Guidelines for the Evaluation of Sexual Abuse of Children," *Pediatrics* 87 (1991): 254-260; J. Beitchman, K. Zucker, J. Hood, G. LaCosta, D. Akman, and E. Cassavia, "A Review of the Long-Term Effects of Child Sexual Abuse," *Child Abuse and Neglect* 16 (1992): 101-118; and L. Young, "Sexual Abuse and the Problem of Embodiment," *Child Abuse and Neglect* 16 (1992): 89-100. Two of these four variables have been minimized by Finkelhor and Browne (D. Finkelhor, *Sexually Abused Children* [New York: Free Press, 1979] and D. Finkelhor and A. Browne, "Risk Factors for Childhood Sexual Abuse: Review of the Evidence," unpublished ms.) but their arguments are severely undermined by the rebuttals of Diana E. H. Russell in *The Secret Trauma: Incest in the Lives of Girls and Women* (New York: Basic, 1988), 142-150.

These same general conditions seem to be the relevant variables in predicting severe trauma in adult victims of sexual abuse as well. (P. Frazier and B. Cohen, "Research on the Sexual Victimization of Women," *The Counseling Psychologist*, 20 (1992): 141-158.)

31. Sheila A. Redmond, "Christian 'Virtues' and Recovery from Child Sexual Abuse," in Joanne Carlson Brown and Carole R. Bohn, eds., *Christianity, Patriarchy, and Abuse: A Feminist Critique* (New York: Pilgrim, 1989). Redmond cites Alice Miller's *For Your Own Good: Hidden Cruelty in Childrearing and the Roots of Violence* (New York: Farrar, Straus, and Giroux, 1984), 131-132; F. R. Schreiber, *Sibyl* (New York: Warner, 1973); Carolyn Black, *It Will Never Happen to Me* (Denver: M.A.C. Printing and Publications Division, 1982); and "Emotional Hangover: Growing Up with an Alcoholic Parent" *McCalls* (October 1984): 161-163.

32. Ronnie Janoff-Bulman and Irene Frieze, "A Theoretical Framework for Understanding Reaction to Victimization," *Journal of Social Issues* 39 (1983): 2, 1-17.

33. Ibid.

34. D. Finkelhor and A. Browne, "The Traumatic Impact of Child Sexual Abuse: A Conceptualization," *American Journal of Orthopsychiatry* 55 (1985): 4, 530-541.

35. Betrayal by persons one loves and trusts is also severely traumatic for adults. It undermines victims' ability to preserve any sense of being worthwhile selves who deserve care and protection. Wives raped by their husbands and women raped by their dates experience a similar sense of betrayal and often come to doubt their own ability to judge who can be trusted. (N. Rynd, "Incidence of Psychosomatic Symptoms in Rape Victims," *Journal of Sex Research* 24 (1987): 155-161; S. Murnen, A. Perot, and D. Byrne, "Coping with Unwanted Sexual Activity: Normative Responses, Situational Deteminants, and Individual Differences," *Journal of Sex Research* 26 (1989): 85-106.) Parent/child incest seems to be the most traumatic variety of incest, because, in addition to other sources of trauma, the child is betrayed by someone in whom she has trusted for love and protection; in fact, her very love and respect for her parent have been manipulated to abuse her. (Russell, *Secret Trauma*, 148-150.)

36. Finkelhor and Browne, "Traumatic Impact of Child Sexual Abuse"; Russell, *The Secret Trauma*, 148-150; V. Felitti, "Longterm Medical Consequences of Incest, Rape, and Molestation," *Southern Medical Journal* 84 (1991): 328-331; M. Massie and S. Johnson, "The Importance of Recognizing a History of Sexual Abuse in Female Adolescents," *Journal of Adolescent Health Care* 10 (1989): 184-191.

37. Diana E. H. Russell, *The Secret Trauma: Incest in the Lives of Girls and Women* (New York: Basic Books, 1988), 172-173.

38. K. Howells, "Adult Sexual Interest in Children: Considerations Relevant to Theories of Aetiology," in M. Cook and K. Howell, eds., *Adult Sexual Interest in Children* (New York: Academic Press, 1981), 80, as quoted in Russell, *Secret Trauma*, 170.

39. Russell, *Secret Trauma*, 171.

40. *Bureau of Justice Statistical Special Report, 1986*, 3.

41. Many sources also include psychological violence in the cycle of violence. The Quebec Assembly of Bishops' "Heritage of Violence" treats psychological violence as one aspect of the cycle of violence, and presents it as part of an often escalating cycle of violence (16-18).

42. Lenore Walker, *The Battered Woman* (New York: HarperCollins, 1980), and *Terrifying Love: Why Battered Women Kill and How Society Responds* (New York: HarperCollins, 1989).

43. Constance A. Bean, *Women Murdered by the Men They Love* (New York: Harrington Park Press, 1992), 139.

44. Ibid., 140.

45. National Coalition Against Domestic Violence Fact Sheet, 1991.

46. Del Martin, *Battered Wives*, 60-61.

47. I. Arias and S. R. H. Beach, "The Role of Social Desirability in Reports of Marital Violence," paper presented at April 1986 meeting of the Eastern Psychological Association in N.Y.C.; also see A. Sachs, "Swinging—and Ducking—Singles," *Time* 132 (1988): 10, 54.

48. C. Fedders, *Shattered Dreams* (New York: Harper and Row, 1987).

49. National Institute of Justice, 1990 Fact Sheet on Domestic Violence Murders.

50. It is significant that Norfolk's population includes a large military population. Shupe/Stacey/Hazelwood's research indicates that while the *rate* of domestic violence does not differ significantly between military and civilian populations, the *degree* of violence varies a great deal. They say: "Instances of violence in military families tend in the more lethal direction. In fact, three-fourths of the military cases were in the dangerously life-endangering category, compared to only about one-third of the civilian cases." (Anson Shupe, William A. Stacey, and Lonnie R. Hazelwood, *Violent Men, Violent Couples: The Dynamics of Domestic Violence* [Lexington, MA: Lexington Books, 1987], 79.)

51. Bean, *Women Murdered*, 6.

52. A. Browne and K. Williams, "Exploring the Effect of Resource Availability and the Likelihood of Female-Perpetrated Homicides," *Law and Society Review* 23 (1989): 1, 76-94.

53. There are, however, some useful recent materials about sexual abuse of children. For example, Joan Golden Mandell and Linda Damon, *Group Treatment for Sexually Abused Children* (New York: The Guilford Press, 1989), deals with child victims, while Kathryn Goering Reid and Marie M. Fortune, *Preventing Child Sexual Abuse: A Curriculum for Children 9-12* (New York: United Church Press, 1989), aims at preventing child sexual abuse by educating children themselves.

54. Fortune, *Sexual Violence*, 143-144.

55. It is, of course, not always easy for police to discern amidst the noise whether they are dealing with a male batterer and a female victim, or two drunken batterers, or even a female batterer and a male victim attempting to defend himself. There has been increasing realization among police that the "typical" case is *not* a spat in which two persons are equally either responsible for assault or likely to be injured.

56. The basic problem in treating batterers is that they refuse to see themselves as responsible for their violence. Bean, *Women Murdered,* 159-161.

57. *Texas Crime Clearinghouse News* 2 (Spring 1985): 2; Shupe et al., *Violent Men,* 48-49.

58. Marvin E. Wolfgang, "Husband-Wife Homicides," *Corrective Psychiatry and Journal of Social Therapy* 2 (1976): 263-71.

59. Robert Crooks and Karla Baur, *Our Sexuality* (Indianapolis: Benjamin Cummings, 1993): 648-649; A. Burgess and L. Holmstrom, "Rape: Sexual Disruption and Recovery," *American Journal of Orthopsychiatry* 49 (1979): 648-657; C. Safran, "What Men Do to Women on the Job: A Shocking Look at Sexual Harassment," *Redbook* (November 1976): 148ff; Felitti, "Longterm Medical Consequences of Incest, Rape, and Molestation," 330-331.

60. Suzanne K. Steinmetz, "The Battered Husband Syndrome," *Victimology: An International Journal* 2: 3 and 4 (1977-78): 499-509.

61. Shupe et al., *Violent Men,* 56-60.

62. Mandell and Damon, *Group Treatment,* 76.

63. Fortune, *Sexual Violence,* 186-189.

64. Bean, *Women Murdered,* 51-55; Quebec Bishops, "A Heritage of Violence," 16.

65. Harrison, "The Power of Anger," in *Making the Connections,* 1.

66. Carol Tavris, "Anger Defused," in Kieran Scott and Michael Warren, eds., *Perspectives on Marriage: A Reader* (New York: Oxford, 1993), 227-228.

67. Harrison, "The Power of Anger," in *Making the Connections*; Fortune, *Sexual Violence*, 204-208.

68. Crooks and Baur survey studies confirming Kinsey's claim that "the physiologic mechanism of any emotional response (anger, fright, pain, etc.) may be the mechanism of sexual response" (Alfred Kinsey et al., *Sexual Behavior in the Human Male* [Philadelphia: Saunders, 1948], 165; Crooks and Baur, *Our Sexuality*, 648-649). Included in those confirmatory studies are: J. Bancroft, "Psychophysiology of Sexual Dysfunction," in M. Dekkar, ed., *Handbook of Biological Psychiatry* (New York: Dekkar, 1980); P. Sarrell and Wm. Masters, "Sexual Molestation of Men by Women," *Archives of Sexual Behavior* 11 (1982): 118; G. Mezey and M. King, "The Effects of Sexual Assault on Men: A Survey of 22 Victims," *Psychological Medicine* 19 (1989): 205-209. All of these references deal with this phenomenon in both sexes.

69. Alice Miller, *For Your Own Good: Hidden Cruelty in Childrearing and the Roots of Violence,* and *Thou Shalt Not Be Aware: Society's Betrayal of the Child* (New York: Farrar, Straus, and Giroux, 1984), and *The Drama of the Gifted Child: How Narcissistic Parents Form and Deform the Emotional Lives of Their Talented Children* (New York: Harper and Row, 1981), 9-17.

70. Miller, *The Drama of the Gifted Child,* Chapter One.

71. Sheila A. Redmond, "Christian Virtues and Recovery from Child Sexual Abuse," in Brown and Bohn, eds., *Christianity, Patriarchy,* 74.

72. Ibid.

73. See Pius XII, Allocution to "Very Young Girls" of Catholic Action, October 2, 1955, in The Monks of Solesmes, ed., *Papal Teachings: The Woman in the Modern World* (Boston: St. Paul Editions, 1959), 246.

74. Rita Nakashima Brock, "And a Little Child Will Lead Us," in Brown and Bohn, eds., *Christianity, Patriarchy,* 54-56.

75. I have dealt with this issue at some length in my *Victimization: Examining Christian Complicity* (Philadelphia: Trinity Press International, 1993), Chapter 3, "Ending the Romanticization of Victims."

76. For example, see James H. Cone, *Liberation: A Black Theology of Liberation* (New York: Lippincott, 1970), Chapter 4.

Chapter 7

1. Dean R. Hoge, *Converts, Dropouts, and Returnees: A Study of Religious Change Among Roman Catholics* (New York: Pilgrim Press/U.S. Catholic Conference, 1981), 10, 23, 83-84.

2. Peter Brown, *The Body and Society: Men, Women, and Sexual Renunciation in Early Christianity* (New York: Columbia University Press, 1988), 202-209.

3. See Charles Kannengiessen, "Early Christian Bodies: Some Thoughts on Peter Brown's *The Body and Society,*" *Religious Studies Review* 19:2 (April 1993): 126-129.

4. This is clearest in "On Marriage" by Clement of Alexandria, often called the "defender of marriage" among the Fathers. See Peter Brown's treatment of Clement in Chapter 6 of *The Body and Society,* especially 132-139.

5. Uta Ranke-Heinemann, *Eunuchs for the Kingdom of Heaven: Women, Sexuality, and the Catholic Church* (New York: Doubleday, 1990; German ed., 1988), Chapter XX ff.

6. I Corinthians 7:9.

7. For a much-cited example, see Martin Luther, "The Estate of Marriage," *Luther's Works,* vol. 45, *The Christian in Society* 2, ed. Walther I. Brandt (Philadelphia: Muhlenberg Press, 1962), Part Three.

8. For a good explanation of the contemporary narrative of therapeutic well-being, see Roger C. Bettsworth, *Social Ethics: An Examination of American Moral Traditions* (Louisville: Westminster, 1990), Chapter Four.

9. I Cor. 15:20-23, Rom. 6:5.

10. I have often thought that were this not so, many of the modern churchmen of the last two centuries would have insisted on the substantive maleness of God in the face of feminist challenges to male language for God, instead of being forced to agree that God is *not* male, that maleness has merely been attributed to God by humans in an attempt to facilitate human ability to be in relation to God.

11. Augustine, *On the Nature of Good,* 1, *Patrologiae Latinae* 42, 551; Thomas Aquinas, *Summa Theologiae,* Iae 9, reply to article 2.

12. Reprinted in Carol P. Christ and Judith Plaskow, eds., *Womanspirit Rising: A Feminist Reader in Religion* (San Francisco: Harper and Row, 1979), 25-42.

13. Genesis 11:4.

14. Gen. 3:22.

15. Not only have Latin American liberation theologians been critical of the transformation of material poverty into evangelical poverty (Gustavo Gutierrez, *A Theology of Liberation* [Maryknoll, NY: Orbis, 1973], 288-289), but some have attacked elements of the tradition regarding evangelical poverty. Hugo Assman stated at the 1975 Detroit *Theology in the Americas* conference, "The epistemological privilege of the poor is a privilege of the struggling poor person—of one struggling in an effective way. Struggling means loving in an effective way with a revolutionary horizon, with strategic goals and practical praxis steps. I cannot accept a general privilege of the poor. Many do, but they forget the poor are oppressed and have the oppressor within themselves." (Sergio Torres, ed., *Theology in the Americas* [Maryknoll, NY: Orbis, 1976], 300.)

16. Augustine, *The City of God*, trans. John K. Ryan (Garden City, NY: Doubleday, 1960), Bk 9, Ch 9, 218-219.

17. Perhaps the best-known scriptural reference on this point is Phil. 2:5-8: "Jesus Christ, who, though he was in the form of God, did not count equality with God a thing to be grasped, but emptied himself, taking the form of a servant, being born in the likeness of God."

18. Paul then wrote of himself as a follower of this Christ: "For though I am free from all men, I have made myself a slave for all, that I might win the more (for Christ)," (I Cor. 9:19).

19. See, for example, 1 Corinthians 9, 2 Corinthians 10-12, Philippians 3, and Galatians 2.

Index

social silence on, as original sin, 18

Sexuality (Avvento), 221 n. 26

Sexuality and Physical Disability (Bullard and Knight), 226 n. 3

Sexuality and the Curriculum (Sears), 247 nn. 29-31

Sexual Language (Guindon), 220 n. 25

Sexually Abused Children (Finkelhor), 251 n. 30

Sexually transmitted diseases (STDs): fear of, and sexual pleasure, 152-55; preventive treatment for, after sexual abuse, 179

Sexual Morality (Keane), 220 n. 23, 238 n. 11

Sexual pleasure: and abuse, 100-101; Augustinian understanding of, 83; costs of ignoring mutuality in, 119-27; dysfunction resulting from sexual ignorance, 149-51; as ethical criterion for evaluating sexual activity, 114-16; and fear of pregnancy, 151-52; and fear of STDs, 152; genital mutilation to prevent, 144-45; importance of mutual, 116-19; mutuality in, as normative, 139-44; power of, 103-5; as premoral good, 89-100; reasons for law status of, in Christian tradition, 82-83; as safe and beneficial, 101-3; sex roles as obstacles to, 146-48; in the sexual response cycle, 107; understanding of, as irresistible, 84-89; women's interest in, 145-46

Sexual Preference (Bell, Weinberg, and Hammersmith), 219 n. 6, 222 n. 30

Sexual purity, and recovery from abuse, 197-98

Sexual relationship, romanticism of, 134

Sexual response cycle: orgasm in, 107-9; resolution in, 109-10; sexual arousal in, 107

Sexual satisfaction, and intercourse, 31

Sexual Selection and the Descent of Man, 235 n. 37

Sexual sin: categories of, 16; recognizing, 17-18

Sexual victimization: avoiding victimism after, 190-93; bodyright and, 170-93; Christian theology as obstacle to recovery from, 196-201; effects of, on women and children, 171-74; healing from, 177-82; of men, 182-84; revictimization of children, 174-75; revictimization of women, 175-77; selfhood and recovery from, 190; theological/ethical advice on, 170-71; trauma-causing factors in children, 173; treatment for, 177-82; victims' innocence in, 184-87; victims' rage in, 187-90

Sexual violence: blindness of sexual ethics texts to, 18; blockages in victims of, 102

Sexual Violence (Fortune), 220 nn. 13-15; 233 n. 21; 242 n. 69; 251 n. 28; 254 n. 54, 63; 255 n. 67

Shattered Dreams (Fedders), 253 n. 48

S974-9